China's Emerging Global Businesses

Also by Yongjin Zhang

CHINA IN THE INTERNATIONAL SYSTEM, 1918–1920

CHINA IN INTERNATIONAL SOCIETY SINCE 1949

ETHNIC CHALLENGES BEYOND BORDERS (*co-editor with Rouben Azizian*)

POWER AND RESPONSIBILITY IN CHINESE FOREIGN POLICY
(*co-editor with Greg Austin*)

Montante Family Library
D'Youville College

China's Emerging Global Businesses

Political Economy and Institutional Investigations

Yongjin Zhang
Department of Political Studies
University of Auckland, New Zealand

© Yongjin Zhang 2003

All rights reserved. No reproduction, copy or transmission of this publication may be made without written permission.

No paragraph of this publication may be reproduced, copied or transmitted save with written permission or in accordance with the provisions of the Copyright, Designs and Patents Act 1988, or under the terms of any licence permitting limited copying issued by the Copyright Licensing Agency, 90 Tottenham Court Road, London W1T 4LP.

Any person who does any unauthorised act in relation to this publication may be liable to criminal prosecution and civil claims for damages.

The author has asserted his right to be identified as the author of this work in accordance with the Copyright, Designs and Patents Act 1988.

First published 2003 by
PALGRAVE MACMILLAN
Houndmills, Basingstoke, Hampshire RG21 6XS and
175 Fifth Avenue, New York, N.Y. 10010
Companies and representatives throughout the world

PALGRAVE MACMILLAN is the global academic imprint of the Palgrave Macmillan division of St. Martin's Press, LLC and of Palgrave Macmillan Ltd. Macmillan® is a registered trademark in the United States, United Kingdom and other countries. Palgrave is a registered trademark in the European Union and other countries.

ISBN 0–333–99934–7

This book is printed on paper suitable for recycling and made from fully managed and sustained forest sources.

A catalogue record for this book is available from the British Library.

Library of Congress Cataloging-in-Publication Data
Zhang, Yongjin.
    China's emerging global businesses : political economy and institutional investigations / Yongjin Zhang.
       p.   cm.
    Includes bibliographical references and index.
    ISBN 0–333–99934–7 (cloth)
    1. Corporations, Chinese.   2. International business enterprises – China.   3. Investments, Chinese – Government policy.   4. Structural adjustment (Economic policy) – China.   5. China – Commercial policy.   6. China – Foreign economic relations.   I. Title.
HD2910 .Z43   2003
338.8′8951 – dc21   2002035787

10   9   8   7   6   5   4   3   2   1
12   11   10   09   08   07   06   05   04   03

Printed and bound in Great Britain by
Antony Rowe Ltd, Chippenham and Eastbourne

HD 2910
.Z43
2003

Contents

APR 15 2004

Part III The Transnationalisation of Chinese Firms: Institutional Investigations

List of Tables, Figures and Boxes

Boxes

Acknowledgements

Writing a book is an intellectual journey, a personal and often formidable one. This is particularly true for me in writing this book. The idea was first conceived in the mid-1990s when I was completing another monograph on *China in International Society since 1949*. I literally bumped into a large number of disaggregated data on China's outward investment activities, and was told bemusing tales of Chinese companies' overseas adventures. Impulse as much as intellectual curiosity was the inspiration for the conception of this project. Little did I expect, however, that it would have been such a challenging and demanding one, accompanied by enormous enjoyment and enrichment as well as by occasional frustrations and irritation. If in completing this project, I have had to stretch myself into a number of unfamiliar territories and have had a testing experience, it is also enriching and enabling. It challenges me to extend my scholarship and learning. It enables me to come to a better understanding of that fundamental economic transformation that China is experiencing today, which I have put down on paper to share with readers of this book.

An intellectual journey would never have been completed without supportive and inspiring companions. I am deeply indebted to a large number of individuals and institutions that have helped me with my interviews and research in China as well as in other parts of the world over the years. I would like to acknowledge my thanks in particular to Bian Yongzhuang, Feng Xiaoming, Guo Shuqing, Natasha Hamilton-Hart, He Jiacheng, Kang Yongping, Lin Ye, Pi Shenghao, John Ravenhill, Shao Binhong, Shi Yutang, Song Xinning, Wang Haijun, Xie Duo, Yu Yongding, James Xiaming Zhan, Zhang Jijing, and Zhang Xiaojin. My debt to many of them goes beyond the intellectual.

I owe many debts of gratitude to a number of institutions, in particular to the United Nations Conference on Trade and Development (UNCTAD) for granting me access to its library and allowing me to conduct interviews at its headquarters in Geneva, and to the Centre for Asian Studies of the University of Hong Kong for sponsoring me as a Visiting Scholar while I was doing my research in Hong Kong. The University of Auckland provided initial financial assistance to kick-start this research project. The Department of International Relations, Research School of Pacific and Asian Studies of the Australian National University, where I was a Fellow between 1999 and 2001, provided a supporting environment and research grant for the completion of this book. I would like to register my gratitude to both these institutions here. At Palgrave Macmillan, I am grateful to my commissioning editors Nicola Viinikka and Amanda Watkins for managing the publication of this book, and to Guy Edwards for seeing through its production.

My ultimate debt is, as always, to my family, who offered unfailing moral and indispensable logistical support throughout this journey. I dedicate this book lovingly to my wife Shanping and to my daughter Jessie, who has grown up into a university student at Cambridge while I was completing this project.

Auckland   YONGJIN ZHANG

List of Abbreviations

ABC	Agricultural Bank of China
ADB	Asian Development Bank
ADR	American Depository Receipts
APEC	Asia-Pacific Economic Cooperation
BOC	Bank of China
CCB	China Construction Bank
CCP	Chinese Communist Party
CIB	CITIC Industrial Bank
CIS	Commonwealth of Independent States
CITIC	China International Trust and Investment Corporation
CNAC	China National Aviation Corporation
CNIFP	Central North Island Forestry Partnership
CNOOC	China National Offshore Oil Corporation
CNPC	China National Petroleum Corporation
COFCO	China National Cereals, Oils and Foodstuffs Import and Export Corporation
COPRI	Comision de Promocion de la Inversion Privada
COSCO	China Ocean Shipping Company
COSTIND	Commission for Science, Technology and Industry for National Defence
CPPCC	Chinese People's Political Consultative Conference
EIU	Economist Intelligence Unit
ENR	Engineering News Record
FDI	Foreign Direct Investment
FEER	Far Eastern Economic Review
FOTIC	China Investment and Trust Corporation for Foreign Economic Cooperation and Trade
GATT	General Agreement on Tariff and Trade
GDP	Gross Domestic Product
GFCF	Gross Fixed Capital Formation
GITIC	Guangdong International Trust and Investment Corporation
GNP	Gross National Product
IBRD	International Bank for Reconstruction and Development
ICBC	Industrial and Commercial Bank of China
ICI	Imperial Chemical Industries

IDA	International Development Association
IDP	Investment Development Path
IISI	International Iron and Steel Institute
ILO	International Labour Organisation
IMF	International Monetary Fund
IPO	Initial Public Offer
ITICs	International Trust and Investment Corporations
LME	London Metal Exchange
M&A	Merger and Acquisition
MIA	Multinational Investment Agreement
MNC	Multinational Corporation
MNE	Multinational Enterprises
MOFERT	Ministry of Foreign Economic Relations and Trade
MOFTEC	Ministry of Foreign Trade and Economic Cooperation
NICs	Newly Industrialising Countries
NIEO	New International Economic Order
NOI	Net Outward Investment
OECD	Organisation for Economic Co-operation and Development
PBOC	People's Bank of China
PICC	People's Insurance Company of China
PLA	People's Liberation Army
PRC	People's Republic of China
RMB	Renminbi
RMRB	Renmin Ribao (People's Daily)
SAFE	State Administration for Foreign Exchange
SAIC	Shanghai Automobile Industry Corporation
SCRES	State Commission for Restructuring the Economic System
SEG	Shenzhen Electronics Group
SEZs	Special Economic Zones
SGNEC	Shougang–NEC
SINOCHEM	China National Chemicals Import and Export Corporation
SINOPEC	China Petroleum and Chemical Corporation
SOE	State-owned Enterprises
SPC	State Planning Commission
SWB	Service of World Broadcast
TNCs	Transnational Corporations
TNEs	Transnational Enterprises
TVEs	Town and Village Enterprises

UN	United Nations
UNCTAD	United Nations Conference on Trade and Development
UNDP	United Nations Development Programme
UNIDO	United Nations Industrial Development Organisation
UNIPEC	China United Petroleum Corporation
UNTCMD	United Nations Transnational Corporation and Management Division
USAC	US Agri-Chemical Co. Ltd
WTO	World Trade Organisation

Introduction

Since the mid-1980s, the economic take-off of China and the impact of such a take-off on the global economy have been much discussed and anticipated as well as contested. Is China going to be Asia's next economic giant? What would it mean to the world if it is (Perkins 1986)? In what sense is the economic reform in China creating a new superpower that is taking the centre stage of the world as No. 1 (Overholt 1993, Brahm 1996b)? How much is the new millennium the dragon millennium (Richter 2000)? What heralds the awakening of the next economic powerhouse, which 'stands poised to alter the global economy' (Brahm 2001)? Or, indeed, does China matter at all for the world economy and for the West (Segal 1999)? The most recent debates on how much China's accession to the World Trade Organisation (WTO) is 'a landmark event' for the global trading system further highlight the contested but growing economic influence of China in the foreseeable future.

Such anticipation and hyperbole apart, these discussions concur with the mainstream literature that explores how the transformation of the Chinese economy has been intimately related to its gradual integration into the global economy through trade, investment and institutional changes, and how this integration is an indispensable part of China's economic revolution (Lloyd and Zhang 2000, Nolan 2001, Lardy 2002). One central focus of these studies is how foreign participation in China's economic reform and opening, mostly through international trade and foreign direct investment (FDI), has profoundly transformed the economic landscape of China and created China's economic power. In both the conventional literature and hyperbole on the emergence of China as an economic power, however, discussions of one salient dimension of China's increasing assertion in the global economy are sadly missing: that is, the significant growing outreach of the

1

Chinese economy through unprecedentedly large amounts of outward investment and the emerging global businesses in China in the reform years.

This economic revolution of another kind created by China's opening and reform, however, has been frequently captured in the news headlines. In 1996, the *Hong Kong Economic Journal* noted that China had become the second largest investor in Hong Kong in 1994, next only to Great Britain (Ding 2000: 121). The *Financial Times* reports increasingly frequent cross-border merger and acquisition activities by Chinese companies throughout the world. More recently, the *Wall Street Journal* wrote on manufacturing operations of the Haier Group, China's largest appliance company, in the United States, and reported acquisitions by the Hangzhou-based Holley Group in America (28 January 2002). Both the *Far Eastern Economic Review* and the *Wall Street Journal* put into their respective headlines recent acquisitions of oil and gas fields by PetroChina and the China National Offshore Oil Corporation (CNOOC) in Indonesia (*Wall Street Journal*, 2 May 2002; *Far Eastern Economic Review*, 28 March 2002). 'Taking on the world' and 'going global' have become catchphrases in reports on transnational operations by Chinese companies carried in newspapers and business periodicals both in China and overseas.[1]

These headlines, fragmented as they are, do indicate that this particular dimension of Chinese economic activities has been substantial and is becoming increasingly significant. The inviting question, which is also an enduring puzzle, is why such a significant outreach of the Chinese economy that potentially has a far-reaching impact on the global economy has been so much neglected in the studies of China's economic transformation, notwithstanding enormous interest in China's integration into the global economy. In stark contrast to the proliferation of studies of reforms of China's trade system, China's entry into the WTO and FDI in China, academic publications in English on Chinese outward investment and China's emerging multinational businesses are few and far between.[2]

If this neglect is unmistakable, it is also inexplicable, on at least three counts, given the compelling interest in the transformation of the Chinese economy in general, and enterprise reform in particular. First is the phenomenal growth of China's outward investment, clearly reported and recorded. As a result of the interactions between the increasingly globalised world economy and economic reform in China since 1978, transnational operations of Chinese firms[3] have advanced by leaps and bounds. Whereas in 1978 China had little investment beyond Hong Kong, twenty years later, in 1998, China's outward FDI stocks, according to *World Investment Report 1999* (UNCTAD 2000: 497), reached $22.079 billion. This puts China – a latecomer among developing countries in outward investment – well ahead of Korea at $21.505 billion and Malaysia at $14.645 billion, but behind Hong Kong, Singapore and Taiwan.[4] The World Bank estimates that already in 1995, 'China's outward investment accounted for 2 percent of global capital flows, making it the eighth largest supplier among all countries and the largest outward investor among developing countries' (World Bank 1997b: 26). At the same time, the estimated Chinese investment in Hong Kong before the British handover in 1997 was between $30 billion and $40 billion. Large-scale investment projects by Chinese firms are now found in North and South America and Australasia as well as Asia and Africa and include a chemical fertiliser manufacturing plant, forestry, fishery, an aluminum smelter, iron ore and coal mines, petroleum exploration and financial services.

Second, as China becomes a significant Third World investor, large Chinese multinationals have already quietly claimed their places among the largest transnationals in the world. Chinese companies have found their places in Fortune Global 500, the top 50 TNCs (transnational corporations) from developing countries ranked by foreign assets in *World Investment Report* (UNCTAD 1998, 1999, 2000) and the top 225 international contractors ranked by *Engineering News Record* (1998, 1999, 2000, 2001).

Third, behind this captivating picture of the emergence and the growth of Chinese multinationals is the intriguing evolution of policy regimes and regulatory framework, as China fast becomes a home country for its own multinational corporations and as Chinese firms transnationalise. For those interested in the political economy of Chinese reform, this poses a number of intriguing questions. How have domestic political and economic institutions changed or resisted to accommodate this rise of Chinese multinationals? In what way does the accelerated integration of China with the world economy promoted exactly by the growth of China's outward investment in turn impact on political changes in China?

Some preconceived ideas about the Chinese economy may be the culprit for such neglect. How could China, a net capital importer, afford to conduct large-scale investment overseas? How is it possible for a state-owned enterprise located in a command economy largely insulated from the world economy until the 1970s to start its international business in the first place? Why should the Chinese government allow and encourage its domestically inefficient firms to engage in outward investment activities? What are the incentives for Chinese firms to transnationalise in the reform process? How could Chinese firms survive and expand in their transnational operations in market economies around the world? These are legitimate questions that need to be addressed seriously. The puzzle is how the transnationalisation of Chinese firms has happened against all these odds.

Explanations for this enigmatic neglect can also be found beyond studies of the Chinese economy. During the decade after 1983 when Louis T. Wells's pioneering work *Third World Multinationals: The Rise of Foreign Investment from Developing Countries* was published, the studies of multinationals from developing economies seem to have largely stalled. As Lecraw observed in 1992, 'Over the period 1977 to 1985 there was a stream of research concerning foreign direct investment by firms based in developing countries. In the last half of the 1980s, since the books by Wells (1983) and Lall (1983), however, little work has been done on this interesting topic (with the exception of Aggarwal (1988)' (Lecraw 1992: 115). Small wonder it is that the transnationalisation of Chinese firms and the emergence of China's global businesses, which took off precisely during this period, should have been mostly over-looked as a large piece in the jigsaw of the rising multinational corporations from developing economies. But even in the mid-1990s, when the revival of studies of multinationals from developing countries was prompted by the increasingly important role of Third World investors in the global economy,[5] China's emerging multinationals remained largely invisible in the literature.

This book examines the emergence and growth of China's global businesses in the years since the launch of China's economic reform. By addressing this important but neglected aspect of China's economic transformation, it aims to fill a yawning gap in the existing literature on China's integration into the global economy and to add a new perspective from which a better appreciation of China's increasing impact on the global economy can be gained. Fred Bergsten warned recently that 'No nation is increasing its impact on the global economy as rapidly as the People's Republic of China at the close of the twentieth century. At the same time, few economies are as poorly understood' (Bergsten 1999: ix). In more than one important aspect, therefore, this study is a direct heed to Bergsten's admonition and lament above: admonition on the rapidly increased impact of the largest emerging market on the global economy, and lament that this economy remains so inadequately understood.

There are two main thrusts of this study. One thrust investigates the changing political economy of the policy context within which China's nascent global businesses have been nurtured and promoted. It seeks to identify the political and economic dynamics that explain the origin and the expansion of transnationalisation of Chinese firms. Rather than looking at the emergence of China's global businesses simply as part of further economic integration of China into the global economy, it posits this intriguing development in the Chinese economy as the response of the Chinese state to the increasingly globalised world economy. The other thrust offers a systematic and analytical account of how China's global businesses gradually emerged and evolved in the process of Chinese economic reforms. Institutional stories of how three Chinese firms transnationalise are told in detail as part of this analytical account. Both thrusts therefore address a less explicit but more challenging puzzle throughout this book: that is, how the Chinese state, in responding to the imperative of economic internationalisation and globalisation, has become internationalised and globalised.

The importance of political economy for the emergence of China's global businesses needs no emphasising. The historical insulation of the Chinese economy, the ongoing transition of its economic system and the nature of its political institutions, however, make the Chinese case appreciably different, if not unique, even among developing countries. Until 1978, the participation of China in the international economy, to say the least, was extremely limited. Foreign investment was strictly barred from China and there was little outward investment from China to speak about. Only in the 1980s did Chinese firms begin engaging in investment beyond Chinese borders. Even among developing countries, China is a newcomer in investing overseas. Further, in spite of obvious successes in reforming its domestic economic structure and in achieving economic growth after 1978, China remains a developing economy and a socialist one at that. How China's global businesses in the form of multinational corporations are initiated and sustained in a socialist developing economy and how transnational firms originating and located in China's institutional landscape and reform experience behave in the global economy are challenging questions to be investigated. Moreover, multinational corporations continue to be 'one of the most controversial economic and political institutions of our time' (Bergsten *et al.* 1978: vii). The fact that socialist China has changed from contesting to embracing this capitalist-dominated institution in China's economic development strategy has significant political as well as economic ramifications for the future of China. What does China's contestation and embracing of this institution inform us about China's acceptance of international economic norms? How does such an acceptance inform us about the internationalisation and globalisation of the Chinese state?

A systematic investigation of the emergence and growth of China's global businesses is therefore more than a study of how Chinese businesses are growing big, though that is part of the story. It provides important additional understanding of China's reform experience and of how China came around to internalise economic norms and to follow 'correct economic behaviour' in pursuing its economic development. The Chinese state, in this way, has been turned inside out, as it becomes increasingly internationalised. Such responses to internationalisation and globalisation by the Chinese state are a quiet revolution of its own kind.

An attempt at systematically tackling the challenging topic of China's emerging global businesses is an ambitious one. It is inevitably subject to some intentional limitations. First, the burden of this study examines the political economy for China's emerging global businesses at both the macro-policy level and the micro-institutional level of firms. These investigations are not seeking to address any economic theories related to multinational corporations in general and those from developing economies in particular. Second, this is not an attempt to establish any economic models of Chinese multinationals. In any case, whatever aggregate data are available now do not warrant such an enterprise yet. Third, this is not primarily a comparative study, though, wherever possible, comparison will be made between China and other developing countries and transitional economies. To the extent that this study is subject to these intentional limitations, its focus is not on evaluating economic performances, such as profitability of individual firms, nor is it on any particular impact that outward investment exerts on welfare and technological development in the home country. The analytical focus is on the political economy of government policy formulation and implementation that significantly foster the emergence and growth of China's multinational corporations and on the institutional story of how some individual Chinese firms transnationalise.

A short explanation about the definition of a key term used in this study, *multinational*, is due here before we elaborate the structure of this book. Throughout this study, we adopt John Dunning's 'threshold definition' of a multinational. In Dunning's words, 'a multinational or transnational enterprise is an enterprise that engages in foreign direct investment (FDI) and owns or controls value-adding activities in more than one country' (Dunning 1981, 1993).[6]

Dunning's definition is adopted here with one caveat. China's investment in Hong Kong (and Macao) has always been regarded as China's outward investment both before and after Hong Kong's handover to China in July 1997 and Macao's in 1999. On the other hand, investment generated from Hong Kong (and Macao) in China has always been without exception regarded as 'foreign investment'. Hong Kong (and Macao), although an integral part of China territorially now, is a distinctive economic entity in its own right.[7] There exist significant economic boundaries in every sense between Mainland China and Hong Kong (and Macao). The two economies are still following two different sets of economic principles. Business corporations in the two economies are still subject to widely different regulations. Moreover, the international business community is treating Hong Kong (and Macao) as a distinctive economic entity, carefully separating, for example, their investment in Hong Kong (and Macao) from that in China. It is warranted therefore that in defining China's multinationals, the phrase 'more than one country' in Dunning's definition is replaced with 'more than one economy'. That is to say that 'Chinese multinational' or 'China's multinational' is taken broadly to mean a Chinese enterprise that makes direct foreign investment and owns or controls value-adding activities in more than one *economy*.[8]

The rest of this book is structured as follows. The two chapters in Part I provide discussions of how and in what sense China's economic internationalisation has happened. Chapter 1 offers a critical interpretation of how economic reform constitutes part of, and is conducive to, the internationalisation of the Chinese state, while Chapter 2 presents empirical evidence of the internationalisation of the Chinese economy. The economic internationalisation of China in both senses provides the context within which China's global businesses were to emerge amidst the trials and tribulations of economic reforms. Part II studies the political economy for the emergence and rise of China's global businesses. In Chapter 3, we discuss how Revolutionary China came to accept multinational corporations as a useful institution to adopt in its developmental programme. We examine policy debates and the evolution of policy regimes with an outline of the emerging regulatory framework, or lack thereof. We also analyse what prompts and constrains China's home country policies towards its own global businesses. In Chapter 4, we situate the emergence of China's global businesses in its historical context and trace the processes and policies through which they are encouraged and promoted. We also profile China's outward investment and aspiring global businesses at the beginning of the twenty-first century.

Part III consists of three empirical and institutional investigations. They investigate in detail how three large Chinese state-owned enterprises (SOEs) have evolved into multinational corporations and what their practices in transnational operations teach us. Chapter 5 studies the China International Trust and Investment Corporation (CITIC) as a pioneer of China's global businesses. China Chemicals Import and Export Corporation (Sinochem) is examined in Chapter 6 as a typical example of how national trading companies go global. Chapter 7 discusses the successes and the collapse of Shougang as China's largest manufacturing multinational. In all three cases, discussions outline the process through which the company concerned goes multinational and highlight the important role of particularistic government policies in promoting the transnationalisation of these firms. They also analyse how firm-level initiatives interact with the dynamics of changing policies in starting and expanding international business, and how the firm concerned exploits, sometimes unscrupulously, the distortions in the Chinese economy in transition for its transnationalisation. The analytical account also examines individually and respectively structural problems, policy hindrances, state intervention and operational obstacles that each firm has encountered in going transnational and in reinventing themselves. The concluding chapter recaptures briefly our findings, reviews the unique context of the political economy of China's opening and economic reform, evaluates different pathways through which Chinese firms transnationalise, and teases out the implications of the emergence and growth of China's global businesses for the internationalisation and globalisation of the Chinese state.

Part I

Revisiting the Economic Internationalisation of China

Since 1978, economic reform in the People's Republic of China (PRC) has profoundly transformed Chinese society and the Chinese economy. Such a transformation was unforeseen at the launch of China's Second Revolution in the late 1970s, and its future as China's 'unfinished economic revolution', to quote Lardy, is still hard to predict. There are many facets of this economic transformation. The opening up of China to foreign trade and investment is a central element in the transformation and a vital part of China's economic awakening. Rapid restructuring of the planned economy and gradual liberalisation of markets constitute part of China's momentous transition to a market economy (see Naughton 1995, Chai 1997). Such a transition has been accompanied by China's increasing participation in, and integration with, the global economy. China's entry into the World Trade Organisation signals not the end of a challenge, but a new beginning of mutual accommodation between China and the global economy.

The two chapters in Part I revisit a particular facet of China's economic transformation, that is, the economic internationalisation of China. China's political isolation and economic insulation prior to 1978 make such investigations particularly relevant and indispensable for setting the context for our understanding of the rise of China's global businesses. Special circumstances pertaining to China in the international political and economic system before its reform and opening also predetermine that economic internationalisation in the Chinese context assumes a distinctive dimension. It does not only mean increased cross-border flows of goods, capital and services and reduction of transaction costs, as conventional wisdom goes. More importantly, perhaps, it means also that China has to learn about, to come to terms with and eventually to internalise generally accepted institutions, norms, standards and rules embedded in the global economy, in spite of its contestations from time to time. China's sustained efforts to enter the World Trade Organisation can be seen as part of this epic story.

Chapter 1 looks at this latter dimension of the economic internationalisation of China. From a critical perspective, economic reforms in China are responses by the Chinese state to first internationalised and now globalised production in the world economy. Radically restructuring economic institutions, principles and policies and adopting 'correct' economic behaviour are but part of that response. Such internalisation of economic norms and institutions amounts to the internationalisation of the Chinese state. In Chapter 2, we discuss another and more conventional dimension of China's economic internationalisation. We line up empirical evidence to demonstrate a dramatic increase in cross-border flows of trade, services and capital between China and the global economy since 1978. China's economic internationalisation thus understood constitutes the context for ensuing discussions of the political economy of China's emerging global businesses and for the institutional investigations we conduct of selected firms.

1
Economic Reform and the Internationalisation of the State

Two main factors combined, the unprecedented globalisation of the world economy and the momentous economic reforms in China, are most responsible for the fundamental economic transformations in China since 1978. These two factors, one endogenous and the other exogenous to the Chinese economy, have also facilitated the emergence and evolution of China's global businesses. This chapter explores a particular aspect of the endogenous factor and examines specifically the dynamics at the interface between Chinese economic reform and the internationalisation of the Chinese state. A number of questions need to be addressed here. Why does internationalisation exert such a strong influence on economic reform in China? How does economic reform promote the internationalisation of the Chinese state? In what sense can economic reform be seen as a process of China's internalising norms, institutions and accepted practices of the world economy? In what way can we interpret this internalisation as China's response to the accelerated globalisation of the world economy?

This chapter, therefore, seeks to do three things. The first section outlines contested definitions of the key concept – internationalisation. On the basis of that, the second section sketches the dynamic interactions between economic reform and internationalisation in China. In the third section, we argue that economic reform in China, even in its most internal manifestation, also aims at internalising norms and institutions prevailing in the global economy. Such internalisation constitutes an indispensable part of the internationalisation of the Chinese state.

Internationalisation: contested definitions

Internationalisation is a troubled and contested concept. The basic problem is that internationalisation, as observed by Milner and

Keohane (1996: 3), 'is a broad concept used by a variety of writers in a variety of ways'. Defining internationalisation is therefore more problematic than controversial. In a broader perspective, the internationalisation of ethnic conflicts and of environmental hazards and, therefore, protection, is now topical in world politics. The internationalisation of education is another subject of intense interest. In a narrower perspective – that of international political economy – the problem is not much mitigated (Hamilton-Hart 1999). In a study of Japan's internationalisation, Ippei Yamazawa simply defines the internationalisation of Japan's economic policy as 'adjusting to international harmony'. He also points out perceptively that

> the definition of 'internationalization' differs between political scientists in Britain and America on the one hand, and those in Japan on the other. The former perceive internationalization as *doing to others*, while the latter perceive it as *adjusting to others*.
>
> (Yamazawa 1992: 119)[1]

There are other definitions to consider. Peter Dicken (1992: 1) argues that internationalisation 'refers simply to the increasing geographical spread of economic activities across national boundaries'. Robert Cox (1987: 253) looks at the internationalising of the state as 'the global process whereby national policies and practices have been adjusted to the exigencies of the world economy of international production'. Milner and Keohane (1996: 4) define internationalisation as referring 'to the process generated by underlying shifts in transaction costs that produce observable flows of goods, services, and capital'. There is, too, a need to differentiate the internationalisation of a national economy and the internationalisation of a firm, which refers largely to 'a process in which the firms gradually increase their international involvement' (Johanson and Vahlne 1977: 23).[2]

It is clear that definitions of internationalisation in different political, economic, cultural and social contexts, and from national and international perspectives, differ sharply. There is no agreed definition. It is, nevertheless, also clear that internationalisation is a multifaceted phenomenon. Any analytically meaningful definition has to take this fact into consideration and has to be contextual.

The above observations suggest that at least three processes of internationalisation have been occurring, at different levels and in different contexts, at the same time, each reinforcing one another. First, the internationalisation of the *world economy* which, as defined by Milner and

Keohane, is chiefly seen in the observable increase of flows of goods, services and capital across national borders, facilitated by what Frieden and Rogowski call the 'exogenous easing of international exchange' (1996: 25). Second, the internationalising of the *state*, which refers, in the Coxian terms, to a process of the state's restructuring its policies and institutions as a response to internationalised production in the world economy. Harmonisation of economic policies and conformity to 'the norms of "correct" behaviour' are believed to be indispensable in this process of restructuring. Through this process, Cox argues, 'the nation state becomes part of a larger and more complex political structure that is the counterpart of international production' (Cox 1987: 253–9). And third, the internationalisation of *firms*. A firm is said to have been internationalised, according to Dunning, when 'first it organises and conducts multiple value-adding activities across national boundaries and second, it internalises the cross-border markets for the intermediate products arising from these activities' (Dunning 1993: 4).

For analytical purposes in this study, when we refer to internationalisation we consider three changing dimensions of the Chinese economy. First is the observable increase of flows of goods, services and capital across once-closed Chinese borders, which both leads to and reflects the progressive integration of China with the world economy. The ever-expanding foreign trade of China and the high level of foreign direct investment in China since the 1980s are prime examples of this dimension. Second, internationalisation refers to the restructuring of China's domestic policies and institutions so that the Chinese economy can be accommodated into the world economy. Economic reform in China in general, which aims to transform the Chinese economy from a planned to a market economy, is no more than a process of 'gearing the Chinese economy to international harmony', to paraphrase Yamazawa (Yamazawa 1992). More specifically, the reform of China's foreign trade system to make it compatible with accepted principles and practices, and that of China's foreign exchange system to make both its current account and its capital account convertible, can be seen as China's adjusting its policies and institutions to accommodate what Cox calls 'the exigencies of the world economy of international production' (Cox 1987: 253). Third, internationalisation means what we call 'do as others': that is, for China to follow the accepted economic practices of the market economies and to accept norms such as liberalisation and interdependence in seeking integration with the world economy. This kind of conformity is both externally enforced and internally induced. China's engagement with the global capital market since the launch of economic reforms to raise funds for its domestic economic development – from accepting and attracting foreign direct investment and exploring various innovative financial instruments, including issuing bonds, to the appearance of China's state-owned enterprises in the stock exchanges in Hong Kong, New York and London – is the most striking expression of this third dimension of China's economic internationalisation. The subject investigated in this study, China's outward investment and the rise of China's global businesses, is but one aspect of this dimension.

Defining economic internationalisation as we do provides a particularly useful and meaningful analytical tool for discussing the changes that have taken place in the Chinese economy. It bears reiterating that until relatively recently China was a historically self-sufficient, large continental economy closed to the international market and dominated by a philosophy of self-reliance. It is only since 1978 that the economic internationalisation of China has evolved from being an economic process to becoming a strategy committed to the development and modernisation of the economy. Essentially, the emergence and ever-strengthening of the first dimension of the internationalisation of the Chinese economy, that is, the dramatic increase in cross-border flows of goods, services and capital, is contingent upon the internationalisation of the Chinese state, which is closely related to the second and the third dimensions of the economic internationalisation of China discussed above. Such a definition, therefore, enables us to revisit and reinterpret the dynamic interaction between economic reform and the internationalisation of the Chinese state.

Economic reform and internationalisation

The pre-reform Chinese economy is often regarded as a model of autarky. The exclusion of China from the world economy was uncompromising before the 1970s. Not only was China excluded from all international economic organisations, but also Communist China was not allowed to use US dollars in settling its international accounts until the early 1970s. Its pursuit of self-reliance in its developmental strategy further closed China to the international economy. No foreign capital was allowed to participate in the Chinese economy, and information of the international market was prevented from interacting with Chinese production. While foreign investment was strictly forbidden and foreign borrowing kept at a minimum, China's limited imports and exports were the only tenuous link between China and the world economy

before 1978. The Chinese economy was among the least internationalised in the 1960s and also much of the 1970s.[3]

Susan Shirk has argued recently that the so-called 'communist coalition of heavy industries, inland provinces, the military and central
agencies of political and economic control' not only 'perpetuate[d]
policies of rapid industrialization and autarky [of China]', but also 'sustained China's self-isolation and blocked' China's opening (Shirk 1996:
205–6). Shirk's main publications in the last few years have employed
an institutionalist approach to explaining how international economic
forces helped create a reformist coalition in the Chinese political landscape for the political and economic successes of the reform programme.
While there are definite merits in Shirk's approach and argument,
it is also painfully noticeable that she has done little to solve the puzzle
of how international political and economic conditions in the 1950s
and the 1960s shaped and sustained the 'communist coalition' in
China in the first place (Shirk 1993, 1994, 1996). This leaves open the
question as to how the changing international political and economic
system in the late 1970s, interacting with the dynamics of China's
domestic politics, made the unwinding of the 'communist coalition'
possible and inevitable. The central questions here are whether the
mutual engagement of China and the world economy as seen in the
1980s was possible, and whether Deng Xiaoping, as a political entrepreneur, could successfully mobilise institutional support for his innovative policies in 1978, had the hostile international environment that
China had been faced with until at least the early 1970s – diplomatic
isolation and virtual exclusion from the world economy – not been
mediated by a series of historical events earlier in the 1970s. Among
these were the recognition of the international legitimacy of the
People's Republic of China, signalled by its admission into the United
Nations in 1971, the Sino-American rapprochement in 1972, and the
normalisation of the diplomatic relations of the PRC with dominant
economic actors, particularly the United States, at the end of 1978.[4]

It should also be noted that China's economic reforms were launched
at a time when the confluence of a number of significant changes in
the world economy was radically transforming the international economic system. Three such changes are important in this discussion.
First, the internationalisation of the world economy was gathering
momentum in the 1970s and accelerated in the 1980s. Cross-border
trade flows, which had already outpaced the growth of global GDP
after World War II, grew at accelerated rates, not only among industrialised economies but also between industrialising and industrialised

economies. Two representative trade statistics presented by Milner and Keohane can be used as examples. Exports of manufactures by six newly industrialising countries (NICs) grew from 1.9 per cent of the world total in 1964–65 to 8.7 per cent in 1983.[5] Between 1964 and 1985, the Organisation for Economic Co-operation and Development (OECD) countries' imports from the NICs 'grew at an average annual rate of 23.6 percent'. Cross-border flows of capital tell a similar but even more striking story. Capital flows to industrialised economies more than quadrupled from the mid-1970s to the mid-1980s – from an annual average of $99 billion in 1975–77 to $463 billion in 1985–89 – while capital flows to developing economies more than doubled in the same period, from $52 billion in 1975–77 to $110 billion in 1985–89 (Milner and Keohane 1996: 11–13).

Second, the 1970s also saw 'the "deindustrialization" of advanced capitalist countries and the shift of production to Third World locations' (Cox 1987: 253) which was characterised by the large-scale transfer of labour-intensive, and later technology-intensive, industries to developing economies. Such a transfer of industries was invariably accompanied by capital flows into the developing countries. In the Asia-Pacific region, the 'spread of industrialization in East Asia' was well under way because of this very process (Vogel 1991). If anything, 'deindustrialization' also perhaps unwittingly promoted the internationalisation of the world economy. Here is an irony. If indeed, as argued by Shirk and many others, the internationalisation of the world economy increased the opportunity cost for China, the dual process of deindustrialisation within the confines of industrialised countries, and the spread of industrialisation beyond, offered rare opportunities for China's ambitious programme of modernisation.

Third, by the end of the 1970s, 'The habit of policy harmonization [among major advanced capitalist countries] had been institutionalized during the two preceding decades and was, if anything, reinforced in the absence of clear norms [with the collapse of the Bretton Woods system].' At the same time, the interstate consensus formation among the leading industrialised economies had all but been completed in 'defining the ideological basis of consensus, the principles and goals within which policies are framed', and 'the norms of "correct" behavior'. Through the power structure in international politics and international production, such consensus was turned into a global consensus, to which national policies and practice of all participating members in the world economy had to be adjusted to comply (Cox 1987: 254–9). China's economic reforms were launched, therefore, at a time when there were already embedded norms, procedures and institutions in the world economy. Accordingly, China's acceptance and contestation of these norms, procedures and institutions constitute part of the experience of China's economic internationalisation.

The broad international context discussed above, in addition to the domestic dynamics of Chinese politics, provides incentives for, and also conditions the content and the extent of, China's economic reform. The opening up of China does not mean knocking down simple barriers. It marks the beginning of a learning and socialisation process for China. It means that China has also to confront how a capitalist world hegemony turns the Chinese state inside out. Inevitably, restructuring national policies and institutions and internalising norms and standards to accommodate the exigencies of the world economy become an inevitable process, in order that China can be incorporated. That is to say that to pursue economic reform, China has to take up a dual challenge: to open up the economy to the trade and investment of the world economy (which has proved to be the easier challenge); and to socialise China into the capitalist-dominated international economy. This latter challenge, as an indispensable component of the Chinese reform package, meant that China would have to internalise the commonly accepted norms and institutions of the world economy. It is such internalisation that leads to the total transformation (even though with 'Chinese characteristics') of the ethics and principles as well as the practices in the economic development of China.

There is little dispute that the internationalisation of the Chinese economy started with the launch of economic reform in China in 1978. No matter how limited that internationalisation looks today, the nature of the Chinese economy at the turn of the twenty-first century is certainly a far cry from that of 1978. The dramatic increase in the flow of goods, services and capital across Chinese borders in the past twenty years is not only observable, but also quantifiable. No other structural reforms have done more than those of the foreign trade system in increasing the cross-border flows of goods and services by reducing the transaction costs. The decentralisation of trade authorities and decision-making from as early as 1979 led to reforms of import and export regimes in the mid-1980s. The reduction of import tariffs and the fading away of the import and export plans in the late 1980s were accompanied by macro-economic reforms such as the devaluation of the Renminbi (RMB), the reform of the foreign exchange retention system and the start of financial reforms (Lardy 1992, 1998). The penultimate example of foreign trade system reform is the promulgation of the first ever Foreign Trade Law of China in 1994. At the same time, a large body of laws and by-laws related to foreign direct investment in China have been promulgated and implemented.

Engagement with international capital and service markets is often regarded as a move towards a higher level of the internationalisation of an economy. One definitive expression of a deeper and broader inter-nationalisation of the Chinese economy is, therefore, China's increas-ingly intensive engagement with global capital. This is not only to be seen in increasing foreign investment in China. Borrowings in the form of intergovernmental loans, and from international economic organi-sations such as the World Bank, the International Monetary Fund (IMF) and the Asian Development Bank (ADB), are not only widely accepted but eagerly cultivated by both the Chinese government and Chinese firms. So, too, are such financial instruments as syndicated loans from commercial banks and the issuing of bonds on international capital markets. It is also largely owing to firm-level initiatives, combined with government approval and undertakings, that a number of China's state-owned enterprises are now floated on stock exchanges from Hong Kong to Sydney, and from New York to London. China began to export capital as early as the 1980s, which led to the emergence of Chinese multina-tional corporations. China's engineering companies have also become a significant force to be reckoned with in the international engineering and labour service markets. At the close of the twentieth century, they were constructing a hydro-electric power plant in Albania, drilling an oilfield in Sudan and building a textile mill in Syria.

China's participation in global and regional economic organisations is also a significant aspect of China's economic internationalisation. China's membership in the World Bank and the IMF since 1980, and its membership in regional economic organisations such as the ADB and Asia-Pacific Economic Cooperation (APEC), ensures that it learns about, and shares in, those common economic institutions. Of more impor-tance is China's participation in the consensus formation taking place at these forums and organisations. China's application to join the World Trade Organisation, and the concessions it is prepared to make so as to meet the demands by other member states for economic liberalisation in line with WTO principles, reflects an enforced conformity and high-lights the direction of Chinese economic internationalisation.

The impact that internationalisation has exerted on China's economic reforms, as Shirk rightly noted (1996: 206), is much more notable as regards making those reforms successful than as regards the decision to launch them. In that sense, internationalisation and economic reform mutually reinforce and enrich each other. It is the economic reforms that make the internationalisation of the Chinese economy possible. Internationalisation, in its turn, makes economic reform both politically and economically successful. In so doing, internationalisation sustains economic reform by ensuring its success. The broadening and deepening of China's economic reform can be seen as both the cause and effect of the internationalisation of the Chinese economy.

Internalisation and the internationalisation of the state

The internationalisation of the Chinese economy is unmistakable. It would be foolhardy to assume, however, that economic internationalisation is *only* related to China's 'international opening' (Womack and Zhou 1994: 145–9). Surely, what can be regarded as the internal facet of economic reform is *not* usually associated with China's economic internationalisation. Agricultural, industrial and urban reforms are normally seen as a series of structural reforms of the Chinese economy in the domestic context. On the face of it, the decentralisation of economic decisions from Beijing to provincial capitals and from ministries to enterprises does not seem to be directly related to internationalisation. By the same token, how could reform of state-owned enterprises and reform of China's domestic tax system be interpreted as a process of internationalisation? It does need a stretch of imagination to see the household responsibility system implemented in rural China as having a significant bearing on China's economic internationalisation.

Yet very few would disagree that the principles and practices prevalent in the Chinese economy in 1978 were incompatible with the norms of good economic behaviour established and accepted in the global economy. Most of them were actually in direct conflict with those norms. Writing in 1999, Rosen poignantly reminded us that 'the dominant legal institutions [in the PRC] in 1977 were even less compatible with Western commercial norms than those that sprouted up during the Republican period (1912–1949)' (Rosen 1999: 200). Further, few would dispute that economic reform in China in general has aimed at, and has achieved, gradual economic liberalisation and marketisation so that the Chinese economy can 'grow out of the plan' (Naughton 1995). By 1993, only 5 per cent of total industrial output was subject to mandatory planning. Price control, on the other hand, was largely dismantled. It was estimated that goods subject to price control in 1993 were 5 per cent, 10 per cent and 15 per cent for retail goods, agricultural goods and means of production respectively (Bell *et al.* 1993). The banking system reforms, on the other hand, were implemented to transform the People's Bank of China (PBOC) into the functioning central bank and to realise the commercialisation of state-owned banks. For that purpose, the Central Bank Law was promulgated in 1995 (Lardy 1998). Attempts have also been made by the Chinese government to introduce greater transparency of the economy, gradual deregulation and freer market access. Even the accounting system has been in a process of total overhaul from the early 1990s to bring it into line with international standards.

From this perspective, the restructuring of China's domestic economy can be seen as a process of internalising policies, norms and institutions already embedded in the global economy. It should also be seen as the response of the Chinese state to the globalisation of the world economy. Such internalisation, however, was by no means a smooth process, and is lengthy. Ling noted a 'pro-internationalizing' shift in China's developmental discourse as early as in the mid-1980s, as the discourse moved from the Marxian economic categories to neo-classical economics (Ling 1996: 11–12). In the late 1980s and the early 1990s, how to make the Chinese economic system compatible with the world economy (*yu shijie jingji jiegui*) in principle as well as in practice was a central question in the intellectual and policy discourses in China about economic reform. However, the ideological obstacle was formidable. Deng allegedly had to go out of his way in saying that 'market economy is not a monopoly of the capitalist system' in order to combat the ideological resistance to acceptance of the market. For many, political reform in China as 'greater internal adaptations', as alluded to by Ling, is essential to facilitate the needs of China's internationalisation (Ling 1996: 9). It was not until 1992 that the Chinese Communist Party (CCP) formally embraced the view that the market system was *not* necessarily incompatible with the ideals of socialism. To establish a 'socialist market economy' was proclaimed to be the ultimate goal of China's economic reforms.

Economic reform, even in its most internal manifestation, has therefore fundamentally changed the principles and practices of the Chinese economy. Moreover, such changes have reshaped specific internal structures in China and created institutional arrangements conducive and complementary to China's economic internationalisation. Domestic economic reforms can equally be regarded as no other than China's adaptations to harmonising economic policies and practices with those widely practised in the global economy, and to learning to adopt general norms of 'correct' economic behaviour. In the Coxian perspective, this is unmistakably internationalisation, the internationalisation of the state. Such conformity, it must be noted, is also partially enforced externally, as Cox argues:

the ideological and political power of global hegemony restricted the forms of state that were tolerated within this world order. A combination of rewards and penalties – access to credit for compatible and political destabilization of incompatible national regimes – enforced conformity.

(Cox 1987: 266)

The process of internalising the basic institutions and principles common to the global economy is of special importance to China, a recent pariah and a revolutionary power in international society. Indeed, if we take a step back to 1978, the pre-reform Chinese economy was based on totally different principles – class struggle and self-reliance – and run by radically different practices from a mandatory plan to arbitrarily set prices. It is small wonder that the acceptance at the end of 1978 of economic development as a primary goal of the Party's work was regarded as an important breakthrough. A prolonged battle has to be waged to overcome the ideological bias, while the internalisation process has been selectively and cautiously carried out with the evolution of reform. The transformation of China since 1978 has seen a gradual convergence between its economy and the world economy, in operating principles, in general norms of acceptable behaviour and in institutional arrangements. China's convergence and conformity are no doubt often reluctant and externally enforced, but they are also sometimes voluntary and enthusiastically embraced. Internalisation in this sense is an indispensable, but also more revolutionary, constituent of China's economic transition since it is an important process for the internationalisation of the Chinese state.

Summary

Economic reform not only makes the internationalisation of the Chinese economy possible and successful. It constitutes part of the internationalisation of the Chinese state, since it represents no less than the restructuring of China's domestic policies and institutions so that the country can accommodate itself to the needs of being incorporated into the global economy. The Chinese experience of internalising norms and institutions embedded in the global economy is also a process of adapting China to fundamentally different ethics, principles and rules in economic development. China's internationalisation experience is arguably unique against the background of its pre-1978 exclusion and isolation from the world economy. The changes that economic reform has brought about are revolutionary because they are transforming China into an internationalised state.

2
The Internationalisation of the Chinese Economy: Empirical Evidence

As discussed in the last chapter, the internationalisation of the Chinese state has been brought about by economic reforms in China. This process of transformation is ongoing and intensifying with China's membership in the World Trade Organisation. At a more tangible level, it is often argued that China has been increasingly integrated into the global economy since the launch of economic reforms (World Bank 1997a, Lardy 2002). Controversies do remain as to how deep or shallow China's integration has been and the nature of China's current trade regimes and economic system (Shirk 1994, Lardy 1998, Naughton 2000). China's commitment to embracing accelerated globalisation is often subject to question and contending interpretations.[1] Interestingly, these controversies confirm, rather than challenge, a simple fact: that is, China's economic integration into the global economy is unprecedented.

From the perspective of this study, underlying China's unprecedented integration is the unparalleled internationalisation of the Chinese economy. It is imperative therefore in this chapter to conduct a brief investigation of how in quantifiable terms the Chinese economy has been rapidly and inexorably internationalised since economic reforms started in 1978. The investigative focus is the dramatic increase of cross-border flows of goods, services and capital in China in the context of the acceleration of globalisation as seen in the widening and intensifying of global linkages in trade, investment and finance. For analytical convenience, we have identified seven areas for discussions below. Together, they present rich evidence to illustrate the extent as well as the limits of China's economic internationalisation.

Growth of foreign trade

Commodity import and export trade is conventionally regarded as the most important indicator of a country's participation in the international division of labour and the internationalisation of production and specialisation. The expansion of China's commodity trade since 1978 has been at a dramatic, and sometimes explosive, rate (see Figure 2.1). In 1978, China's total foreign trade amounted to only $20.64 billion with its exports at $9.75 billion and its imports at $10.89 billion. In 2001, they were respectively $509.77 billion, $266.15 billion and $243.62 billion.[2] From 1992 to 1998, the average annual growth was 15.1 per cent, over 6 per cent higher than China's GDP growth, and 8 per cent higher than the growth rate of world trade in the same period (Shi 1999). In the late 1990s, China overtook Korea, Taiwan and Hong Kong in terms of annual trade volumes. The World Trade Organisation reports that in 2000, China was the seventh largest trading country in the world (WTO 2002: 21, Lardy 2002: 4).[3]

Other indicators are equally significant in illustrating China's remarkable trade growth. China's share in the world trade total also grew from 0.7 per cent in 1977 to 1.8 per cent in 1990, 2.77 per cent in 1996 and 3.7 per cent in 2000[4] (Lardy 2002: 178, WTO 2001: 37). In 2001, China

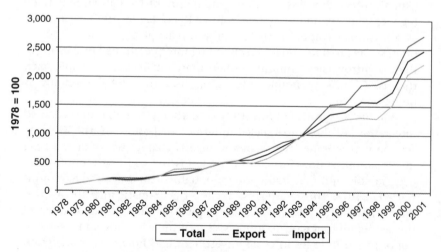

Figure 2.1   The growth of China's foreign trade, 1978–2001

Sources: State Statistics Bureau (various years),
www.moftec.gov.com.cn/moftec_cn/tjsj/jcktj.

accounted for 3.9 per cent of exports and 3.4 per cent of imports of the world total (WTO 2002: 21). There has been also a sharp increase in the ratio of China's trade to its GDP. A World Bank report in 1997 puts this in an interesting historical perspective. 'In 1975–79 China's international trade was 10 percent of GDP, the lowest among 120 countries studied. By 1990–94 this ratio has risen to 36 percent, placing China in the top third' (World Bank 1997a: 2).[5] The structural change in China's export composition is, on the other hand, an indicator of China's intensified participation in the global production networks (see Figure 2.2).

Foreign direct investment

A direct and close correlation exists between the rapid growth of China's manufacturing exports and foreign direct investment flows into China. China's manufactured exports, as Figure 2.2 shows, increased sharply in the 1990s. So has FDI in China (see Figures 2.3 and 2.4). Not surprisingly, exports by foreign-funded enterprises have captured an increasingly larger share of China's total exports. In 1992, they accounted for only 20.4 per cent of the total at $17.36 billion.[6] In 1999, they exported a total of $88.63 billion and their share in China's total exports increased to 45.47 per cent (*Beijing Review*, 6 March 2000: 27).[7] Nicholas

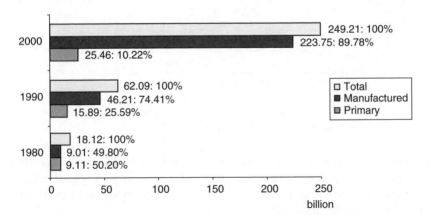

Figure 2.2 Composition of China's exports, 1980, 1990 and 2000

Sources: *State Statistics Bureau* (various years), Shi (1999), www.moftec.gov.com.cn.

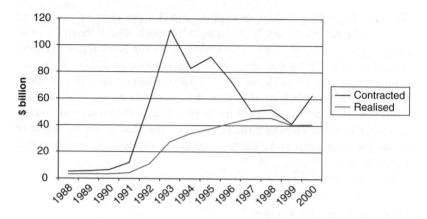

Figure 2.3   FDI flow into China, 1988–2000

Sources: State Statistics Bureau (various years) and *International Monetary Fund* (various years).

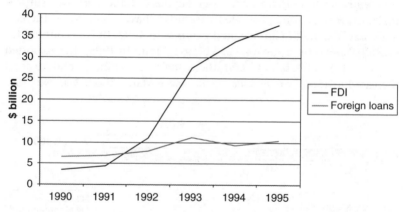

Figure 2.4   FDI and foreign loans used by China, 1990–95

Sources: State Statistics Bureau (1991–1996) and MOFTEC (1997).

Lardy put this into a more illustrative picture when he noted that 'By 2000 foreign-invested firms, which accounted for only one eighth of all manufacturing output, were responsible for almost one-half of all of China's exports' (Lardy 2002: 6, 179).[8]

China's opening up to FDI is arguably the most fascinating aspect of China's economic reforms. There are historical reasons for this. Before 1949, China had been one of the major destinations for foreign direct investment from, among others, the British, the Americans and the Japanese. From 1949 to 1979, China was virtually closed to any foreign direct investment. However, it was not until the 1990s, more than a decade after China's opening up, that foreign direct investment in China really took off.

A recent World Bank study puts China's FDI inflow in the 1990s into an interesting comparative perspective. China was the largest recipient of FDI amongst the developing countries, attracting around 40 per cent of total FDI flows to those countries.[9] While before 1979, FDI to China was 'virtually non-existent', it rose to 3.5 per cent of China's GDP in 1990–94, the ninth highest ratio among the 120 countries surveyed by the World Bank. In 1993–95, FDI inflow increased to 6.0–6.5 per cent of GDP, which is, the World Bank believed, likely to be exceptional. The World Bank further estimated that for the first five years of the 1990s, 'FDI accounted for 25 percent of domestic investment, 13 percent of industrial output, 31 percent of exports, 11 percent of tax revenue [of China]' (World Bank 1997a: 8, 19–21). In 1997, the ratio of FDI (stocks)/GDP reached 23.5 per cent (UNCTAD 2000: 521), similar to the ratio of export/GDP.[10]

By the end of 2000, the accumulated total of FDI in China was around $623.76 billion in contract value and $346.64 billion in realised value (*China Statistical Yearbook* 2001: 602).[11] The significant participation of international capital in China's economic transformation is clearly reflected in Table 2.1.

Table 2.1 Share of foreign-funded enterprises in China's exports, industrial output and investment in fixed assets, 1990–99 (percentage)

	Exports	Industrial output	Investment in fixed assets*
1990	12.58	2.28	N/A
1991	16.75	5.29	4.15
1992	20.44	7.09	7.51
1993	27.51	9.15	12.13
1994	28.69	11.26	17.08
1995	31.51	14.31	15.65
1996	40.71	15.14	15.10
1997	41.00	18.57	14.79
1998	44.06	24.00	13.23
1999	45.47	27.75	11.17

* Calculated on the basis of realised FDI.
Source: www.moftec.gov.cn/moftec_cn/tjsi/wztj.

Loans from foreign governments and international organisations

FDI, if the most notable, is but one form of cross-border capital flow into China. Loans that China has received from foreign governments and international organisations constitute another.

In its national economic development strategy before 1978, China prudently and purposely avoided any long-term indebtedness to any foreign countries. The only exception was the Soviet offers of credits in the 1950s which China did not pay off until 1964. In the 1970s, China occasionally used short-term commercial credits and loans, all from non-communist countries, and deferred payments to facilitate the flow of imports of capital goods and industrial supplies into China (Barnett 1981: 225–6).[12] As a matter of principle, however, China did not accept any intergovernmental loans, or any loans from international organisations. There was a near total insulation of China from international finance.

Fundamental changes took place in 1978 when the Chinese government submitted an application to the United Nations Development Programme (UNDP) for technical assistance, the first ever application by that government for aid from an international organisation. In 1979, the government officially announced that China was 'ready to accept loans from all friendly countries and financial organisations provided they do not affect China's sovereign rights'. In April 1980, an official agreement between the Chinese and Japanese governments was signed in Beijing, whereby the Japanese government was to provide a loan of 50 billion yen to China in 1979 alone. This was the first intergovernmental loan that the PRC had ever received from a capitalist country.

From 1979 to 1985, the Chinese government signed a series of loan agreements with eight countries for a sum total of $4.862 billion, around 25 per cent of China's total borrowing of the period. By 1985, $3.403 billion of this total had actually been used (Shi Lin *et al.* 1989: 346–53). The importance of intergovernmental loans to China's capital inflow in the initial period of China's reforms can be illustrated by a simple comparison. By 1985, the accumulated total of realised FDI in China was only $4.72 billion (*China Statistical Yearbook* 1997: 605), not much larger than the intergovernmental loans China received and used. In 1999, however, China used only $3.32 billion intergovernmental loans, whereas the FDI realised was $40.32 billion (*China Statistical Yearbook* 2001: 602–3).

Table 2.2 Loans from foreign governments and international organisations to China, 1992–96 (in $ billion)

	Intergovernmental		International organisation	
	Loans[a]	Loans[b]	Loans[a]	Loans[b]
1992	4.39	1.50	2.17	1.58
1993	2.89	2.65	3.81	2.14
1994	1.25	3.38	4.41	3.30
1995	4.78	3.47	3.68	1.99
1996	4.20	2.49	1.68	2.52

[a] Contracted, MOFTEC statistics.
[b] Utilised, PBOC capital account balance statistics.
Sources: *China Statistical Yearbook* (1994: 550, 1996: 620, 1997: 627).

China's membership in global and regional international economic organisations opened more channels for China to contract loans internationally. China obtained its membership in two important global economic organisations in 1980, namely, the IMF and the World Bank. The World Bank group has since played an important role in channelling concessionary loans into China. In June 1981, the World Bank and the International Development Association (IDA) together provided $200 million for their first project in China: the University Development Project. From 1981 to 1988, a total of $7.4 billion in loans and credits was committed by the World Bank group to China, with the IDA providing an average of $600 million 'soft loans' annually. The World Bank quickly became the second largest lender to China, after the Japanese government, in the 1980s. Since 1992, China has been the largest borrower of investment financing from the World Bank. As of 30 June 2001, the cumulative lending of the World Bank group to China amounted to $35.52 billion, of which $25.57 billion is from the World Bank, and $9.95 billion from the IDA (*World Bank Annual Report*, 2001: 127).[13] Since China became a member of the Asian Development Bank (ADB) in 1986, it has received by the end of 2001 91 loans totaling $6.9 billion from the ADB (*Asian Development Bank Annual Report*, 2001: 61–3). It is particularly worth noting that before FDI really took off in the early 1990s, these capital inflows constituted the bulk of cross-border capital flows into China.

Commercial borrowings

Commercial borrowings and private flows of capital into China further reflect the intensified integration of China into the world economy. China has used, and diligently cultivated, commercial instruments for borrowing since the 1980s. Ironically, its insulation from the international capital markets before the end of the 1970s, which rendered it virtually debt-free, gained China by default ready access to international capital markets.[14] According to the OECD, China's borrowing from commercial banks from 1983 to 1990 was $19.291 billion, as China's total borrowing went up from $1.137 billion to $24.082 billion in the same period (OECD 1992: 109). The World Bank, on the other hand, claimed that China accounted for 10 per cent of total syndicated loans to developing countries in 1990–95. In 1996 alone, China borrowed $12 billion from commercial banks (World Bank 1997a: 24–5).

Most noteworthy, however, is the cultivation by Chinese banks and financial organisations of such instruments as the issuing of bonds on the international capital markets to raise funds. Bond issuing on international capital markets was repudiated in China after 1949. However, in 1982, China reappeared on the international bond market when the China International Trust and Investment Corporation issued a batch of 10 billion yen bonds in Tokyo. From 1982 to the end of 1985, a total of twelve issues were made by Chinese institutions on the Japanese, Hong Kong and West German markets (Morrison 1986: 18–20). According to IMF statistics, China borrowed $44.5 million through international bond issues in 1982, $20.5 million in 1983, $81.7 million in 1984, and $959.9 million in 1985. In the first three quarters of 1986, China issued international bonds worth $1,307.8 million (Watson *et al.* 1986: 50). In 1986 and 1987, China became the most significant borrower among the developing countries through bond issues on international capital markets (see Table 2.3). In 1986, China issued, in value terms, 32.3 per cent of the total bonds issued by developing countries. In 1987, the percentage was 38.1 per cent (Goldstein *et al.* 1992: 75). From 1982 to June 1989, China issued altogether more than forty batches of international bonds.

The significance of China's activity on the international bond market lies not in the number of batches it had issued, nor in the amount it had raised, which is after all quite small in comparison to other forms of capital inflow. Given China's inexperience and its political constraints at the time, the significance lies rather in China's rapid entry

Table 2.3 International bond issues by selected developing countries, 1985–90 (in $ million)

	1985	1986	1987	1988	1989	1990
China	972.8	1,362.1	1,415.2	911.6	150.4	–
India	417.8	323.2	377.0	714.6	668.3	523.0
Indonesia	–	300.0	50.0	221.1	175.0	825.0
Korea	1,730.9	783.0	332.3	130.0	328.2	1,515.4
Thailand	861.7	50.0	–	261.0	231.7	50.0
Algeria	500.0	125.6	49.2	433.3	159.0	–
Total*	8,113.3	4,210.3	3,711.4	6,436.7	5,810.7	6,609.5

* Total international bond issues by all developing countries and regions.
Sources: Goldstein *et al.* (1992: 75), International Monetary Fund (1991: 65).

Table 2.4 China's international bond issues, 1991–94 (in $ million)

1991	1992	1993	1994	Total
115	1,359	3,047	4,077	8,598

Source: Folkerts-Landau and Ito (1995: 42).

and in its readiness and willingness to explore options and instruments to raise capital on international financial markets.

China disappeared from the international bond market after mid-1989, partly as a result of the international sanctions imposed on China in the wake of its military crackdown in Beijing in June 1989. It returned to the international bond markets only in 1991, but with a vengeance (*Beijing Review*, 5–11 August 1991: 29).[15] In 1993, the total amount of capital raised by China through seventeen issues of bonds reached $2.3 billion (*South China Morning Post*, 2 February 1994).

China also became active as a sovereign borrower. China first made such an appearance tentatively in 1987 on the West German market, when it issued 300 million Deutschmark five-year bonds. In September 1993, China returned to the Eurobond market as a sovereign borrower by issuing 30 billion Yen bonds (*China Daily*, 13 September 1993). In October 1993, China became the first sovereign borrower on the fledgling market for Dragon bonds by launching a $300 million issue in Hong Kong (*China Daily*, 16 October 1993). In 1994, the Chinese government appeared on the American and the Japanese markets as a

Table 2.5 China's issues of sovereign bonds, 1987–97

Time of issue	Amount	Type	Maturity
Oct. 1987	300 million Deutschmarks	Deutschmark bond	5 years
Sept. 1993	30 billion Japanese yen	Euro–yen bond	5 years
Oct. 1993	300 million US dollars	Dragon bond	10 years
Feb. 1994	1 billion US dollars	Global bond	10 years
July 1994	30 billion yen	Samurai bond	5 years
	30 billion yen	Samurai bond	10 years
Dec. 1995	30 billion yen	Samurai bond	7 years
	10 billion yen	Samurai bond	20 years
Jan. 1996	300 million US dollars	Yankee bond	7 years
	100 million US dollars	Yankee bond	100 years
July 1996	700 million US dollars	Global bond	5 years
	300 million US dollars	Global bond	10 years
June 1997	500 million Deutschmarks	Deutschmark bond	5 years

Source: Li Jianguo (1997: 15).

sovereign borrower for the first time. In February, it placed its first global bonds offering in New York worth $1 billion (*Xinhua*, 3 February 1994). In July, the government issued two lots of Samurai bonds in Tokyo, with a total value of 60 billion yen (*China Daily*, 8 July 1994).

From September 1993 to June 1997, the Chinese government issued twelve batches of sovereign bonds, and raised a total of just under $4 billion (see Table 2.5) and tested the bonds markets worldwide, as a sovereign borrower, including Dragon bonds in Hong Kong, Yankee bonds in the United States, Samurai bonds in Japan, Japanese Yen bonds in Europe and global bonds (*China Daily*, 26 January 1997). In 1996, however, China only accounted for 5 per cent of international bond flows to developing countries (World Bank 1997a: 25). According to the *China Daily*, by the end of April 1997, China had placed altogether 110 batches of bonds on international capital markets and raised a total of $18.7 billion (7 May 1997).[16] The Bank of China (BOC) alone floated 23 international bonds and raised over $6 billion (EIU 1997: 39–40). The Asian financial crisis of 1997–98 greatly affected the international bond market, which remained subdued in 1999 (Mathieson and Schinasi, 2000: 51). China's interest in the international bond market seems to be also subdued in the same period. In 1999, for example, China raised only $0.8 billion through external bonds (*China Statistical Yearbook*, 2001: 603).

Other portfolio inflows

The above discussions suggest that while China reaches out for capital on global markets, international capital is keen to embrace China as an emerging market. If an intensive two-way engagement between China and international capital has taken place, we need to look at other portfolio capital flows into China. Large portfolio flows into developing countries are a new phenomenon of the 1990s. If they are still concentrated on a score of countries, their growth is rapid and remarkable. In the case of China, the World Bank notes in 1997 that 'Such flows were negligible in 1980–84, rose to around 0.5 percent of GDP in 1986–88, and collapsed in 1989 because of political tensions. Flows revived modestly in the 1990s (to 0.7–0.9 percent of GDP in 1993–94) before slipping back in 1995 and 1996.' It further notes that China attracted 10 per cent of international equity flows to developing countries (World Bank 1997a: 8, 21).

The emergence of China's securities markets and the government's decision to float selected state-owned enterprises on international stock exchanges, both in the 1990s, provided new and additional channels through which international capital flowed into China. International equity flows in these forms are different from, but complementary to, bond issues as portfolio inflows. The two stock exchanges in China, the Shanghai Stock Exchange and the Shenzhen Stock Exchange, came into full operation in 1990 and 1991 respectively. In 1992, both began to offer the so-called B-shares specifically targeted at international equity investors.[17] By the end of 1993, the capitalisation of B-shares in the two stock exchanges had already reached around $2.5 billion. An increasing number of foreign brokers were granted licences to trade in both stock exchanges, but by the beginning of 1996 there were altogether only 66 B-shares listed in Shanghai and Shenzhen (Lees and Liaw 1996: 65–70).

China's international equity placement was first tried in 1993 when the Chinese governments decided to float nine state-owned enterprises on the Hong Kong Stock Exchange (Liu Hongru *et al.* 1998).[18] According to the IMF, from 1990 to 1994, Asian companies' international placements amounted to nearly $25 billion. The leading issuers were Chinese companies which accounted for more than 20 per cent at $5.6 billion. They were followed by Indian companies at $3.6 billion, and Hong Kong and Indonesian companies at about $3 billion each (Folkerts-Landau *et al.* 1995: 38).[19] According to a Chinese researcher, by the end of 1996, 25 Chinese state-owned enterprises had been floated on international stock markets, 23 in Hong Kong and two in New York.[20] The total of H-shares and N-shares[21] raised more than HK$36.76 billion ($4.77 billion), more than China's actual use of foreign capital in 1991, which was $4.4 billion (Liu Yan 1997: 29–30).[22] It should not be surprising that international capital inflow into China in the 1990s, led by FDI, increased more than fivefold (World Bank 1997a: 21).

In October 1997, the floating of China Telecom (HK) in Hong Kong, the largest IPO (initial public offer) of a Chinese company on the Hong Kong Stock Exchange, raised $4.2 billion (*Renmin Ribao*, 2 December 1997). Even during the Asian financial crisis in 1998, two new China issues were placed on the Hong Kong market (EIU 1999: 35). It is reported in the *Financial Times* (5 February 1999) that China had raised about $13 billion by the end of 1998 through its international equity placement, although 'China's international issues have suffered from a lack of liquidity and poor standards of disclosure'.[23] In 2000, the floating of China Mobile (HK), PetroChina, Unicom and Sinopec in both Hong Kong and New York raised more than $15 billion through equity sales (Lardy 2002: 7).

The limited opening of China's securities market to foreign investors and a steady stream of listings of state-owned enterprises on international stock exchanges have undoubtedly complemented FDI inflows. More importantly, they have become part of China's strategy to seek the participation of international capital in China's economic development and modernisation from diversified channels.

Capital outflows

International capital flow has not been just a one-way traffic into China in its reform decades.[24] Less well-known is China's capital outflow. In 1993, it was reported that 'Since its open-door economic policy in 1979, outflows of FDI [from China] have been constantly increasing; cumulative flows during 1982–1991 accounted for 15 percent of outflows from developing countries during this period' (UNTCMD 1993: 52). The World Bank believed that in 1995, China accounted for '2 per cent of total export of capital by all economies in the year and was the seventh largest capital exporter of the world' (World Bank 1997a: 26). Largely because of the opaque nature of information on these flows, the full story of China's capital outflows has so far never been told, and is likely to be unknowable.

A better indicator, but not always reliable, of China's capital outflow, is the balance of payment statistics that the Chinese government issues

Table 2.6 Long-term capital outflows from China, 1990–96 (in $ billion)

	1990	1991	1992	1993	1994	1995	1996
Long-term outflow	5.157	5.188	26.986	22.943	25.03	27.82	28.17
FDI from China	0.83	0.913	4.0	4.4	2.0	2.0	2.11
Purchase of foreign bonds and stocks	0.241	0.33	0.45	0.597	0.38	0.079	0.628
Omissions and errors	−3.131	−6.792	8.274	−9.804	−9.774	−17.81	−15.56

Sources: State Statistics Bureau (1995: 578–9, 1996: 620–1, 1997: 627–8).

every year in the *China Statistical Yearbook*. Statistics entered in Table 2.6 provides strong indications as well as interesting readings of China's increased capital outflow in the 1990s.

The increasing outflow of capital from China in the 1990s can be partly explained by the growing size of China's foreign debt, the amortisation and interest payments of which have to be serviced. As China's international debt significantly rises, the amount of capital for debt servicing also increases. That is, however, at best only part of the story. The long-term capital outflow in official Chinese statistics also includes two large categories of China's outward investment. One is China's FDI and the other is Chinese purchases of foreign bonds and stocks. It should be noted that China's outward FDI registered here differs significantly from the figures provided by the Ministry of Foreign Trade and Economic Cooperation (MOFTEC), but agrees largely with those published by UNCTAD (United Nations Conference on Trade and Development).[25] On the other hand, China's purchase of foreign bonds and stocks seems to have been most significantly underrepresented in the official statistics. By the end of 1992, for example, China's total investment in US bonds had risen to a gross value of $3.4 billion. China reportedly bought $490 million US treasury bonds and $700 million enterprise bonds in 1992 alone (see SWB 1993: A/6). There was a report in China in early 1997 that according to the statistics published by the Treasury of the United States, from September 1995 to September 1996, China's purchase of American stocks, bonds and other securities reached $12.1 billion, larger than Japan's purchase of $11.6 billion (*International Financial News*, 19 February 1997).

The most intriguing reading is the increasingly larger 'omissions and errors' in the Chinese official statistics of the balance of payment.[26] These are entered to cover/capture the gaps between China's trade surplus plus net capital inflow and the rate of increase of its foreign exchange reserves. To all intents and purposes, they can be categorised as capital flight from China, as these transfers of capital to overseas destinations are without the ratification of Chinese foreign currency regulators. As Fredrich Wu observed in 1994, economists generally agree that 'inordinately large statistical discrepancies in a country's international transactions data imply the plausible existence of covert movements of fugitive funds across national borders' (Fredrich Wu 1994: 23–4).[27] Much of the capital outflow unaccounted for is most likely to be 'fugitive funds' across Chinese borders. There is strong evidence to suggest that the official Chinese statistics have significantly understated China's FDI in Hong Kong, for example. Wu noted that the Nomura Research Institute estimated that, by 1994, China's accumulative investment total was over $30 billion in Hong Kong – 'most of which lacks the official seal of approval' (Fredrich Wu 1994: 22).[28] Shen Jueren, Chairman of the Association of Chinese Enterprises in Hong Kong, claimed in 1996 that China's direct investment in Hong Kong reached $42.5 billion by the end of 1994 (Institute of Developing Economies 1996: 14).

Evidence from China's investment in Hong Kong seems to support David Wall's observations on illicit capital outflows from China. Although the capital flight from China can be partly accounted for by 'theft for the personal enrichment of corrupt officials and enterprise managers', 'most of the outflows are likely to be on behalf of enterprises on one or other level of public ownership'. They are 'illicit flows' because they occur 'without the approval of the government' (Wall 1996: 41–3).[29] This is backed up by a more recent study which examines the illicit transfer of property ownership of the state assets to privately registered offshore Chinese businesses through internationalisation (Ding 2000).

The amount of capital flight from China is difficult to estimate, but it is certainly not captured correctly in the entry of 'omissions and errors' in the official statistics of the balance of payments. For example, estimates by the World Bank are at $24.9 billion in 1992 and $20.9 billion in 1993, much higher than the comparable figures in Table 2.6 (Lardy 1995: 1071). That gap seems to have grown in the late 1990s. While the 'omissions and errors' in official statistics are $22.1 billion, $18.9 billion and $11.7 billion respectively in 1997–99, estimates of capital flight from China in the same period vary from $53 billion to more than $90 billion (*China Daily – Business Weekly*, 28 May 2002). Regardless of how accurate these figures are, capital flight continues to present a serious challenge to China's macro-economic managers. Capital outflow from China is certainly much larger than the official statistics suggest.

International engineering and labour service trade[30]

Last but certainly not least, China's participation in the international service trade is another important thrust of its economic internationalisation. Two groups of statistics are systematically entered in the official Chinese record: construction and engineering, and labour services, vaguely referred to as international economic cooperation. A large number of Chinese multinationals have grown out of their engagement with international engineering and the labour service market.

China did not enter the world construction and labour service markets in any meaningful way until the end of 1978, when the State Council sanctioned the establishment of Chinese companies specialising in engineering projects and labour services overseas.[31] At the time of its entry, however, China had unwittingly, through its extensive aid programme to Third World countries in the previous decades, already laid a solid foundation for its participation. Before 1978, Chinese engineers had completed a large number of construction projects, from a textile factory in Burma to roads in Nepal and Rwanda and a large railway project in Tanzania and Zambia. This may, indeed, partly explain why and how China's construction and labour service trade developed so rapidly in the following years. By the end of 1989, the completed value of China's construction and labour service trade reached $7.8 billion. In 1992, it was reported that 130,000 Chinese engineers and labour service personnel were working in foreign countries fulfilling China's service contracts (Ma and Sun 1993: 305). In 1999 alone, Chinese construction and engineering companies signed contracts valued at $13 billion and fulfilled $11.23 billion worth. The comparable statistics in 2001 were $12.14 billion and $16.45 billion (*www.moftec.gov.cn/moftec_cn/tjsj/hztj*).

The acceleration of the expansion in China's construction and engineering and labour service trade in the 1990s has been accompanied by substantial outward investment by the Chinese companies concerned. According to a recent *World Investment Report*, the China State Construction and Engineering Corporation has accumulated $2.81 billion in foreign assets by 1996, and was accordingly ranked ninth in the top

Table 2.7 China's construction, engineering and labour service trade, 1991–2001 (in $ billion)

	Contracted	Realised
1991	3.609	2.363
1992	6.585	3.049
1993	6.80	4.538
1994	7.988	5.978
1995	9.672	6.588
1996	10.27	7.696
1997	11.37	8.383
1998	11.77	10.13
1999	13.00	11.23
2000	14.94	11.33
2001	16.45	12.14
Total	112.454	83.425

Sources: State Statistics Bureau (various years),
www.moftec.gov.cn/moftec_cn/tjsj/hztj/hztj_menu.html.

50 transnational corporations from developing countries. Its annual foreign sales in 1996 were $1.59 billion (UNCTAD 1999: 48). China has thus diligently cultivated its comparative advantage of an abundance of skilled labour and expertise in construction and engineering in fostering this group of specialised non-manufacturing multinationals. As will be discussed in Chapter 4, these companies are among China's emerging global businesses and have become an important vehicle for China's overseas investment.

Summary

The empirical evidence surveyed above suggests that measured in cross-border flows of trade, finance and services, the internationalisation of the Chinese economy since 1978 has been rapid and unmistakable. But it is not just the pace of change that is exceptional. It is rather the fact that China, as a developing economy that had been tightly closed to others and had its own philosophical reasoning for such closure up till 1978, has been so fundamentally transformed in such a short period of time. And it has been integrated into the global economy like never before. In terms of both economic internationalisation and integration, China is catching up quickly with other developing economies of East Asia. The empirical evidence indicates, too, the limits of the internationalisation of the Chinese economy. The real trade–GDP ratio, excluding China's processing trade, is still relatively low. Equity flows into China are still much smaller than into many other Asian developing economies. And the liberalisation of China's capital account is yet to happen. For the purpose of the investigation conducted in this study, it is important to remember that the emergence of China's multinational businesses is predicated upon the achievements and conditioned by the limits of China's economic internationalisation as well as the internationalisation of the Chinese state, two mutually reinforcing transformative processes.

Part II

The Political Economy of China's Emerging Global Businesses

As Part I illustrates, the Chinese state has been going through a transformative process of internationalisation. China's all-out engagement with the global economy is only recent, after thirty years of virtual exclusion from the international economic system. These are two significant dimensions of the changing political economy in China's economic internationalisation. Against this broad backdrop, Part II investigates how China's aspiring global businesses emerge and grow within or in spite of the constraints imposed by China's political system and economic transition. The nature of China's political and economic systems – particularly centralised political control, economic planning and public ownership – predetermines two important conditions for the emergence of China's global businesses. First, the central government plays a preeminent role in formulating and implementing China's home-country policies related to its own multinational corporations. And second, the administrative intervention in and intrusion into corporate decision-making and management with regard to both domestic operations and international business is ubiquitous.

As has been well-acknowledged in the existing literature, home-country policies are of overriding importance for the emergence and growth of multinationals from both developed and developing countries alike. In the case of China, this insight assumes added significance. The particular features of China's transitional politics and changing economic governance make it inescapable that government policies become the most significant explanatory variable for the transnationalisation of Chinese firms. The key to grappling with the intriguing question of the emergence of China's aspiring global businesses is therefore to examine the political economy of the evolution of critical government policies that either foster and encourage or restrict and regulate the transnational operations of Chinese enterprises.

Discussions in Part II, which consists of two chapters, are centred on such an examination. Chapter 3 conducts an investigation of how China's home-country policies first evolved amidst intense domestic debates about the virtues of outward investment and transnationalisation of Chinese firms. The making of China's home-country policies are preceded, however, by an agonising process through which China learns to accept intellectually that multinational corporations, though a capitalist-dominated economic institution, play an important role in promoting the economic development of developing countries like China. Not surprisingly, throughout the 1980s, domestic debates about China's development strategy and the general orientation of economic reform constitute part of the general milieu within which Chinese government policies towards outward investment gradually unfold.

The chapter also highlights how a general regulatory framework has been gradually put into place and continuously modified to encourage, to regulate and to control outward investment by Chinese firms. One particular policy regime, which we call particularistic policies, plays an unusual role in facilitating the transnationalisation of Chinese firms. They are used by the Chinese government to help designated firms overcome systemic constraints on transnational operation associated with the nature of a transitional economy and distortions therein. The irony is that such policies are a double-edged sword, as they tend to reinforce the existing distortions of the economic system and discourage the firms concerned from developing their own competitiveness. Their limits as a means to promote the transnationalisation of Chinese firms have been belatedly exposed.

Chapter 4 follows the trail of the speedy emergence and rapid growth of multinationals from the PRC and profiles its outward investment and emerging global businesses. We note in particular that the Chinese government is not entirely non-conversant with transnational operations prior to 1978. Its extensive foreign aid programme to Asian and African countries carried out from the 1950s through to the late 1970s has unwittingly left some transferable assets such as expertise about the local market and reputation of Chinese workers for the would-be Chinese engineering companies to cultivate in their commercial operation after 1978. Business operations run by the ministries of the Chinese government in Hong Kong after 1949 have allowed limited but valuable exposure of Chinese officials to commercial transnational operations in a market environment. The rapid take-off of transnational operations of state-owned enterprises, on the other hand, owes most to a number of policy innovations in 1978–79, which are examined in detail.

In the 1980s, China's outward investment takes off quickly to catch up with what is now called the 'first-wave Third World investors'. It also marks the beginning of a systematic entry of Chinese firms into business operations beyond the Chinese borders. By the second half of the 1980s, large Chinese investment projects are found in Australia, Canada and the United States, in addition to Hong Kong. In the 1990s, China's outward investment goes through a period of adjustment and growth induced by the faltering of economic reform in 1989–92 and by the Asian financial crisis 1997–98. It is also affected by intensified economic globalisation, which compels and creates more open economies and therefore more investment opportunities. In addition, China's accession to the World Trade Organisation is reconstituting China's economic institutional landscape, which has significant implications for China's outward investment.

3
Towards the Transnationalisation of Chinese Firms: Policies and Debates

This chapter discusses the political economy that conditions and promotes the evolution of China's home-country policies towards its own multinationals and examines debates within China about the pros and cons for Chinese firms to engage in transnational operations. Because of the nature of its political and economic system, China's home-country policies emerged out of very special circumstances and were accompanied by controversies and continuous debates as to whether, why, how, where and for what purposes transnational operations should be conducted by Chinese enterprises, most of which are state-owned. The controversies and debates are as much about economics as about politics. For one thing, the role that the Chinese government plays in the economy predetermines state intervention in promoting or prohibiting the emergence and growth of China's own multinational corporations. Policy debate is naturally a focal point of contention. For another, until 1992 controversies abounded as to whether and in what way transnational operations and Chinese investment overseas were compatible with China's socialist planned economy with public ownership and how they could be incorporated into China's national development strategy. For yet another, intellectually and politically, China had initially to come to terms with the operations of multinational corporations across national borders, and to accept that multinational corporations play a positive role in the developmental process and in the modernisation of the world economy.

The political economy of policy evolution is therefore particularly interesting, as it underlies the emergence and growth of Chinese multinational corporations. It is also a process whereby China reconciles itself with this capitalist-dominated institution as the globalisation of the world economy accelerates. Debates within China are inevitable and intense because of controversy drawn from ideological opposition, as well as from practical considerations. They are concurrent with, and constitute part of, debates about the nature and direction of the transformation of the Chinese economy. They also concern themselves with the role of the state in the economy and with the possibility of reconciling the socialist system with capitalist rules. In more practical terms, the political and economic determinants of outward investment and the transnational operations of Chinese firms have to be identified, and issues such as lack of funds and managerial expertise and the management of state assets have to be addressed. It is out of these debates that China's policy and regulatory framework for the transnational operations of Chinese firms have gradually evolved and been modified, albeit in a haphazard, rather than well-coordinated, way.

China travelled a long and winding road from 1979 to 1992 in accepting the market orientation of its economic reform. This is also a period in which Chinese officials, economists and emerging entrepreneurs alike grappled with the full political and economic implications of Chinese firms engaging in transnational operations. As early as 13 August 1979, one State Council document announced that '[investing] to set up [Chinese] enterprises overseas' (*chuguo ban qiye*) was to be one of thirteen measures to open up the Chinese economy to the world. But it was only in September 1992, at the Fourteenth National Congress of the Chinese Communist Party, that transnational operations by Chinese firms were officially incorporated into China's national economic development strategy. In publicly endorsing the transnationalisation of Chinese firms, the Chinese leader Jiang Zemin stated that 'we should encourage enterprises to expand their investments abroad and their transnational operations' (*Beijing Review*, 26 October–1 November 1992: 20). The transnationalisation of Chinese firms has since been seen as one major thrust in China's economic integration into the global economy.

After September 1992, the question of whether Chinese firms should engage in transnational operations was largely resolved in theory. With considerations of political correctness out of the way, the enthusiastic embrace of multinational corporations as a viable institution in China's economic development has prevailed and has been followed up by discussions which turned to focus on more substantive matters related to the transnationalisation of Chinese firms, such as finance and management of outward investment, M&A (merger and acquisition) operations by Chinese firms, and issues related to the loss of state assets. The changing context of political economy for China's emerging global businesses in the 1990s has been defined, therefore, by China's bid for WTO membership, further liberalisation of China's trade and investment regimes, and the deepening of structural reform of the Chinese economy, particularly the reform of the financial system. Internationally, the Asian financial crisis in 1997–98 and accelerated economic globalisation serve as a catalyst for China's 'unfinished economic revolution' and provide challenges and opportunities that China has to take up. It is perhaps not surprising that in the tenth five-year plan most recently articulated in May 2001, Premier Zhu Rongji took a step further to pronounce that China should implement a strategy for Chinese enterprises to 'go out [and invest beyond Chinese borders]'. In Zhu's formulation, this constitutes one of the four thrusts intended to deepen China's reform and opening (Zhu 2001).

Understanding multinationals in the world economy

Revolutionary China's image of transnational corporations

China's historical aversion and ideological opposition to transnational corporations was emphatic prior to 1978. The classical denunciation of multinational corporations emanating from Revolutionary China in the early 1970s was that multinational corporations were an expression of neo-colonialism in the unjustifiable international economic order; and that they were tools of capitalism for the oppression and exploitation of the Third World. At the United Nations in 1974, Deng Xiaoping articulated in blunt terms Revolutionary China's perception of the international economic order. In his words,

> As we all know, in the last few centuries colonialism and imperialism unscrupulously enslaved and plundered the people of Asia, Africa and Latin America. Exploiting the cheap labour power of the local people and their rich natural resources and imposing a lopsided and single-product economy, they extorted super-profits by grabbing low-priced farming and mineral products, dumping their industrial goods, strangling national industries and carrying on an exchange of unequal values.
>
> (*Peking Review*, 12 April 1974, Supplement: iii)

Deng's words are not only a reflection of the ideological bias of Revolutionary China against the capitalist-dominated international economic order in which multinational corporations played an important role. They are also expressions of the Chinese version of the dependence relationship between the South and the North and China's understanding of such distorted dependence, partly from China's history of being a 'semi-colonial country'. In the 1980s, China's economic reforms would gradually and inexorably change such perceptions of the international economic system prevalent in Chinese official statements in the 1970s.[1]

There was another inhibitive factor in China's understanding of multinationals in the world economy. Because of China's isolation in world politics and its insulation from the world economy, until the 1970s not only did China have little physical contact with operating multinational corporations in the sense that no multinational operated in the Chinese economy, but also, since it was largely isolated from the epistemic community of international economics at the time, it had no intellectual contact with the existing literature on multinational corporations that happened to be flourishing in the 1970s. For China, understanding the nature and the role of multinational corporations in the world economy is a learning and adaptation process in both political and intellectual terms.

Towards changing perceptions

China's membership of the United Nations may be incidentally responsible for its initial interest in understanding multinationals. In the 1970s, intensive studies were carried out both within and outside the UN framework on multinational companies and on what is called 'transnational relations' (see, for example, Modelski 1972, Keohane and Nye 1972, United Nations 1973, Barnet and Muller 1974, UNCTC 1977, Bergsten *et al.* 1978). Research undertaken by UN organisations on multinational corporations was made available to China as a member state. UN studies of the role of multinationals in economic development, in particular, attracted China's attention. In 1975, in the twilight years of the Cultural Revolution and one year before Mao's death, the government-controlled elite publisher, the Commercial Press, published the Chinese version of *Multinational Corporations in World Development*, a publication of the UN Department of Social and Economic Affairs in 1973.[2] This is widely regarded as the first publication in China on multinationals (Kang *et al.* 1996: 5–6).[3] The fact that it is a UN publication and concerns world development issues must have contributed significantly to easing political opposition to such publications. China was thus launched into learning about the role and operation of multinationals.

This publication represents, in essence, an exploration of unknown territory, one that carries some political hazard. In the Chinese edition, multinational corporations were still described as 'the imperialist tool for economic exploitation and plundering'.[4] Such an image of multinational corporations persisted throughout the late 1970s. An entry in *A Dictionary of Political Economy*, published in 1980, while acknowledging multinational corporations as 'a significant force in international relations, which exercises strong influence on the politics and economy of the host countries', insisted that 'their monopoly and speculative activities impair the normal international economic relations and erode the sovereignty of the host countries' (Kang *et al.* 1996: 6–9).[5]

The publication in 1975, nevertheless, signalled the beginning of China's engagement in the discourse on multinationals. The translation of the UN book was helpful in legitimising such studies. Nankai University, which had organised the translation, was to become in the years to come a major research centre in China for the study of multinationals in the world economy. As China's opening and economic reforms unfolded in the 1980s, continued discourse on multinational corporations would exercise a strong impact on China's acceptance of multinationals and their role in the developmental process of developing countries. At the same time, as China was opened to foreign investment, multinational corporations entered China and began to engage in a variety of investment operations in the Chinese economy. The legitimacy of China as a host country to foreign multinational corporations was a broad acknowledgement of the positive role of multinationals in economic development. It promoted also the legitimacy of China as a home country to transnational businesses.

It is only natural that it is in the coastal areas, where FDI flow into China made a significant impact in the 1980s, that the question of initiating China's own multinationals was first raised. As early as 1984, Shanghai hosted what we know now as the first seminar on China's overseas investment, 'Symposium on Developing China's Investment Overseas'. It was also in Shanghai that Louis T. Wells's pioneering work, *Third World Multinationals: The Rise of Foreign Investment from Developing Countries*, was translated into Chinese by Ye Gang, a professor at Fudan University, in 1985. It was published by the Commercial Press in 1986.[6]

The publication of Wells's book in Chinese may have helped overcome China's ambivalence and antipathy towards multinationals. The emergence and the success of Third World multinationals, as reported by Wells, challenged the prevailing preconception in China that multinational corporations are but a tool for the West to engage in imperialistic exploitation and aggression. Wells's analysis also registered support of international institutions, including the International Labour Organisation (ILO) and UN subsidiaries such as the United Nations Industrial Development Organisation (UNIDO), for the development of Third World multinationals. Such support suggests possible economic and political benefits brought about by Third World multinational corporations to their home countries as well as host developing countries, particularly in South–South cooperation.

Political acceptance

The publication of *Third World Multinationals* in Chinese facilitated the study of the roles and function of multinationals in the global economy in China. Towards the end of the 1980s, a 'new understanding' (*zai ren shi*) of multinational corporations in the world economy was clearly under way.[7] China was going through 'a learning curve in its relations with transnational corporations' (Wang 1988: 251–65). In October 1986, the first international conference on transnational corporations ever held in China was convened at Nankai University.[8] It was at the conference that China's changing perception of multinational corporations was publicly voiced. Professor Chen Yinfang of Nankai University argued that 'transnational corporations play an important role in promoting the development of the world productive forces through moving factors of production and technology [across the national borders]'. He urged that China 'should view from this perspective the positive function of transnational corporations [in the world economy]' (Chen Yinfang 1988: 33–46).

By 1988, it was possible for some to claim that 'the Chinese attitude toward transnational corporations has changed dramatically' and 'transnationals are no longer viewed as tools of capitalist exploitation but as agents and resources that can serve the purposes of Chinese development' (Teng and Wang 1988: iv).[9] The ideological prejudice against multinational corporations nevertheless lingered on.[10] In the 1990s, there continued to be agonising attempts to reconcile the emergence of China's multinationals with Marxism, Leninism and socialism (see, for example, Yuan 1991: 50–5, and Zhang 1991: 43–9). Scepticism about, and opposition to, China's outward investment remained a serious concern in China's policy-making, at least in the first half of the decade (Teng 1997: 5–6).

Nevertheless, the late 1980s did indicate gradual and increasing political acceptance in China, not always without misgivings, of the positive role of multinational corporations in the development of the global economy. Studies of multinational corporations were no longer a 'forbidden area'. The lowering of political and ideological barriers permitted an open debate on the role of multinational corporations in world economic development, which in turn stimulated studies of China's overseas investment and the emergence of China's own transnational businesses. The early 1990s saw a flurry of publications on these two subjects.[11] The political and ideological compromise reached in China's understanding of multinationals is particularly important for China's home-country policy-making. As Ma Hong, an eminent official economist,[12] remarked in 1994:

> Only a few years ago, 'MNC' was a strange name in China. As China's opening continues and as the investment from MNCs in China increases, we began to learn about MNCs. It is encouraging to see that academics no longer simply criticize MNCs from a biased and parochial perspective and that the research on MNCs is making encouraging progress.
>
> (Ma Hong 1994: 1)

In the 1990s, political and ideological opposition to developing China's transnational businesses became increasingly muted. Significantly, in the debates during 1990–92 discussed later in this chapter, the political correctness of outward investment was largely off the agenda.

Initiating general and particularistic policies, 1979 to 1988

In spite of China's ambivalence and political antipathy towards multinational corporations in the 1980s, in practice, transnational operations of the Chinese firms associated with large-scale outward investment were already under way during that period. Because of the historical circumstances, and given the nature of China's planned economy, the state assumes an unusual role in facilitating the emergence of Chinese multinational corporations, particularly in their first decade. Changing policies become an exceptionally important explanatory variable.

The Chinese government seemed to have adopted a purposely ambivalent stance towards the transnational operations of Chinese firms from the very beginning of economic reform, particularly when they were linked with outflow of capital. The early approach by the Chinese government to dealing with China's investment overseas may be characterised as eclectic and *ad hoc*, and sometimes clearly half-hearted. This, one could argue, was largely due to both ideological opposition and practical considerations. From 1979 to 1988, a set of policies, not always consistent and coherent and very often ill-defined, evolved not only to permit, and sometimes to encourage, the transnational operations of Chinese firms, but also to regulate and to control outward investment.[13] Although not so pronounced and clearly articulated as China's host-country policies for multinational corporations, they are nevertheless observable, and some are well-documented. For analytical purposes, we divide those policies into two sets: general and particularistic. General policies refer to those that apply to all cases of transnational operations and outward investment, which are usually recorded in official documents. Particularistic policies refer to special policies applicable only to specific cases and firms and very often initiated by China's top leadership. These are always preferential. They are not always documented in the official policy record and tend to have a shorter lifespan. The two sets of policies are not necessarily compatible with each other. Taken together, these two sets of policies constitute an emerging policy regime for outward investment and for the transnational operations of Chinese firms.

Evolution of general policies

Three signposts could be observed in the evolution of the government's general policies towards transnational operations of Chinese firms from 1979 to 1988. The starting point was the State Council document issued on 13 August 1979 in which '[investing] to set up [Chinese] enterprises overseas' (*chuguo ban qiye*) was pronounced as one of thirteen official policies for opening the Chinese economy. The second signpost was the release of a MOFERT (Ministry of Foreign Economic Relations and Trade) document in July 1985. *Provisional Regulations Governing the Control and the Approval Procedure for Opening Non-trade Enterprises Overseas* was among the first and is still one of the major central government documents that attempted to guide and regulate China's overseas investment. Policies elaborated in that document with regard to application and approval procedures for Chinese firms to establish overseas subsidiaries are still largely applicable today.[14] And the third was the State Council's approval of the application by Sinochem, the largest import and export corporation in China, for experimenting with large-scale transnational operations in 1987. By then, the transnational operations of Chinese firms and overseas investment were firmly on the policy agenda of the government.

Because of China's state trading practice at the time and because the state literally owned all firms, state intervention in the economic decisions of firms was ubiquitous. All Chinese firms, without exception, must operate within the straitjacket of government policies. As in many other Third World countries, however, China's general policies emerging in this period were made to perform three different but interrelated functions. It is, therefore, possible to classify them into three categories: that is, policies to *encourage*, to *regulate* and to *control* transnational operations of Chinese firms and overseas investment.

Export promotion seems to be the key to a series of policies that emerged to allow, as well as to *encourage*, Chinese firms to engage in transnational operations. On 4 December 1978, the Foreign Trade Ministry and the Foreign Ministry made a joint submission to the State Council, proposing to allow China's foreign trade companies to open offices abroad. By early 1979, this proposal was sanctioned by the State Council.[15] Together with the sanction authorised by the State Council on 13 August 1979 mentioned earlier, it opened the gate for Chinese trading firms to go abroad. Twelve national import/export corporations, which had until 1979 monopolised China's foreign trade but had no foreign presence by then, quickly seized this opportunity and opened offices in Hong Kong and a number of China's trading partner countries.[16] They also made initial investments, mostly trade-related, in offices and other facilities (Shen *et al.* 1992: 109–10).[17] What Jones calls 'multinational traders' (Jones 1998) was emerging in China.

A policy innovation aimed at promoting the export of labour and engineering expertise was also initiated in 1978 to cultivate China's comparative advantage in the international construction and labour market. A group of companies specialising in labour and engineering projects were set up, with the special approval of the State Council, particularly to tap the international market for engineering and construction works. The first of such companies, China State Construction and Engineering Co. Ltd, was established in 1978. In the 1980s, a host of ministerial, provincial and municipal international economic and technical cooperation corporations mushroomed to engage in such service trade.

The second set of general policies was made to *regulate* Chinese firms' transnational operations and overseas investment. Four official documents, circulated in the period 1984–88, laid down the foundation of these policies. Of these four documents, the most central is the MOFERT 1985 document *Provisional Regulations Governing the Control and the Approval Procedure for Opening Non-trade Enterprises Overseas*. Not

---

Box 3.1   The MOFERT documents on outward investment

The four MOFERT documents are:

1   *MOFERT Circular concerning the Approval Authorities and Principles for Opening Non-Trade Joint Venture Overseas as well as in Hong Kong and Macao* issued on 19 May 1984.
2   *Provisional Regulations Governing the Control and the Approval Procedure for Opening Non-trade Enterprises Overseas* issued in July 1985.
3   *MOFERT Circular on the Approval Procedures for International Economic and Technical Cooperation Corporation to Set up Overseas Subsidiaries*, issued also in July 1985.
4   *Regulations Governing the Approval of Setting up Trade-related Enterprises Overseas*, circulated in July 1988.

Sources: Li Yuesheng *et al*. (1993: 123–39), Liu Xiangdong *et al*. (1993: 1276–9).

---

only were a series of government policies clearly and systematically articulated for the first time, but a number of important changes were also introduced.

One of the most significant changes embodied in the 1985 document was that it clearly stipulated that *all economic entities* (not just the foreign trade corporations and specially designated enterprises) 'could apply to open overseas ventures as long as it has its own financial resources to do so, possesses some technological advantage and expertise, and had foreign joint venture partners'. Between 1978 and 1984, only a limited number of designated entities, such as the import and export corporations and the newly established international economic and technical cooperation corporations at the provincial and national levels, were permitted to engage in overseas investment activities. The approval of such investment was centralised in the hands of the State Council. From the perspective of the twenty-first century, this simple policy change represented a significant step towards liberalising the policy environment for outward investment. In the 1990s, not only state-owned enterprises, but township enterprises and even the private sector have engaged in investment overseas (Kang *et al*. 1996, Zhu and Ye 1993).

Box 3.2 Government-specified requirements for the approval of outward investment

1 It helps import advanced technology and equipment that are difficult to import through other channels.
2 It helps provide a long-term reliable supply of raw materials needed for China's domestic economic development.
3 It helps generate foreign currency income for China.
4 It is conducive to exporting Chinese machinery and materials; and to the expansion of China's engineering and labour service contracts overseas.
5 It helps provide the local market with Chinese products needed and make foreign currency earnings.

The 1985 document further laid down explicitly the basic requirements for an overseas investment project to be approved. While affirming that the government encouraged enterprises to engage in overseas ventures, it also clearly stipulated that the investment project must meet at least one of the specified requirements by the government as shown in Box 3.2.[18]

These requirements are surprisingly similar to those laid down by the Taiwanese government as summarised by Wells.[19] They reflect three main purposes that the government would like to see outward investment serve: namely, to promote export so as to increase foreign exchange earnings, to import advanced technology, and to gain reliable access to raw materials badly needed in the economy (Zhang Yangui 1997: 58). In other words, the regulations aim at promoting and rationalising, as well as guiding and directing, China's outward investment so as to realise economic benefits for the home country. It is also clear that even at this very early stage, Chinese government policies for overseas investment aimed at market-seeking, technology-seeking and resource-seeking. They are among the four major motivations for outward investment by Third World multinationals as identified by the UNTCMD study of 1993 (UNTCMD 1993).[20] These requirements also make it clear that the regulations and control of non-trade-related outward investments are more stringent than those on trade-related investments.[21]

How well these policies and regulations have served the economic interests of China is extremely difficult to determine. The limited empirical evidence available, however, does suggest that they have generally guided a large amount of Chinese investment into designated industries and sectors. Take, for example, China's investment in natural resources. Because of China's relative lack of natural resources and its huge demand due to the size of its population and the stage of its economic development, the government has always emphasised the importance of investing overseas to secure supply of, and to gain access to, raw materials and food. China's investments overseas in the 1980s were, therefore, made in fisheries in Africa and New Zealand, in forestry and its products in the United States and Canada, and in minerals in Australia.[22] Increasingly and more recently, they are poured into oil exploration and petroleum production sectors. China's investment in the resource sectors remains the largest sector of China's non-trade investment overseas in value terms.

A third set of general policies could be identified as those trying to *control* direct capital outflow from China. The basis of this set of policies is again found in the four official documents mentioned in Box 3.1. Additional documents in the 1990s only modified some previous arrangements, not the principles.[23] It is interesting to note that it is *not* primarily through a set of macro-economic policies, such as a strict foreign exchange control policy, that outward investment was regulated. Foreign exchange control is at best only a supplementary measure in controlling the outflow of capital from China. This is clearly demonstrated in the State Administration of Foreign Exchange (SAFE) document in 1989 regulating the foreign exchange control of China's overseas investment (Li Yuesheng *et al.* 1993: 129–30). Further, until very recently, the central bank, the People's Bank of China (PBOC), had little say in these matters.[24] Rather, it is through devising and implementing an elaborate process of application and often cumbersome bureaucratic procedures for screening and approval that outward investment from China was, and to some extent is still, controlled.

What is important to our discussion here is the fact that hand in hand with the decentralisation of economic decision-making in China's economic reform, there emerged layers of decentralised authority in screening and approving China's overseas investment projects. This may partly be responsible for the first upsurge in China's overseas investment in 1986–87. In 1992, the State Council would expand the authority of MOFERT to approve projects involving Chinese investment of up to $30 million and would concern itself only with projects with more than $30 million of Chinese investment (Zhang Yangui 1997: 58–9, Lu Jinyong *et al.* 1996: 45–6). Such decentralisation and expan-

---

Box 3.3 The bureaucratic control of China's outward investment

The State Planning Commission (SPC) and the MOFERT, or the relative authorities at the provincial level, are to screen and approve overseas investment projects. The bureaucratic procedures for governmental approval were only institutionalised when they were clarified in the two MOFERT documents in 1984 and 1985 mentioned earlier. The State Council then delegated most of its authority for approving overseas investment projects to MOFERT, reserving only the authority to approve projects involving large-scale Chinese investment of more than $10 million. The MOFERT in turn delegated authority for approving projects involving Chinese investment up to but not including $1 million to the provincial government and the ministerial authorities under the State Council. It reserved to itself, however, the authority to approve projects involving Chinese investment between $1 million and $10 million. Those projects that need to apply to the central government for guarantee of loans from foreign banks or for loans from Chinese banks in foreign currency or in RMB, or in both, were also to be screened and approved by MOFERT in consultation with the State Planning Commission.[25]

Source: Li Yuesheng *et al.* (1993: 125).

---

sion of authority seem to have undermined the central government efforts to control the outflow of capital from China. As discussed in Chapter 2, in the 1990s China's current account statistics continuously record large amounts of unaccountable capital outflow each year.

The three sets of policies discussed above constituted what may be called the emerging regulatory framework for China's outward investment in the 1980s. In the 1990s, the government moved towards further liberalisation of the regulatory framework, but did not radically change it.

A series of government preferential policies that foster and support transnational operations by Chinese firms should also be noted as general policies. Like many other developing countries, the government introduces a number of policies to offer incentives for Chinese firms to invest overseas with capital equipment made in China. These include the provision of preferential loans associated with export of machinery manufactured at home, exemption from export tax and a much simplified procedure for approval. Other incentives for Chinese firms investing abroad include exemption from home taxes for the first five years of their overseas operation, cheap credit subject to the approval of the State Planning Commission, and a preferential tariff for importing raw materials produced by China-invested firms overseas and included in the official import plan (Zhan 1995, Zhang Yangui 1997).[26] For China's invested ocean-going fishery operations, the government offers guaranteed market access and zero tariffs for all the catch of those operations (Li Yuesheng *et al.* 1993: 29–30, Liu Xiangdong *et al.* 1993: 1268–9).[27]

There is, however, a clear deficiency in this policy environment which is yet to be overcome. In the emerging general policy regime of the Chinese government, little is extended beyond the process of screening and approval. There was, and still is, no clear policy regime that is aimed at monitoring and, even less so, servicing China's outward investment and the transnational operations of Chinese firms.

Characteristics of particularistic policies

In addition to these general policies, some particularistic policies emerged as part of a policy environment for the growth of China's multinational corporations. These policies are best seen as examples of state intervention to foster China's overseas investment. The irony is that it is the distortion in the Chinese economic system, the highly centralised control and lack of market mechanism, for example, that makes these particularistic policies not only possible, but also necessary in fostering specific thrusts and firms in internationalising. In the short term, these government policies seem to be able to achieve their objectives by assisting the firms concerned to overcome particular systemic or bureaucratic constraints embedded in the unreformed economy. They also help the firms concerned to gain 'created assets', some of which are transferable into their transnational operations (Zhang and Van Den Bulcke 1996: 388). The problem is, however, that in the long run, privileges afforded by these policies may prevent the firms concerned from developing their capacity to compete in a market environment both at home and abroad.

These policies are particularistic in that they are either firm-specific, that is, applicable only to appointed firms, or case-specific, that is, applicable to only one-off nominated cases. Particularistic policies may, for example, refer to ready access to loans, possibly at a lower than normal interest rate, granted by state-controlled banks to particular firms and on particular projects as one-off cases. They may refer to exceptional decision-making power granted to the management. These policies are usually not institutionalised and are very often biased against other Chinese firms engaged in similar transnational operations. In the Chinese policy discourse, this is sometimes called *zhongdian fuzhi* (offering preferential support). All three firms examined in Part III of this book have benefited from, and been eventually hampered by, particularistic policies.

Without preempting detailed investigations later, a brief sketch of particularistic policies that these three firms enjoyed is due here. A special decision of the government in 1979 led to the establishment of the China International Trust and Investment Corporation (CITIC) as a ministerial-level organisation to engage in investment activity both at home and abroad. For that purpose and from the very inception of CITIC, special permission was given by the State Council for CITIC to engage in certain activities that were not permitted to other enterprises. In 1982, CITIC was given special permission to explore the international bond markets for capital. It successfully pioneered China's first issue of bonds on the international capital market to raise funds for domestic industrial projects.[28] CITIC's large investment projects overseas in the mid-1980s did not seem to have gone through the screening and approval procedures of MOFERT, and were certainly not registered in MOFERT statistics. The high-level autonomy granted by the State Council to the Shougang Corporation for its domestic operations in the early stage of China's economic reform proved highly beneficial to the internationalisation of Shougang. In the early 1990s, this high-level autonomy was extended to Shougang's transnational operations. Sinochem, on the other hand, was singled out by the government as an experiment for the internationalisation of Chinese firms in 1987. In 1995, Sinochem was designated by the State Council to implement a pilot project for conglomeration and transnationalisation. Both experiments have been carried out with special policy incentives and purposes.

The formulation and granting of particularistic policies are often associated with the top Chinese leadership and with their personal relations with the top management of the firm. Deng allegedly told Rong Yiren in 1979 when Rong was asked to head the newly created CITIC, 'In the assignment to you, you may accept what you think is rational, and may refuse what you think is irrational. You are in charge of managing [CITIC] with your full power . . . You should manage the economics with economic methods and sign contracts in a commercial manner. Sign what can bring in profits and foreign exchange . . . As long as what you do is for the betterment of building socialism, do not hesitate' (Brahm 1996a: 43–4). Deng's patronage is also often suggested as being what underlies the special autonomy that Shougang gained and maintained throughout the 1980s and part of the 1990s.[29]

From 1979 to 1988, therefore, a preliminary policy environment for China's overseas investment and the transnational operations of Chinese firms tentatively emerged. The general orientation of the regulatory framework seems not so different from that of other developing countries. It encourages and guides the transnational operations of Chinese firms for the fulfilment of the government's economic developmental goals. It tries at the same time to restrict any direct outflow of capital from China. What is really different is the ubiquitous and heavy presence of the state in the operations and decision-making of Chinese firms. This is, as Zhan commented, 'in [sharp] contrast to the Republic of Korea where the role of the government in the economy is more discreet, to Brazil and Singapore where it is more selective, and to Hong Kong where it is largely absent' (Zhan 1995: 80). It is also worth noting that not only are general policies not well-defined, apart from screening and approval procedures, but that particularistic policies tend to interfere with, and therefore erode, the general regulatory framework.

National economic development strategy and transnational operations: earlier debates

It is sometimes argued that for developing countries, 'national policies on outward FDI are largely an extension of a general development-promoting strategy' (UNTCMD 1993: 86). By the same token, the policy evolution described above is conditioned by China's national economic development strategy. In the first decade of economic reform, the search for such a strategy appropriate to China was painstaking, and sometimes agonising. Ongoing debates among Chinese economists and officials on what is the best strategy for China's opening to the outside world accompanied this painful search. It is therefore instructive to look briefly at how these debates influenced Chinese policy-making on outward investment.

The search for a new and appropriate national economic development strategy began at the onset of China's economic reform and opening up to the outside world.[30] With economic reform proceeding in the 1980s,

Chinese economists came under the increasing influence of developmental economics.[31] As a late-developmental state, China was presented with three strategies practised, with varying degrees of success, by the developing countries of Latin America, Eastern Europe and East Asia. There are, in other words, three models for China to choose from: the import substitution strategy, the export-upgrading strategy and the export-led growth (promotion) strategy. They set the parameters of the debate on China's economic development strategy in the first decade of economic reform.

Contending strategies for economic development

The contention in these early debates was mainly between the import substitution strategy and its critics. The essence in contention was whether China should adopt an inward-looking development strategy. The advocates of the import substitution strategy argued that import substitution should be the long-term development strategy for China for the following reasons. First, China is a large country. Judging from international experience, all large countries have inward-looking economies with low export dependence for their industries. At the same time, the extensive domestic market is conducive to pursuing a long-term import substitution strategy for the industrialisation of large countries. Second, China's existing economic system, the planned economy, was more compatible with the import substitution strategy, which offered protection for domestic industries and minimised the impact on the domestic economy of the fluctuations in the international market. Third, China was yet to develop an export-oriented industrial sector that was competitive on the international market. Fourth, the 1980s offered opportunities for China to modernise its heavy and chemical industries, which were vitally important in the industrialisation of the country, as the developed economies were gradually transferring these industries offshore. Fifth, China could not hope to expand its exports continuously because of the increasingly strong protectionism by industrialised countries. Finally, pursuing an export-oriented strategy would also mean China would have to liberalise further its trade regimes and capital markets. It could not afford such liberalisation as yet.

The critics of the import substitution strategy pointed out that, first, pursuing the import substitution strategy would call for high tariffs and over-valuation of the Chinese currency, which would enhance the existing distortion of the market. Such a policy would tend to protect inefficient industries in the domestic economy, further impeding the competitiveness of the Chinese economy on the world market. Second, such a strategy was not financially sustainable, as China still had a foreign exchange shortage. Extensive borrowings on the international capital market would not only create an unacceptable dependence relationship between China's economic development and international credit, but might also lead to a debt crisis as in the case of Latin American countries. And third, the import substitution strategy was incompatible with the opening up of the Chinese economy and the gradual liberalisation of China's trade regimes, and ultimately with the long-term goal of ongoing economic reform. China's application for GATT membership in 1986 further strengthened this criticism.

These critics could be further divided into three groups, advocating three different strategies and approaches. The first group argued for an export-upgrading strategy. This strategy called for the import of machines and raw materials in order to produce high-quality consumer products for the domestic market rather than importing them, and to increase the export of manufactured goods instead of traditional primary products, particularly natural resources. Such advocates claimed that this strategy was an effective way not only to solve China's problem of foreign exchange shortage, but also to enable China to capitalise on both domestic and international markets. It would also help Chinese enterprises to adapt themselves to, and eventually participate in, competition on the international market.

The second group looked to the successful development models in East Asia for inspiration. They argued that first Japan and then the four mini-dragons (Hong Kong, Korea, Singapore and Taiwan) had all successfully adopted an export-led growth strategy in their industrialisation. China's economic reform since 1978 and its export promotion policies had created positive conditions for the adoption of an export-led growth strategy. China's coastal areas in particular possessed comparable advantages that the four successful NIEs (newly industrialising economies) used to have: namely, cheap labour, a skilled workforce, serviceable communications and infrastructure, and most importantly of all, scientific and technological capacity to attract foreign investment. In a word, China should follow the example of Japan and the four mini-dragons in its economic development strategy.

The third group adopted what is sometimes called an eclectic and neutral position (Hsu 1991: 137). They criticised strongly the inefficiency and inadequacy of the import substitution strategy. At the same time, they argued that an all-out export-led industrialisation strategy might create unnecessary dependence on foreign markets and on the international price, and even constraints on Chinese foreign policy.

They also questioned the practicability of China adopting an export-led industrialisation strategy, when the spectre of trade protectionism was again raised in the world economy in the 1980s, and when most Chinese enterprises were not prepared for competing on the international market. This group strongly recommended a strategy that combined import substitution with export promotion. Some in this group argued that import substitution and export promotion were not mutually exclusive and could be looked at as two phases of the same process, or as mutually complementary (Liu Guoguang 1984: 527–48, Duan 1995: 1–12).

The great international cycle

In 1988, controversies about the theory of the great international cycle (*guoji daxunhuan lilun*) put forward principally by Wang Jian, a researcher in the State Planning Commission, pushed the debates on China's economic development strategy to a new level.[32] Space forbids discussion on the details of the theory of the great international cycle here.[33] Originally proposed as an escape from China's dual dilemma in its economic development – massive transfer of surplus labour from the agricultural sector and a severe shortage of capital with which to invest in and upgrade its ageing industries – the great international cycle was a frontal assault on an economic system still characterised by half-baked reforms and on the thus far half-hearted and hesitant participation in international production and the international division of labour. The emphasis on the link between foreign trade and China's long-term economic development strategy and on China's full participation in international competition represented an early realisation by Chinese economists of the possibility, as well as the necessity, of facilitating economic development through internationalisation of the Chinese economy.

Even more important is the swift adoption by the government of the coastal development strategy (*yanhai fazhan zhanlue*), obviously inspired by the theory of the great international cycle. Already in January 1988, Zhao Ziyang, then the Chinese Premier, reportedly said during his tour of coastal areas, 'China should seize the current opportunity, take part in international competition, and push the coastal areas into the international market' (quoted in Fewsmith 1994: 215). He further indicated that if the coastal areas could successfully develop an export-oriented economy, that would facilitate the same development in central and western China. In February 1988, the Politburo of the CCP formally adopted the coastal development strategy.[34] The State Council then proceeded to open another fourteen coastal cities as special economic zones (SEZs).

The so-called great international cycle was flawed in theory and controversial in practice. The advance of such a theory and the adoption of a coastal development strategy were, nevertheless, important as they both unreservedly encouraged China's all-out participation in the world economy and in international competition (*quanmian canyu*). It was during discussion of the great international cycle that the call for putting the establishment of China's own multinationals on the agenda of national development strategy was first made (Duan 1995: 6–23). There are good reasons to believe that they facilitated the approval by the State Council of Sinochem's application to internationalise its operations in December 1987. Sinochem's application and the State Council's approval popularised the term *guojihua jingying* (internationalised operations). In the government work report submitted to the Seventh National People's Congress in 1988, *guojihua jingying* of large-scale state-owned enterprises was for the first time written into the economic reform programme (Zhao and Li 1991: 265).

Clearly, earlier debate on China's national development strategy was inconclusive. Further, it did not address the question of what role, if any, transnational operations of Chinese enterprises could play in this strategy. Nor did it necessarily see outward investment and the transnational operations of Chinese firms as an integral part of national economic development strategy. The debate is pivotal, however, in China's eventual discarding of import substitution strategy in favour of an export-led growth strategy. In so doing, it helped put the question of fostering transnational operations of Chinese enterprises on the agenda as indispensable to China's outward-looking economic policies. It paved the way for the debates in the 1990s on developing China's own multinationals and for making overseas investment an integral part of China's economic development strategy.

Policy debates, 1989–92 and beyond

A snapshot of discussions and debates nationwide

It may seem ironic, but it is true that from late 1989 to 1992 when economic and political sanctions imposed by the West against China were in full swing in the wake of the violent crackdown in Beijing in June 1989, a new wave of lively and vigorous discussions and debates were taking place in China on many policy issues with regard to China's overseas investment and the establishment of Chinese multinationals. From

October 1989 to December 1992, a number of symposiums and seminars were held in different localities and hosted by either research institutes, firms, government organisations, or a combination of these. If up till the late 1980s, public discussions about the transnational operations of firms had been limited, the period of 1989–92 was marked by intensified public debates involving high-ranking government officials, the top management of Chinese firms and senior economists. The Fourteenth CCP Congress in 1992 gave further momentum to these discussions and debates by explicitly affirming an official policy of encouraging Chinese firms to invest abroad as part of China's overall strategy of opening itself up to the world economy. Transnational operations by Chinese firms have since been firmly incorporated into the economic developmental strategy.

A research seminar, 'China's Overseas Ventures', was convened by the China Association of International Economic Cooperation and the Research Institute of the World Economy of Fudan University in Fuzhou in October 1989. In October 1990, Sinochem hosted in Beijing a symposium, 'Internationalisation of Chinese Firms', with a focus on Sinochem's experiment from 1987 to 1990. In November 1991, 'A Symposium on Policies Concerning the Transnational Operations of Chinese Firms' was organised in Beijing by the Editorial Board of *Guanli Shijie* (Management World), an influential bimonthly in Beijing, jointly with the Division of Industries and Transportation of the State Council's Research Office, the Department of International Cooperation of MOFERT, and the University of Foreign Economic Cooperation and Trade. In December 1992, an international conference held in Nanjing, 'Multinational Business Management and Internationalisation of Chinese Enterprises', saw the participation of UN officials and scholars from the United States, Germany, Japan and Hong Kong. Two other seminars on the same topic in this period, one in Shanghai in 1991 and the other in Qingdao in 1992, should also be put on record here.[35] The list goes on.

A closer examination of the holding of these public forums is revealing on two accounts. First, such frequently held seminars and conferences on the topic of transnational operations and internationalisation of Chinese firms were all invariably followed by the publication and distribution of conference papers either in a journal or in edited volumes.[36] These seminars and their publications both helped institutionalise the discussions and debates on the transnational operations of Chinese firms in the period and led to a booming publication on such topics in 1993 and 1994.

Second, there were clearly local initiatives in these discussions and debates. Most seminars were held in localities other than the capital Beijing. Of the six listed above, three were held in the coastal cities of Fuzhou, Shanghai and Qingdao respectively. Even the one held by Sinochem in Beijing could be regarded as a local initiative in the sense that the initiative came from a specific firm. The question as to why most of these initiatives should be local elicits both political and economic answers. Away from Beijing, participants, both officials and academics, could speak more freely, and the political atmosphere was less restrictive for discussions and debates on issues for which the government was yet to pronounce clear policies. But more significantly, it is clear that in the first decade of China's transnational operations, local authorities had already built up a substantial stake in overseas investment, even if this is only confirmed by the very raw data available. For example, from 1980 to 1990, Shandong Province invested $17 million to establish 47 trade- and non-trade-related ventures and subsidiaries overseas, and in 1991 alone thirteen overseas ventures were opened by the province (Wang and Wu 1993: 144–5). Shanghai, on the other hand, had 201 overseas ventures and subsidiaries with a total contract investment from Shanghai standing at $41.36 million by the end of 1991 (Wang and Wu 1993: 158–9). In the same period, Guangzhou accumulated a total of over $30 million in overseas investment, and Liaoning around $19 million (Zhu and Ye 1993: 155, 203).

The 1991 Beijing symposium

If local initiatives are clear, the importance of the central endorsement of such discussions and debates could hardly be overemphasised. Such endorsement came in the form of a government-sponsored symposium in Beijing in 1991. The organisation of 'A Symposium on Policies Concerning the Transnational Operations of Chinese Firms' involved the State Council's own think tank, the State Council's Research Office and MOFERT. The State Commission for Restructuring the Economic System (SCRES) also had a significant presence at the seminar, though was not officially involved in its organisation.[37] Further, the participation of ministers and vice-ministers in this symposium, and their substantive presentations in a personal capacity at such a public forum on policy issues, was also unusual. More than anything else, they testify to the importance that the central government attached to the issues addressed.

The timing of this symposium is extremely intriguing. The year 1991 experienced severe stagnation in the reform process. It would be three months after the symposium that Deng Xiaoping's tour of southern China in February 1992 would relaunch this process. On the other hand, it was almost one year before the Fourteenth Party Congress in October 1992 when encouraging overseas investment by Chinese firms was announced by Jiang Zemin as a component of the national economic development strategy. In Jiang's words, 'to open wider to the outside world', 'we should encourage enterprises to expand their investments abroad and their transnational operations' (Jiang 1992: 20). For all intents and purposes, however, presentations by three ministerial-level officials at the symposium had already foreshadowed this government policy.

It is of great interest to note how the three ministers at the symposium addressed issues relating to transnational operations of Chinese firms from three different perspectives. Yuan Mu, Director of the State Council's Research Office and close to the decision-making of the time, spoke of a recent Central Committee Working Conference and its emphasis on encouraging Chinese enterprises to 'develop the international market in a multidimensional manner'. He argued that attracting foreign investment in China and encouraging Chinese firms to invest overseas were two sides of the same coin. Transnational operations would not only make natural resources in foreign countries available and accessible to China, they would also help revitalise large and medium-size state-owned enterprises by introducing new and advanced technologies and management expertise, and by transferring China's traditional skills and surplus production capacity overseas (Yuan 1992: 29–32).

Li Lanqing, the Minister of MOFERT, seemed to be more concerned about the pluralisation and diversification of China's export markets, given the sanctions on China imposed in particular by the United States at the time. He looked on the transnational operations of Chinese firms as a way to cultivate new markets for trade.[38] What is most interesting in Li Lanqing's presentation is his candid admission that as transnational operations by Chinese firms were still at an early and exploratory stage, policy and management issues were 'very important but at the same time very difficult'. They need to be further explored and studied, as 'we [the government] do not yet have well-considered proposals'. Further, China could not follow any precedent in establishing its own multinational corporations in either theory or practice, because no state-owned enterprise from a socialist country had successfully built itself into a multinational corporation (Li 1992: 35–7).

Both Yuan Mu and Li Lanqing, however, did emphasise the political considerations in encouraging the growth of Chinese multinational corporations. For both Yuan and Li, fostering China's own multinational corporations would help promote South–South cooperation and, more importantly, help break the sanctions and even the blockade imposed on China by 'Western hostile forces' and 'resist the political and economic pressures of the West' (Yuan Mu 1992: 31, Li Lanqing 1992: 34).

Gao Shangquan, Vice-Minister of the SCRES, conceded that while the government took early steps to attract foreign investment into China, it only belatedly and slowly realised the importance of outward investment in the establishment of overseas ventures. The sluggish development of China's outward investment was, in his words, 'incompatible with the deepening of economic reforms and expansion of opening of China'. Gao argued that structural problems existed in the Chinese economic system that hindered the development of transnational operations of firms. In his 'personal opinion', to facilitate these operations on an appreciable scale, reform of the domestic economic system was a prerequisite. The entrenched structural problems of the economy he identified include the separation of foreign trade from domestic trade, the lack of inter-enterprise lateral linkage because of administrative boundaries and departmentalism and segmentation of the economy. The need for reform and for sound management of an investment regime for overseas investment, he argued, was also an essential requirement (Gao 1992: 38–40).

It is clear that the central concern of the symposium was not whether Chinese firms should engage in outward investment and transnational operations. As indeed the executive summary of the symposium affirmed:

> international economic competition will take its main form in the competition between multinational corporations [in the 1990s and in the twenty-first century]. Faced with such new development and competition pattern, China should prepare itself at an early date and draw up a plan so as to be able to make significant progress in the next five to ten years [in establishing China's own multinationals].
>
> (Song Ning *et al.* 1992: 54)

Post-1992 debates

After 1992, public debates on whether Chinese firms should actively seek transnationalisation were increasingly couched in terms of economics rather than politics. This should not be a surprise, given the virtual official sanction at the 1991 Beijing symposium and the endorsement by Jiang Zemin at the Fourteenth Party Congress in 1992. If this endorsement, together with the symposium, cut short the debate on the political correctness of transnationalising, it stimulated at the same time the discussion on how far and how fast the Chinese enterprises should develop their transnational operations, and what government policies would be conducive to the promotion and facilitation of such an endeavour. The major concerns articulated were the need of funds for China to invest overseas, the lack of competitive edge of Chinese firms in international production, and the poor return of most transnational operations already conducted by Chinese firms. There was also the problem of the loss of state assets (Zhang 1997: 67–8). Rather intriguingly, though, some common concerns for the developing economies as home countries of multinational corporations, especially the socio-economic impact of multinational corporations on home countries, such as the export of jobs, have never been seriously featured in Chinese discussions and debates, although the shortage of exportable capital in China for outward investment was sometimes discussed extensively.[39]

The discussions and debates in the early 1990s therefore turned to address the questions of how rather than why or whether. How did the Chinese firms perform in their transnational operations in the past decade? How should they conduct overseas investment in the future in establishing multinationals with 'Chinese characteristics'? How could and should domestic economic reforms facilitate transnational operations? How could government policies support and foster the growth of China's multinationals? And how could China learn from the experiences of other countries in developing its own multinational corporations?

It is in this process of looking back and looking forward that a number of policy and management issues were identified and raised. A list of inhibiting factors was identified as detailed in Box 3.4.

The implications are clear. The construction of a policy regime conducive to China's overseas investment and the transnationalisation of Chinese firms entails not only the creation and continuous improvement of a regulatory framework. It is also closely bound up with the structural reform of the Chinese economy and its marketisation. The government's macro-economic policies are the key to cultivating the potential development of transnational operations. Further growth of China's multinationals is, therefore, contingent upon broader liberalisation and restructuring of the Chinese economy, in particular reform of the financial sector. To understand the evolution of Chinese multi-

---

Box 3.4   Inhibiting factors for the transnationalisation of Chinese firms

- The dearth of laws and by-laws governing outward investment and the absence of legal and institutional frameworks to manage and facilitate such investment activities
- The segmentation of the Chinese economy by administrative barriers: for example, the separation of domestic trade from foreign trade, and the traditional division of line ministries in managing specialised and specified industries[40]
- Bureaucratic inefficiency
- The ubiquitous intervention of government at various levels in management decisions of firms, and consequently the lack of autonomy of firms in making business decisions
- The lack of macro-economic policies and the inadequacy of existing policies in support of transnationalisation
- A severe shortage of expertise and human resources as well as entrepreneurial spirit
- The incompatibility of China's socialist system wherein the parent company is located and the capitalist market environment wherein the subsidiaries have to operate

---

national corporations in the 1990s, we need to look beyond the regulatory framework to see what macro-economic policies in China promote and prohibit the development of Chinese multinationals.

Institutionalisation of policy regimes and globalisation

In 1993, China was noted as 'an exception', which UNTCMD found difficult to classify either in a group of outward-oriented, export-oriented countries or in a group of inward-looking countries. This is simply because 'Since its open-door economic policy in 1979, outflows of FDI have been constantly increasing; cumulative flows during 1982–91 accounted for about 15 per cent of outflows from developing countries during this period' (UNTCMD 1993: 52). UNTCMD's difficulty in pigeonholing China lies largely in the rapid increase of China's overseas investment, which in turn ranked China as among the most important of the second-wave Third World investors (Dunning *et al.* 1998).

However imperfect and rudimentary they were, China's home-country policies initiated in the 1980s played an important role in promoting the growth of its own multinationals. In the 1990s, this policy environment continued to evolve with the accelerated globalisation of the world economy. Two large components constituting this changing policy environment are worth our attention. One component involves the fine-tuning of Chinese policies and the regulatory framework that specifically addresses, or is closely related to, the transnational operations of Chinese firms and overseas investment. The other component concerns the interplay between globalisation and further restructuring of the Chinese economy, particularly seen in China's sustained economic growth and in the reform of the financial sectors and state-owned enterprises.

Institutionalisation of policy regimes

In short, in the 1990s Chinese policies *per se* and the regulatory framework have undergone appreciable but not radical change. The overall goals of the government in pushing for overseas investment remain the expansion of China's exports, securing and obtaining access to raw materials, and the promotion of international economic cooperation with both developing and developed nations.[41] Modifications of China's home-country policies in the 1990s, however, can be found in a number of official documents released by the State Council and MOFTEC (Zhang Yangui 1997: 59; Liu Xiangdong *et al.* 1993: 1272). State Council document No. 13 of 1991 raised the ceiling of approval for MOFERT and the State Planning Commission. The two ministries can now approve projects with Chinese investment up to $30 million, not just up to $10 million as pronounced in the 1985 document.[42] It also established a new threshold for outward investment projects that require borrowing from state-owned banks, or the products of which need to be incorporated into the national economic plan for market access into China. Such investment projects up to $1 million no longer need the approval or screening of MOFERT and the State Planning Commission. Belatedly, in March 1992, MOFERT promulgated its *Regulations for Approval and Control of Non-Trade Related Overseas Investment by Chinese Enterprises* (*guanyu zai jinwai juban fei maoyi qiye de shenpi chengxu he guanli banfa*), which formally incorporated the changes outlined above (Liu Xiangdong *et al.* 1993: 1276–9). State Council document No. 33 of 1992 addressed the question of Chinese firms investing in neighbouring countries newly opened to China, particularly those successor states of the former Soviet Union. It stipulated that investment in kind by

Chinese firms, such as capital equipment, could be decided by the firms concerned and would need no approval by government authorities. Investment projects that required the export of capital of less than $1 million only needed the approval of provincial and ministerial authorities. These documents obviously aimed more at modification than radical overhaul of previous policies (Li Yuesheng *et al.* 1993: 131–3).

One set of policies specifically related to the administration of China's outflow of capital for investment purposes was formally pronounced in 1989 and 1990 by the SAFE, which was not only responsible for making these policies, but also for implementing them. The broad objective of these policies was clearly to control the export of capital in foreign currency for investment and to regulate the remission back to China of foreign currency earnings of overseas subsidiaries of Chinese multinationals. Increasingly in the 1990s, an added objective in administrating this policy was to guard against state-asset losses.

The two documents in 1989 and 1990 – the *Regulations on the Foreign Exchange for Overseas Investment (jinwai touzi waihui guanli banfa)* and *Implementation of Regulations on the Foreign Exchange for Overseas Investment – Administrative Procedures (jinwai touzi waihui guanli banfa shishi xize)* respectively – form the foreign exchange control regime for overseas investment by Chinese firms (see Liu Xiangdong *et al.* 1993: 1283–7). These belatedly announced regulations constitute part of the regulatory framework. Two major areas of policy concern are addressed. One is the export of capital for investment, which must be approved by the SAFE or related foreign exchange control authorities. Reinvestment from profits earned by foreign subsidiaries are subject to the same approval procedure. The other is the remission back to China of profits made by foreign subsidiaries. To guarantee this, 5 per cent of the original investment from the parent company is to be held by the bank until profit remission from the overseas subsidiary is fulfilled. A heavy penalty is also stipulated for the parent company in China if its subsidiaries do not remit their profits in violation of the regulations above (Liu Xiangdong *et al.* 1993: 1283–7). How effective these policies have been in serving their purposes remains an open-ended question. Anecdotal evidence suggests that the control regime for export of capital has largely been either circumvented or compromised, whereas the regulatory regime for the remission of profits of subsidiaries of Chinese multinationals has been almost totally ignored (Interviews).

These new documents together represent the Chinese government efforts to formalise and institutionalise, but not significantly to alter, the previous regulatory framework for, and the administration of, overseas investment activities. Zhan observed in 1995, not without criticism, that 'Outward FDI has been regulated through about ten *provisional* regulations and administrative procedures' and with the absence of any formal law, 'the regulatory process [of China's outward investment] is far from perfect' (Zhan 1995: 69, emphasis in original). No systematic efforts have been made by the Chinese government to construct new policy regimes for outward investment in the 1990s in its bid for the WTO membership.

One particular policy that may have unwittingly promoted China's outward investment is worth mentioning here. Largely in the context of trying to attract foreign investment into China, the government has since 1979 signed a number of bilateral and multilateral treaties and agreements as investment promotion measures. One study claims that from 1982 to 1992, bilateral investment protection agreements with 54 countries were signed, and agreements on double taxation with 35 (Li Yuesheng *et al.* 1993: 30; for texts see: 123–450). According to another study, by 1995 China had 'concluded 71 such treaties, 46 since January 1990 alone' (Zhan 1995: 96). China has also participated in the negotiations on the controversial Multilateral Investment Agreement (MIA).

There is no doubt that these treaties have been negotiated and signed first and foremost to promote China as a host country for foreign investment and foreign multinationals. Even now, there is no clear evidence to suggest that the government has started to actively promote the existing treaties and agreements as beneficial to China's outward investment or demonstrate how Chinese firms investing overseas could benefit from these agreements. It is important to note, though, that through the signing of those treaties, the institutional foundation has already been laid for protecting Chinese investment overseas.

It is clear that the principal purposes for the regulatory framework for China's outward investment in the 1990s remain little changed. They are to encourage, regulate and control such activities. Appreciable changes in the regulatory framework itself are best seen in terms of its formalisation and institutionalisation. Yet, even towards the end of the 1990s, the Chinese government did not seem to have a well-coordinated policy package. Various government institutions are involved in screening and approving outward investment projects. MOFTEC's approval, for example, may not necessarily agree with SAFE's policy. Different layers of approval authorities – provincial, ministerial and central – may interpret the central government's broad and sometimes ambiguous policies in different ways.

Screening, monitoring and servicing are often said to be the three major functions of government institutions in facilitating inward foreign direct investment (Wells and Wint 1991). If the same is applicable in describing government policies with regard to outward investment, then Chinese policies seem to aim at and to fulfil only one function – screening. Even in the late 1990s, very little in the policies discussed above were purported to monitor or service China's overseas investment. The deficiencies in China's domestic policies towards its own multinationals are particularly outstanding when compared to its policies as a host country for foreign direct investment. In the two decades since 1979, hundreds of laws have been promulgated with regard to foreign investment in China and a legal framework has been institutionalised.

WTO, globalisation and further restructuring of the Chinese economy

Acceleration and deepening of the structural reforms of the Chinese economy in the 1990s, it has been often argued, have been prompted and sustained by China's bid for its WTO membership, and by the unprecedented globalisation of the world economy. China's accession to the WTO is sometimes seen as a new frontier of economic globalisation. What is important in our discussions here is to recognise the dialectic relationship between economic globalisation and the transformation of the Chinese economy. It is the forces behind the globalisation of the world economy that have worked to keep the momentum of economic reforms in China going. On the one hand, they make further economic liberalisation imperative for China to benefit from the globalisation of the economy in its developmental process, thus rendering the economic reforms irreversible. On the other, they provide more opportunities and greater markets for sustained growth of the Chinese economy in transformation, conditional on the acceleration of economic reforms. Such is the broad context of political economy for the making of China's strategies and policies on outward investment and the expansion of China's emerging global businesses.

It has been widely noted that in 1992 FDI incentives were extended beyond SEZs and the coastal areas to inland provinces and cities in the Yangtze Valley as well as to border cities in the north-east and the west. New sectors, previously 'prohibited and protected' from foreign investment, were also opened, such as real estate, telecommunication, insurance and infrastructure. Enterprise reform in the 1990s sought to diversify the ownership structure by introducing what is sometimes called 'mixed ownership' to dilute, but not to fundamentally change, the dominance of state ownership in an effort to bring in elements of market mechanism. Together with the continued marketisation of the Chinese economy, it helped transform the government business relationship 'from administrative governance into contract-based dependence' (Zhang and Van Den Bulcke 1996: 407).

The financial sector reforms in the mid-1990s are worth particular attention, too. As 'China's unfinished economic revolution' unfolded,[43] establishing effective macro-economic management became the main thrust in the marketisation of the economy. To all intents and purposes, the Fourteenth Party Congress in 1992 brought to an end the political and ideological controversies as to the general orientation of Chinese economic reform. This enabled the presentation and the approval of the substantive reform package at the Third Plenum of the Fourteenth Central Committee in November 1993.[44] The Party decision at this plenum not only explicitly reaffirmed that establishing a socialist market economy is the goal of economic reform, it also mapped out various programmes for the realisation of that goal (*Beijing Review*, 22–28 November 1993: 12–31). One IMF study identified the initiatives taken at this plenum as 'the break with the past reforms' (Mehran *et al.* 1996: 1). What is particularly pertinent to our discussion is that the decision stipulates the necessity of establishing a 'sound macro-economic control system' as the key for the transformation of the Chinese economy into a market economy. This signalled the reluctant willingness of the Party and the state to reduce, and to retreat from, unnecessary intervention in the macro-economic management of the Chinese economy.

In a very unconventional and also unprecedented way, the Party decision detailed the priority and goals of financial sector reform. Five areas are singled out in financial sector reform, namely:

- enhancing the central bank's independence
- realising RMB convertibility
- developing money and capital markets
- establishing policy lending banks
- commercialising state-controlled specialised banks (Mehran *et al.* 1996: 2).

Within three years of the decision being announced, substantial progress was achieved towards these goals. In January 1994, as a step towards RMB current account convertibility, exchange rate reform was carried out. Two previous exchange rates merged into a single, devalued rate; the exchange retention scheme for enterprises was abolished; and an exchange surrender system was adopted (Girardin 1997: 100). In December 1996, the current account convertibility of Renminbi was achieved. At the same time, three policy lending banks were established in 1994.[45] In March 1995, the Law Concerning the People's Bank of China was adopted and enacted to provide the legal foundation of the independence of the PBOC as China's central bank. On 1 July 1995, the Commercial Banking Law also came into effect. In the wake of the Asian financial crisis in 1997–98, financial reform in China was accelerated. In 1998, the PBOC reorganised its 31 provincial branches into nine centres, following the model of the Federal Reserve System in the United States. In 1998 and 1999, it also took action to close a number of non-banking financial institutions, including the high-profile closure of the Guangdong International Trust and Investment Corporation (GITIC). Also in 1998, the Chinese government injected RMB 250 billion to reca-pitulate the four big commercial banks. Asset management companies were set up to deal with the perennial problem of the huge amount of non-performing loans that had bedevilled the four biggest state-owned banks.

Concurrent with these reforms was continuous liberalisation of trade regimes and of China's host-country policy towards foreign invest-ment. Throughout the 1990s, for example, China continuously reduced its import tariffs. From April 1996 to January 2001, five tariff cuts were implemented to reduce the import duties of thousands of lines. As a result, on the eve of China's accession to the WTO, the average statutory import duty rate is only 15 per cent, much lower than many other developing countries. Only 4 per cent of all tariff lines are subject to restrictions of import quotas and licences (Lardy 2002: 22–3, 34–5).[46] China also began to open limited retail and service sectors to foreign investment in the mid-1990s. The limited opening of 'new doors', such as those to China's banking and insurance market, has led to an intensified foreign presence of both banking and non-banking financial institutions, as well as foreign participation in China's capital and securities markets (Lees and Liaw 1996).[47] In 1997 and 1998, the People's Bank of China began to open the domestic currency business to foreign banks, issuing a limited number of licences to selected foreign banks in Pudong and Shenzhen (*People's Daily*, 1 December 1999). China's commitments to open its telecommunication and financial services sectors to foreign investment after its WTO accession are sweeping.

The reasons why the Chinese leadership, fully aware of short-term political, economic and social costs, chooses to make broader and deeper commitments of economic reforms for its WTO accession are likely to remain contentious (Lardy 2002: 10–20). Using foreign competition to stimulate the domestic economy, Premier Zhu Rongji repeatedly said, is one major objective in seeking China's WTO membership (Chow 2000: 428). What Yang Xiaokai branded as 'state opportunism' hijacking economic reforms (Yang 2000: 437–9) may have also contributed to the leadership decision. Regardless of these arguments, radical restructuring of the Chinese economy both before and after China's accession to the WTO means, as I have argued in Chapter 1, China's further internalising norms, principles and rules in the global economy, leading to deeper internationalisation of the Chinese state. Such internationalisation is conducive to positioning China to meet the challenge of globalisation associated most closely with greater openness of markets, shrinking economic space and advance of information, communication and transportation technologies.

It is not surprising that in the most recent five-year plan (the tenth five-year plan) announced in 2001, Premier Zhu Rongji justified the deepening of China's opening to the outside world on the basis of the need for China to 'adjust itself to the trend of economic globalisation'. In that context, Zhu articulated four thrusts of China's new levels of opening, one of which is to 'implement a strategy [for Chinese enterprises] to go out [and invest beyond Chinese borders]'.[48] Zhu is more specific that

Those enterprises that have comparative advantage should be encouraged to invest overseas to conduct processing trade and engage in cooperation [with foreign partners] in developing natural resources. They should be encouraged to further develop international engineering contracts, expand the export of labour. We must establish and perfect our system of policy support so as to create favourable conditions for Chinese firms to invest overseas. At the same time, we should strengthen supervision so as to prevent the loss of state assets.

(Zhu 2001)

From Jiang Zemin's endorsement of China's outward investment in 1992 to Zhu's explicit call for implementing a coordinated strategy for such investment in 2001, China has realised a quantum leap in embracing economic internationalisation and in creatively responding to globalisation.

Summary

China has travelled a long way in coming to terms with multinational corporations, not only in terms of accepting intellectually and ideologically this capitalist-dominated institution, but also in terms of embracing it into the Chinese economic development strategy. The creation of a number of companies specifically aimed at tapping the international engineering and construction service markets and also CITIC in 1979 was the first step in this embrace. In the late 1980s, China's domestic policies emerged amidst active debate on the role of overseas investment in the overall economic development of China and against the backdrop of the active engagement of Chinese firms in business operations beyond Chinese borders. As in many other Third World countries, the emerging regulatory framework sought to encourage, regulate and control China's outward investment activities. It was not until September 1992 that the transnationalisation of Chinese firms through outward investment was finally and officially endorsed by the Chinese leadership. While the debates in the 1990s turned to more substantive matters of transnational operations, official efforts seem to have concentrated on institutionalising or otherwise fine-tuning the regulatory framework already in place in the 1980s. In the 1990s, however, a policy regime that is conducive to China's outward investment and the transnationalisation of Chinese firms is more dependent on further liberalisation of China's trade and investment policies and, on a broader scale, on the transformation of the Chinese economy into a market economy. Increasingly, the forces behind accelerated globalisation make further liberalisation of the Chinese economy both imperative and desirable.

The reform politics and the changing political economy of China's economic reforms make it inevitable that the prototype of China's nascent multinational corporations is to emerge from circumstances that are very different from what conventional theories speculate for the Third World multinationals. The state and government policies play an unusual role in fostering and facilitating such emergence. The raging debates about China's developmental strategy, the disagreement on the ultimate goal of China's economic reforms, unresolved until at least 1992, and the ubiquitous intervention by the state in micro-economic management and its eventual withdrawal set the context and limits for the evolution and effectiveness of the policy regimes. To the extent that the transnationalisation of Chinese companies is promoted by government policies, politics, more than economics, is in command, in most of the period of our discussions.

4
China's Multinational Corporations: Then and Now

Discussions of policy evolution and debates in the last chapter show how China has wrestled with its changing attitude towards multinational corporations in the global economy, from looking at them as part of the problem for world economic development to embracing them as part of the solution for its economic modernisation. It is at best, however, only half of the story of the political economy of China's emerging global businesses. This chapter examines transnational operations conducted by the Chinese government and enterprises before 1978, and discusses specific policy innovations significant in the early transnationalisation of Chinese businesses. In this chapter, we also tell the story of the steady growth of China's outward investment and rapid emergence of transnational businesses headquartered in China. Accordingly, this chapter seeks to address a number of questions that are of great interest. Were there any transnational operations and investment activities by the Chinese government and enterprises before 1978? When and how did the Chinese multinational corporations first emerge? And to borrow from Raymond Vernon, 'Where are they coming from? Where are they headed for?' (Vernon 1992). How does China's outward investment promote the transnationalisation of Chinese firms? What is the scale of China's investment overseas now and where is it distributed? Why should Chinese state-owned firms seek transnationalisation and how do they do it? Which group of enterprises are at the forefront of China's transnational business operations at the start of the twenty-first century?

To seek answers to the questions above, this chapter starts with an examination of a variety of economic activities beyond the Chinese borders conducted by the Chinese government as well as Chinese enterprises before 1978. It is important to note that transnational economic

81

and investment activities carried out by Chinese enterprises directed by the Chinese government between 1949 and 1978, though limited in scope, serve as precursors to the rise of China's multinational corporations after 1978. For analytical convenience, in the discussions that follow, we divide the post-1978 years into two periods. The first period, the decade of 1978–87, saw a modest but steady growth in China's overseas investment and the rapid inception of transnational operations by Chinese firms. A series of Chinese government policy innovations at the beginning of economic reform, it is argued, promoted and stimulated the internationalisation of Chinese firms.

The second period, from 1988 to 2000, is identified as a period of adjustment and growth of China's emerging global businesses as the firms respond to opportunities offered and constraints placed on them by ongoing economic reforms, the end of the Cold War and intensified and accelerated economic globalisation. Changes in the policy environment for the operation and growth of these emerging global businesses have been introduced throughout the period, sometimes domestically, sometimes internationally, but more often both. The retrenchment of transnational operations towards the end of the 1980s, when economic reform faltered, is a good example. The Asian financial crisis of 1997–98, to give another example, dictated a rethinking about China's domestic financial governance and the SOE reforms. It also affects the corporate strategy for transnationalisation. To complete our picture, in the latter part of this chapter, we also provide a brief overview of China's outward investment since 1978 and profile China's emerging global businesses today.

Transnational operations before 1978

Studies on Third World multinationals published in the early 1980s rarely mention any multinationals from the People's Republic of China (Kumar and McLeod 1981, Wells 1983, Lall 1983). Neither does Geoffrey Hamilton's volume on multinationals from socialist countries in 1986, nor the volume by a group of French scholars on state-owned multinationals (Hamilton 1986, Anastassopoulos *et al.* 1987). There are obvious explanations. The opening of China to international trade and investment started only towards the end of 1978. Even at the beginning of the 1980s, overseas investment from China, if any, was mostly restricted to Hong Kong. The transnational operations of Chinese firms were yet to begin in any meaningful way, although some national trading corporations had opened their offices in major trading partner countries. There was a bias, too, prevailing in the existing literature at the time, towards what is sometimes called 'classic' multinational corporations: that is, manufacturing multinational corporations.[1]

Some unwarranted presumptions, however, may also be responsible for the absence of discussion of the transnational operations of Chinese firms in the literature of the 1980s. Given China's relative isolation from the international community and the insulation of China from the international economic system up to the 1970s, it would seem unthinkable that either the Chinese government or Chinese firms *could* engage in any transnational business operations. Neither would it seem possible for Chinese firms to do so, given China's self-reliant economic development strategy in the same period.

Early outward investment

The real picture is more complicated. Even before 1978, that is, before the government officially announced its policy of economic reform, some Chinese enterprises had already been involved in transnational business and investment operations. An officially sponsored publication in 1989, which provides a detailed account of what it calls China's foreign economic cooperation from 1949 to 1986, mentions briefly but specifically that

> In the early years of the People's Republic of China, China already started investing overseas. From the 1950s to the 1970s, China had set up some joint ventures or wholly-owned firms engaged in ocean shipping, financial service and trading in foreign countries.
>
> (Shi *et al.* 1989: 450)

This may be referring, for example, to the Chinese–Polish Joint Stock Shipping Company known as CHIPOLBROK, established in June 1951 with each government holding 50 per cent of the shares. From four old vessels in the early days of its establishment, CHIPOLBROK now has a fleet of 21 multipurpose ships (Shi *et al.* 1989: 319, www.cosco.com.cn/about/overseas.asp).[2] It may also be referring to a limited number of Chinese enterprises established in Hong Kong in the period, including, in particular, China Resources Co. Ltd in 1950, the Hua Chiao Commercial Bank in 1962 and the Po Sang Bank Ltd in 1964. In 1975 and 1976, two provincial-level authorities, Fujian and Tianjin, also established trading subsidiaries in Hong Kong (Tseng 1994).[3]

Foreign aid programmes

One special kind of transnational operation that the Chinese government was engaged in before 1979 is particularly worth mentioning here. From the 1950s to the end of the 1970s, the Chinese government ran extensive foreign aid programmes in Third World and socialist countries, particularly in Asia and Africa. More than seventy countries received Chinese aid. Projects built by Chinese firms under the aid programmes ranged from the Tanzam Railway to a textile mill in Cambodia and from a sugar factory in Mali to bridges in Iraq. The total number of Chinese aid projects from 1954 to 1978 was 1,307, ten of which were large projects of more than 100 million yuan (Duan 1995: 44–7). Tens of thousands of Chinese aid workers were dispatched to work in Third World countries from Afghanistan to Zaire (see Bartke 1989).

These aid projects, strictly speaking, were not transnational commercial operations. Indeed, they were looked upon and largely discussed as part of China's foreign economic cooperation.[4] Nevertheless, they enabled Chinese firms to acquire knowledge of local conditions and expertise in working with a wide range of aid-recipient countries, as well as project management. Almost inadvertently, they afforded Chinese firms some ownership advantages to cultivate for its transnationalisation later. They also established the presence and, in some cases, the reputation of Chinese engineers and workers in Third World countries. They proved to be invaluable experience for China's entering the international labour and engineering services markets in the 1980s, when Chinese firms quickly turned these assets to the advantage of their commercial transnational operations.

The emergence and expansion of China's multinational corporations specialising in engineering and construction services were literally built upon the knowledge, expertise and experience that Chinese companies had acquired through their involvement in aid programmes in Third World countries before the end of the 1970s. The Ministries of Railway and Communications, for example, had by then already accumulated significant human resources for tapping into the international engineering and construction services markets. The two largest Chinese construction and engineering transnational corporations, the China Civil Engineering and Construction Corporation and China Road and Bridge Engineering Co. Ltd, were established in 1979 on the basis of the Foreign Aid Office of the Ministry of Railways and the Foreign Aid Office of the Ministry of Communications, respectively. By the mid-1980s, both were among the top thirty of the 225 largest firms in the international engineering and construction markets.[5]

Investment in Hong Kong

The most intensive, and perhaps also most interesting, transnational operations in the period, however, were conducted by state-owned firms in Hong Kong under direct instructions from the central government. The four largest firms merit particular attention here. Three of the four, the China Merchants Steam Navigation Company, China Travel Ltd, and the Bank of China Hong Kong Branch, had all been established and state-owned well before the establishment of the PRC in 1949.[6] With the British recognition of the PRC in January 1950, these firms passed into the hands of the PRC government and eventually became subsidiaries of various ministerial-level institutions. The China Merchants came under the Ministry of Communications. The Bank of China Hong Kong Branch was managed by the People's Bank of China, while China Travel Ltd was controlled by the Overseas Chinese Office of the State Council. The fourth, the China Resources Company Ltd, was established in 1950 as the trading arm of the PRC's Ministry of Trade. Accordingly, all four were directly controlled by the central government in Beijing.

Before 1978, these four firms, with their prominent presence in Hong Kong, served strategic purposes for the Chinese government in the period when the economic embargo was imposed on the PRC and when Beijing shunned intensive engagement with the world economy. As arms and vehicles of the Chinese government in Hong Kong, they provided essential services for PRC-related economic activities such as banking, finance, transportation, tourism and trade. These operations facilitated China's trade and foreign currency earnings. This was particularly valuable when China was largely isolated and insulated from the world economy, particularly before 1970. These firms were, nevertheless, largely restricted in their operational geographical areas to Hong Kong and Macao, as well as in their business scope. None of them, for example, was actively involved in the prosperous real estate market in Hong Kong in the 1960s (Lin and Jian 1995: 9).[7]

Towards the end of the 1970s, however, things began to change. Take the Bank of China Hong Kong Branch, for example. As one study pointed out, 'In 1977, Beijing prodded the BOC to expand and compete in the Hong Kong market. Expansion took the form of aggressive branching and the BOC Group overtook the Chartered bank as the second largest banking group in Hong Kong in the late 1970s' (Sung 1996: 20). In the 1980s and the 1990s, all four firms were to become dominant economic entities in Hong Kong and were to evolve into multinationals in the true meaning of the term.

A number of other firms in Hong Kong were also gradually transferred into the hands of the PRC government through different means.[8] Nanyang Brothers Tobacco Co. Ltd, for example, became state-owned when its parent company in China went from private ownership to joint public–private ownership and then to total public ownership by the state. Apart from this, the PRC also made some modest investments in Hong Kong prior to 1979. Three Chinese investments in the manufacturing industries in Hong Kong before 1970, as identified by Sung Yun-wing, were in 'Yien Chu Chemicals, Nanyang Tobacco and one other', which, in his words, 'were large and worth a total of US$311 million at original cost'. From 1970 to 1979, five other small investments were also made by the Chinese government. The investment total at the original cost by China in Hong Kong for the period of 1970–79, according to Sung, was $358 million (Sung 1996: 21, 41). One estimated value of the total stocks of China's investment in Hong Kong in 1981 was between $3 and 5 billion.[9] In Macao, an investment was made in establishing the Nan Tung Bank as early as 21 June 1950. The Nan Tung Bank, similar to the BOC Hong Kong Branch, was controlled by the PRC government and 'had long been acting somewhat like a representative of BOC in Macao'. It was renamed BOC Macao Branch on 1 January 1987 (Tam 1995: 45).

History as precursor

Several points in the above discussion merit our attention. First, Chinese firms directed by the government had been clearly involved in transnational operations before 1979. Second, China had exported capital either through its investments in Hong Kong or through its government aid programme. Third, the government, therefore, was not completely absent from operating economically and commercially beyond Chinese borders and it was by no means non-conversant with transnational economic operations. Fourth, in spite of all this, multinational corporations as defined, and with the PRC as the home country, did not exist.

China's involvement in economic operations beyond its borders discussed above can best be seen as a precursor of the transnational operations of Chinese firms. This is not only because it established the presence of Chinese firms beyond the national boundaries of the PRC, but, more importantly, because it provided some institutional basis upon which the transnational operations of Chinese firms could be built. As mentioned earlier, the institutional origin of the China Civil Engineering and Construction Corporation is the Foreign Aid Office of the Ministry of Railway, and that of the China Road and Bridge Engineering Co. Ltd is the Foreign Aid Office of the Ministry of Communications. By the late 1980s, the former had sixteen branches and representative offices in foreign countries, including Japan and Europe, and the latter had ten branches and representative offices in Asia and Africa (Interviews).

Transnational operations conducted by the Chinese government in Hong Kong are equally illustrative. The Bank of China Hong Kong Group, the China Merchants (Holding) Group the China Resources (Holding) Group and the China Travel (Hong Kong) Group – the Four Heavenly Kings, as they are nicknamed in Hong Kong – are the dominant forces in the Hong Kong economy at the time of writing. The exposure, though limited, of the Chinese government to the Hong Kong market and the experience of its officials in running businesses in Hong Kong prior to 1978 afforded the government rare, but nevertheless invaluable, expertise in operating firms abroad in a market environment.

Moreover, after 1979 Hong Kong proved to be the ideal location for Chinese firms to experiment with and experience transnational operations before expanding into the wider world market. Geographical proximity and cultural similarity are important factors. Of equal importance, Chinese firms established in Hong Kong before 1978 provided good examples for latecomers to learn managerial skills and strategic planning in transnational operations. Many of China's would-be multinationals, therefore, took their first tentative steps towards transnationalisation by establishing a foothold in Hong Kong and used Hong Kong 'as a springboard for further transnationalisation'. Zhan gave two telling examples:

> Fujian Enterprise (Holdings) Ltd. has used Hong Kong as a base to establish affiliates in Argentina, Australia, Canada, Japan, Peru, Thailand and the United States. Similarly, Guangdong Enterprise (Holdings) Ltd. based in Hong Kong has established 15 ventures in Australia, Canada, France, Germany, Thailand, the United Kingdom and the United States.
>
> (Zhan 1995: 89–90)

A new and modest start, 1978 to 1987

Policy innovations

Three policy innovations in 1978–79 directly promoted transnational operations and are of particular significance. First, the central government took the initiative to sanction the establishment of a number of firms whose main business activities were specifically directed at transnational operations. A number of purposely built multinational corporations began to emerge.[10] In November 1978, the CCP Central Committee and the State Council jointly approved the establishment of the China State Construction Engineering Co. Ltd specialising in overseas engineering and construction works and labour services. This was followed in 1979 by the establishment of three other such companies also sanctioned directly by the State Council, namely the China Civil Engineering and Construction Corporation, the China Road and Bridge Engineering Co. Ltd and the China Complete Set Equipment Import and Export Co. Ltd. These four companies became pioneers in the introduction of China to international construction, engineering and the labour service trade. They are now among the largest 225 engineering and construction firms.[11] From 1979 to 1982, 29 such specialised companies were established with the approval of the State Council. In the same period, they operated in 45 countries, and won 755 contracts worth about $1.2 billion (Duan 1995: 48). By 1985, a total of 63 engineering and construction firms were established. By June 1992, the number more than doubled to 133 (Liu Xiangdong 1993: 1234–9).

This policy innovation of the government is also illustrated, perhaps more significantly, in the State Council's sanctioning of the establishment of the China International Trust and Investment Corporation. In October 1979, CITIC was inaugurated with the blessing of the State Council as a ministerial-level organisation and as an investment vehicle for the government, which established and affirmed the special status of CITIC in the evolution of Chinese firms' transnational operations. CITIC has pioneered many aspects of transnational operations and has grown to be perhaps the most successful Chinese multinational. The next chapter discusses in detail the evolution and operation of CITIC as China's pioneering multinational.

Second, as part of its strategy to promote trade, the government not only allowed but actively encouraged the established national trading corporations to open offices in Hong Kong and in foreign countries, at the same time that it tried to decentralise China's trade regimes. All twelve national trading corporations under the Ministry of Foreign Trade quickly took advantage of this policy and branched out worldwide. By the end of 1980, all of them had opened offices overseas and made initial investments in offices and trading facilities in their respective trading partner countries. Sinotrans[12] (China National Foreign Trade Transportation Corporation), for example, set up its first overseas joint venture, the International United Shipping Agency, with Y. K. Pao in Hong Kong in early 1980. In December 1980, less than two years after the establishment of diplomatic relations between China and the United States, Sinotrans set up its first wholly owned overseas subsidiary in the United States, USA–China Interocean Transport Incorporation (Yan 1994: 18).

The initial investments made by these companies were understandably mostly trade-related. It was, nevertheless, a significant first step towards the transnationalisation of those firms. MINMETAL UK, for example, was to grow out of the MINMETAL UK Representative Office established in 1979. These initial steps, therefore, laid the foundation for those corporations to develop into fully fledged multinational corporations. In early 1994, the *Beijing Review* reported that by the end of 1993, 2,839 trade-related subsidiaries had been established overseas with a total investment of over $3.46 billion (*Beijing Review*, 21–27 March 1994: 18).

The government policy of encouraging established firms to set up subsidiaries and open representative offices was not restricted to trading firms. The Bank of China, for example, opened a branch in Luxembourg in 1979, the first overseas branch ever opened since 1949. Similarly, COSCO, China's national ocean shipping company, opened its new branches also in 1979, first in Hong Kong and then the United Kingdom.

Third, and closely associated with the above-discussed activities of Chinese firms, is the government policy regarding China's outward investment. It is generally overlooked that one of the earliest reform policies adopted by the Chinese government was to allow Chinese firms to conduct outward investment. As discussed earlier, on 13 August 1979, the State Council issued a circular on fifteen measures of economic reform, the thirteenth of which specifically and explicitly stated that Chinese firms should be encouraged 'to set up Chinese enterprises overseas' (*chuguo ban qiye*). Admittedly, this was not the main thrust of China's opening up in the early years. There were no clearly defined policies on China's outward investment, either, for years to come. It is important to note, however, that at such an early stage, the government already considered outward investment as part of its economic reform package and that this announcement laid down an important principle from which a series of government policies were to evolve.

Finally, though not directly a measure to promote the transnational operation of firms, one other policy innovation was introduced. The establishment of the special economic zones in the early 1980s represented an unusual decentralisation of economic decision-making in China's early reform period (see Oborne 1986, Jao and Leung 1986). This innovation, among other things, facilitated the early expansion of firms located in SEZs into operations beyond the Chinese borders. Many enterprises in Shenzhen, for example, took advantage of geographical and historical connections, as well as preferential policies, to establish a foothold quickly in Hong Kong and Macao.[13]

With hindsight, it is clear that these policy innovations were particularly important in encouraging the emergence of China's multinational corporations. China's engineering firms broke into the world market. National trading corporations took important first steps towards the transnationalisation of their activities by gaining and establishing a firm foothold abroad. Chinese investment overseas also began to take off.

Outward investment

The Chinese government, however, was at best ambivalent towards overseas investment, though it did pronounce a general policy in principle to encourage firms to engage in economic activities beyond Chinese borders. As discussed in the last chapter, even in the mid-1980s, Chinese academics were still embroiled in a debate about the nature and the role of multinational corporations in the world economy. Ideological and political legacies of three decades of political isolation and economic insulation are not easy to overcome. Moreover, attracting foreign investment *into* China dominated the Chinese leadership's political and economic agenda at the time.

There were other considerations, too. Could China afford to export capital for outward investment, given the shortage of funds, particularly foreign currency reserves, needed for such investment? Did Chinese firms have a competitive edge, and what comparative advantage, if any, did they have for competing on the international market? How could China overcome its dearth of expertise in transnational business operations? Was there any successful formula for Chinese firms to follow when they were still lacking the necessary managerial skills and entrepreneurial spirit for operating at home, not to mention overseas? There was also the uncompromising tension between the socialist economic system of China and the capitalist market economies. Was it possible for a state-owned parent company in a largely command economy to effectively operate subsidiaries in a market economy environment, and how? These questions kept coming back to haunt Chinese policy-makers and the top management of Chinese firms. The domestic economic system further hampered the growth of overseas investment. In the mid-1980s, the liberalisation of China's trade regimes was at best limited. Foreign exchange controls were harsh. And the liberalisation of China's financial system and institutions was yet to start in earnest. Looking back from the perspective of the twenty-first century, economic reforms that had been implemented by then were, at most, half-baked.

Given these political and economic constraints, China's non-trade-related outward investment activity in the first ten years of China's opening to the world economy, as seen in Table 4.1, is instantly instructive. From a cautious and tentative start in 1979–83, it grew steadily in 1984–86. The first great leap outward in terms of China's overseas investment was in 1987.[14]

How do we interpret these raw statistics in the table? First, they are only indicative of the trend of China's outward investment. The statistics are by no means accurate, or comprehensive. The IMF database shows, for example, that in 1988 alone, China's direct investment abroad amounted to $850 million. From 1982 to 1988, an investment total of $2,845 million was made by China (*International Financial*

Table 4.1 China's non-trade-related outward investment, 1979–88 (in $ million)

	Number of ventures*	Total investment	Chinese investment**
1979	4	1.21	0.53
1980	13	68.01	30.90
1981	13	6.78	2.56
1982	13	5.87	3.18
1983	18	19.32	8.70
1984	42	102.6	80.86
1985	77	92.17	50.51
1986	92	75.51	53
1987	108	1,373	410
1988	141	118	75.00
Total	521	1,862.47	715.24

* Number of ventures are those approved by MOFERT.
** Investment values are approved contract values, not realised values.
Sources: Duan (1995: 52–5), Zhang Yangui (1997: 29), Shi Lin *et al.* (1989: 453).

Statistical Yearbook, 2001: 356–7). It has been widely observed that there are huge discrepancies between different sets of Chinese statistics and between Chinese statistics and the statistics released by international organisations such as UNCTAD and the IMF.[15] One example of these notoriously inaccurate Chinese statistics is that in 1986, one single investment made by CITIC was A$120 million in the Portland Aluminium Smelter in Australia. However, the MOFERT statistics recorded only $75.71 million outward investment in that whole year for 92 projects! One possible explanation for this wild discrepancy is that MOFERT figures only recorded the actual capital export by Chinese firms it approved. CITIC's investment in the Portland Aluminium Smelter in Australia was funded by the capital it raised through the lease-leverage financing on the international capital market. It did not involve a large amount of actual capital export from China.

Second, the overall investment figure is insignificant, either compared to China's GDP, which was $206.21 billion in 1986, or to FDI flow into China, the accumulated total of which stood at the end of 1988 as $28.2 billion in contracted value and $12.1 billion in realised value. In 1988 alone, the contracted foreign investment inflow was $5.29 billion, whereas the contracted outward investment by Chinese firms was only $75.71 million, a bare 1.4 per cent of the inflow total. Further, it is negligible in terms of world FDI investment flow total. For example, according to MOFERT, in 1985 the total of world FDI was $650 billion, whereas that from China was only $50.51 million.

Third, these incomplete statistics collected and published by MOFERT are nevertheless clear indications that China was emerging as a significant investor from the developing countries. The total of $715 million of China's non-trade-related outward investment from 1979 to 1988 represented around $71.5 million per annum throughout this decade. In a comparative perspective, Korea invested a total of $110.85 million overseas from 1967 to 1978. That is to say, in the first twelve years of Korea's overseas investment activities, Korea's outward investment per annum was on average less than $10 million. It was only in the period 1981 to 1985 that Korea's annual overseas investment, including both trade-and non-trade-related, reached $77 million per annum. In another comparison, Brazil invested around $78 million on average per annum in its peak years of outward investment from 1970 to 1978 (Kumar and MacLeod 1981: 54, Duan 1995: 53). It should also be noted that the Chinese statistics do not include either trade-related investment or the bulk of its investment in Hong Kong. Should those be included, the annual average in 1979–88 would be much higher.[16]

Table 4.2 China's large overseas investment projects, 1980–87 (in $ million)

	Investment	Investor	Destination
1980	22.25	China Ship Building Industrial Corp.	Hong Kong
1981	17	MINMETAL	Hong Kong
1984	36	China National Fishery Corp.	USA
1984	13.14	CITICFOR	USA
1984	3.85	China Forestry Int. Co. Corp.	Brazil
1984	30	China Fishery Co. Ltd.	USA
1986	120	CITIC	Australia
1986	47*	CITIC	Canada
1987	117	China Metallurgical Industrial Corp.	Australia
1987	38.15	China Metallurgical Imp./Exp. Corp.	Australia

* Figures here are in Canadian dollars.
Sources: Zhan (1995: 78–9), Zhang Yangui (1997: 32), Wall (1996: 56).

To further understand China's overseas investment activity in this period, it is instructive also to look at some large investments made by Chinese firms in 1980–87. As Table 4.2, which is by no means exhaustive, clearly illustrates, even in its first stage the amount of investment in single projecs was not insignificant.

In the mid-1980s, there were large Chinese acquisitions in Hong Kong, too. In 1986, CITIC Hong Kong acquired substantial stakes in the Ka Wah Bank. In 1987, China Merchants acquired the Union Bank. These two acquisitions were believed to be 'rescue' operations launched by the two Chinese firms concerned under the instruction of the central government.[17] They turned out to be, by default, the beginning of Chinese company investment in firms listed on the Hong Kong Stock Exchange through indirect listing. In 1987, some provincial subsidiaries in Hong Kong also began acquisition operations. Yue Hai Investment from Guangdong acquired Union Globe Development, and Hua Min from Fujian province bought the Min Xin group (Lin and Jian 1995: 30–2).[18]

During the first decade of China's economic reform, significant outward investment was therefore made. Chinese firms had made tentative yet bold moves towards experimenting with transnational operations all over the world. What could be regarded as a prototype for Chinese multinationals was emerging. The importance of policies and policy innovation was tested in this period. Whereas the consolidation of and reaffirmed commitment to economic reform in the mid-1980s was behind the surge of outward investment in 1987, it is the limits of economic reform that set the context for the transnationalisation of Chinese firms. By the end of 1987, the liberalisation of China's trade regimes was still relatively limited. State trading was still characteristic of China's foreign trade system. The government still exercised strong foreign exchange control. Macro-economic policies remained basically unchanged. The command economy was largely in place. In other words, serious policy impediments as well as systemic constraints in the Chinese economy provided a not so hospitable environment for the emergence of multinationals. In addition, lack of expertise and world market information, a paucity of managerial skills and the absence of entrepreneurial spirit were challenges that firms had to face in building their international businesses.

Important attributes of state-owned firms

One other explanation for the rapid take-off of transnational operations by Chinese firms is to be found in the attributes of large state-owned enterprises. First, after thirty years of growth, a number of China's national corporations, such as the twelve national trading companies, had already grown fairly large even by international standards, with expertise and experience, albeit limited, in international operations and an extensive 'relational network' all over the world, an important asset for traders to go multinational.[19] Once the inhibitive policies and conditions were lifted, they all strove to experiment and to engage in transnational operations. Second, it is worth mentioning that there are ownership advantages for Chinese firms associated with government ownership, among which are a high political profile and rapid resource mobilisation, pivotal in initiating outward investment in the government-controlled investment scenario (Zhang and Van Den Bulcke, 1996: 387). Third, creative firm-level initiatives are not entirely absent even among the state-owned enterprises. They are crucial in determining the direction, the nature, the scope and the size of the development of early international business of individual firms. Different responses to the changing policy environment by China's trading corporations, for example, resulted in variations in the initial transnationalisation of those firms.

This was also true for the newly established construction and engineering companies. Almost by default, these firms acquired ownership advantage partly through their valuable experience and expertise in running government aid programmes in Third World countries prior to 1978. The government policy of restructuring and organising specialised companies in this sector, first implemented in 1978–79, amounted to policy support and ensured the successful and aggressive entry of Chinese firms into the world market. This group of purposely built transnationals, together with the newly established CITIC and provincial ITICs (international trust and investment companies), spearheaded China's non-trade-related overseas investment and transnational operations. Again, the combination of the new policy milieu and the creative response of Chinese firms to economic liberalisation proved critical in the emergence of China's own multinational corporations in the first period of our discussion, and in sustaining their growth in the second.

Adjustments and growth, 1988 to 2000

The transnational operations of Chinese firms in the second period of our discussion have a mixed record of sustained growth with constant adjustments and consolidation. The faltering of economic reform towards the end of the 1980s and changing macro-economic conditions in the mid-1990s, for example, seriously affected the policy milieu set up by the government for the internationalisation of Chinese firms. Sanctions imposed on China by major economic powers in the wake of the government crackdown in Beijing in June 1989, the Asian financial crisis in 1997–98 and economic globalisation accelerated by technological revolution throughout the 1990s provided constraints as well as incentives and opportunities for firms to engage in transnational operations. China's renewed aggressive bid for membership first of the General Agreement on Tariffs and Trade (GATT) and then of the World Trade Organisation after 1992 is another broad context within which China's official policy towards transnational operations of firms has been made and implemented. So was the incorporation of the transnationalisation of Chinese firms into the overall economic development strategy at the CCP's Fourteenth National Congress in 1992. In other words, the emergence and growth of China's global businesses in the second decade had to respond to changes and transformations in domestic economic conditions, as well as in the international context.

The great surge of China's outward investment in 1987, both in terms of contract value and the number of projects approved, marked the end of one period and the beginning of another. Approval by the State Council in December 1987 of Sinochem's application to internationalise its operations is symbolically the starting point of the second decade of the transnationalisation of Chinese firms. China's bid for GATT and WTO membership, first submitted in 1986, was to provide the impetus for the continuous and further liberalisation of China's trade regimes throughout the period.

The faltering of economic reform

The beginning of the second decade of transnationalisation of Chinese firms coincided with the biggest ever stumble in the economic reform process. From mid-1987 to mid-1988, the twelve-month inflation rate reached 30 per cent, an inflationary pressure that the PRC's economy had never experienced. The socio-economic impact of this hyperinflation[20] was clearly seen in the streets of Beijing in early 1989. Already in late 1988, the government had introduced a rectification programme to control inflation and to stabilise the economy. A more stringent austerity programme would be more rigorously implemented after the second half of 1989. The political repercussions of these economic difficulties would eventually lead to the downfall of the reform-minded Zhao Ziyang. But even before the student protests and the eventual crackdown in Beijing in May and June of 1989, reform had largely stalled. After the June crackdown, the government tightened political control at the same time as it retrenched and recentralised part of the economy. To all intents and purposes, structural reform in the Chinese economy largely stagnated after the second half of 1989.

If 'some earlier reforms were reversed' (Mehran *et al.* 1996: 12), the Chinese government did not seem to have reversed its overall policy on the transnationalisation of firms, though a retrenchment in transnational operations of Chinese firms was apparent in 1989–91. The government suspended its approval of trade-related investment overseas. It also tried to overhaul China-funded enterprises in Hong Kong and Macao (Zhang Yegui 1997: 30). Take Shenzhen as an example. By the end of 1988, Chinese firms in Shenzhen claimed 110 non-trade-related subsidiaries in Hong Kong. But by the end of 1990, only 53 remained (Zhu and Ye 1993: 170). Domestically, the government took drastic measures to restructure and rationalise the trust and investment companies, as it believed that credit creation by some irresponsible ITICs was partly responsible for the rising inflation. Internationally, because of the sanctions imposed on China in the wake of June 1989, China suddenly disappeared from the global bond market.[21]

At the same time, however, trade liberalisation seems to have continued. There are good reasons why Lardy contended in 1992 that trade reforms 'by no means floundered' after 1989.[22] The contract responsibility system, which selected foreign trade enterprises were experimenting with in 1988, was implemented by all trading firms in

1991 (Kang *et al.* 1996: 50–1). The RMB was twice devalued in less than a year, by 21.2 per cent in December 1989 and by 15.4 per cent in 1990. The foreign exchange retention system underwent further reform (Lardy 1992). Also in 1991, the organisation of foreign trade enterprise groups began its experimental phase, first with Sinochem and MINMETAL (Qiu 1992: 13–15).

But it was Deng's relaunch of economic reform in the spring of 1992 that breathed new life into the transnationalisation of Chinese firms. Not only were political controversies surrounding the transnational operations of firms eventually resolved when the transnationalisation of Chinese firms was incorporated into the national development strategy at the Fourteenth CCP National Congress. Equally importantly, further liberalisation of the Chinese economy transformed macro-economic conditions for the further integration of China into the global economy. In June 1992, preferential policies for attracting FDI were granted to eighteen inland provincial capital cities and a number of border cities along the newly opened frontiers in south-west, north-west and north-east China. Some sectors previously forbidden for foreign investment such as airport construction, power plant and telecommunications were tentatively opened.

More directly relevant are the enterprise reforms in 1992–93. *Regulations for Transforming the Operating Mechanism of the State-Owned Enterprises* was promulgated. The government conceded a wide range of decision-making power to the enterprises. Management autonomy was extended to most key managerial areas, including production, pricing, distribution, purchasing, import and export, and investment and finance. More importantly, this autonomy was now protected by law. Further, enterprise groups directly controlled by the central government ministries were given 'separate planning status' in order to prevent them from bureaucratic intervention (Zhang and Van Den Bulcke, 1996).

Internationally, sanctions against China after June 1989 were gradually relaxed and then largely lifted in 1992–93. Not surprisingly, the contracted FDI in 1992 alone reached $58 billion, which was more than the total commitment of FDI China received from 1979 to 1991. In 1993, it reached a historical high of $111.43 billion – a record unlikely to be surpassed in the near future (State Statistics Bureau 1997b: 132). The annual growth of the Chinese economy in those two years reached 13 per cent.

In 1994–95, financial sector reforms were introduced, which aimed at improving the macro-economic conditions within which firms operated domestically and transnationally, as discussed in the last chapter. At the same time, the government began to engineer a 'soft landing' of the economy after two years of overheating and overexpansion. The austerity programme introduced a severe credit squeeze and the government resorted mostly to administrative measures to ensure compliance with its 'soft landing' policies, in Beijing as well as at the provincial level. The austerity programme affected China's outward investment, probably most clearly illustrated by the MOFTEC figures of the period (see Figure 4.1).

Responding to challenges and expansion

The transnational operations of Chinese firms in the early 1990s, therefore, had to respond to a series of complex changes in the political and macro-economic policy environment and broad transformations of the Chinese economy. It is interesting to note that a combination of factors – fear of loss of state assets, demands of the domestic economy, concerns to keep foreign currency reserves high, severe credit control and the austerity programme – seem to have slowed down MOFTEC approved overseas investment. Overall, however, the outward investment from China grows rapidly.

Two features are striking in Table 4.3 and Figure 4.1. One is that the figures released by the State Statistics Bureau and MOFTEC have huge discrepancies. It is obvious that MOFTEC only monitors a small portion of outward investment projects. The other is that, as seen in China's balance of payment statistics, China's outward FDI took off in 1992. The 1993 record of $4.4 billion remains. The annual average in 1991–2000 is over $2.36 billion. Compared with the previous decade, the growth of China's outward FDI in the 1990s is striking. According to Zhan, the annual average FDI outflow from China in 1980–84 is only $52 million, and in 1985–89 is $671 million (Zhan 1995: 71).

The expansion and growth of transnational operations of Chinese firms is closely related to such a jump in outward investment in this period. A number of large-scale investments overseas were made.

Table 4.3   China's outward investment, 1991–95 (in $ million)

	1991	1992	1993	1994	1995
MOFTEC	367	195	96	804	131
UNCTAD	913	4,000	4,400	2,000	2,000

Sources: MOFTEC (1997: 454), UNCTAD (2000: 370).

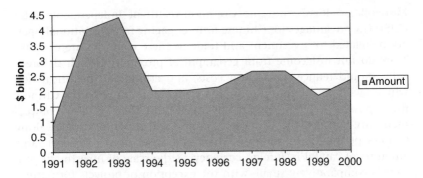

Figure 4.1 China's outward investment, 1991–2000

Sources: State Statistics Bureau (various years), *World Investment Report 2001: Country Sheet: China*,[23] *International Monetary Fund* (2001: 356–7).

Sinochem's $122 million investment for the acquisition of the US Agri-Chemical in Florida in 1989, Shougang's $312 million investment in an iron ore mine in Peru in 1992, CITIC Australia's acquisition of Metro Meat with A$100 million in 1994, and CITIFOR's purchase of 37.5 per cent of assets of the Forest Corporation of New Zealand with over $500 million in 1996 are but a few examples that will be examined in Part III. Other examples include Sinotrans's $87 million investment in New Zealand forestry in 1990, China's National Petroleum Corporation's (CNPC) $441 million investment in oil exploration in Sudan in 1996, and China's commitment to invest $4 billion in Kazakhstan for oil exploitation and oil pipe-line construction (*International Herald Tribune*, 6 June 1997; UNCTAD 1999: 200).

Aggressive M&A operations by Chinese firms in Hong Kong are another main thrust of Chinese transnationalisation. Suffice it here to mention CITIC Hong Kong's acquisition of 20 per cent of Hong Kong Telecom in 1989 and 20 per cent of China Light and Power in 1996. These are the two largest utilities companies in Hong Kong. Each acquisition involved an investment of over HK$10 billion. Shougang, too, went on a spree of aggressive M&A in 1993–95 in Hong Kong, as will be discussed in detail in Chapter 7.

Chinese firms have also actively cultivated hitherto untouched territories for outward investment and transnational operations. With the end of the Cold War and China's opening of its borders for trade, favourable geopolitical and geo-economic conditions created opportunities for operations in countries bordering China, from Burma and

Mongolia to Russia and the Commonwealth of Independent States (CIS). The advantages for Chinese firms engaging in transnational operations related to investment and trade in these countries are obvious. They do not just come from geographical proximity, which theoretically should reduce transaction costs, and ethnic and historical ties, which facilitate communication and trade. More importantly, Chinese firms possess a technological advantage and there is also complementarity between the Chinese economy and those economies along China's periphery. In addition, there is a lesser need to export large amounts of capital in foreign currency, as the scale of investment projects is comparatively small, with the exception of projects for natural resources exploration. According to MOFTEC statistics, in China's eighth five-year-plan period, that is, from 1991 to 1995, its approved outward investment in Russia was $70.11 million in 206 enterprises. This accumulated total was in fact the second largest to a single foreign country in that period, second only to Canada, but larger than that to the USA (MOFTEC 1997: 454).[24] China's investment in Kazakhstan's oil industry, as mentioned above, is another example.

Last but by no means least is the growth of China's multinationals specialising in construction and engineering services. In 1996 alone, they fulfilled $7.696 billion of contract value and won contracts worth more than $10 billion. In comparison, in 1987, the respective figures were $1.22 billion and $1.733 billion. Four contract projects secured by Chinese firms in 1996 were worth over $100 million, including a power station in Malaysia, a textile factory in Syria and a railway construction project in Nigeria (MOFTEC 1997: 127).

The impact of the Asian financial crisis, 1997–98

The Asian financial crisis broke out in 1997, when the transnationalisation of Chinese firms reached a new plateau. The impact of this crisis on the Chinese economy was profound and multifaceted. In the throes of the financial crisis, the growth of China's exports literally stalled in 1998.[25] In the wake of the financial crisis, FDI flow into China in 1999 declined, only to pick up again in 2000. More importantly, perhaps, the crisis exposed a number of serious weaknesses in China's financial system. Among them were irresponsible lending resulting in an unacceptably high percentage of non-performing loans from the state-owned banks and the poor governance structure of the banking system. The question of the viability and vulnerability of China's financial system was put on line. In its own way, the crisis persuaded the Chinese leadership to conduct urgent and more sweeping reforms of its banking system. It seems to have also convinced the Chinese leadership and elite alike of the desirability of more actively participating in economic globalisation (Pang 1999).[26] Efforts to negotiate for and to obtain China's WTO membership began to be seen as an indispensable part of China's embrace of globalisation.

It is not clear why the crisis does not seem to have had an immediate effect on China's outward investment. The *International Financial Statistics Yearbook 2001* reports that China's outward investment actually rose from $2.114 billion in 1996 to $2.563 billion in 1997 and $2.634 billion in 1998. It only declined in 1999 to $1.775 billion and further to $0.916 billion in 2000 (IMF 2002: 356–7).[27] It is clear, though, that it seriously affected the international capital market for Asia. Research conducted by the IMF found that even in 1999, total new financing in Asia from the international bond and loans markets remained merely 40 per cent below the peak levels in 1997, whereas the syndicated loans market remained 50 per cent below its historical peak, also in 1997 (Mathieson and Schinasi 2000: 51). The effect of foreign banks' retreat from Asia in the wake of the crisis was exacerbated by the bankruptcy of the Guangdong International Trust and Investment Corporation in 1998. Not only did foreign banks' lending to China as a whole decline sharply in the period of 1997–99, but also Hong Kong banks reduced their loans to China-related non-banking red chips in 1998 and 1999 by at least $12 billion (Lardy 2002: 17).

The crisis also critically affected the reform of large-scale SOEs. As will be discussed in Chapter 6, in the wake of the crisis, *chaebol* (conglomerate) and *sogo shosha* (general trading company) were ditched as a model for the conglomeration of large SOEs. It is also noteworthy that in 1997 and 1998 the 'omissions and errors' in China's balance of payment account reached historical highs respectively at $22.12 billion and $18.90 billion.[28]

A new thrust of transnationalisation of Chinese firms?

Towards the end of the 1990s, China began to seek to list parts of its largest state-owned enterprises on the international equity markets. For example, in 1997, the sale of China Telecom (Hong Kong) raised $4 billion. In 2000 alone, four of the largest Chinese companies – three oil giants, the China National Petroleum Corporation, the China Petrochemical Corporation (Sinopec) and the China National Offshore Oil Corporation (CNOOC), and one Chinese telecom giant, China Unicom – listed their subsidiaries in Hong Kong and New York and raised a total of $15 billion. The Bank of China (Hong Kong) is due to be listed in July 2002. Large Chinese firms seeking foreign listing to raise funds on the international equity markets is nothing new. As discussed in Chapter 2, since the early 1990s a number of Chinese companies have been successfully listed on both the Hong Kong and New York stock exchanges. What is different in these recent listings is not only that they are among the largest Chinese state-owned enterprises. More importantly, unlike many previous listings, the funds sought and raised are not entirely for these companies' domestic operation and expansion. This is most clearly demonstrated in the case of CNPC and CNOOC. Both have sought aggressive cross-border mergers and acquisitions through its listed arms. CNPC already owns oil assets in Sudan, Peru, Venezuela and Thailand. Its listed arm PetroChina is most recently reported to be in the market for overseas oil and gas assets, possibly in Russia and Canada, to compensate for its domestic operations in the future (*Far Eastern Economic Review*, 28 March 2002; www.asia.cnn.com/2002/business/asia/02/20/china.husky.biz).[29] CNOOC, on the other hand, has acquired substantial oil and gas assets in Indonesia in January 2002 from a Spanish company (*Far Eastern Economic Review*, 28 March 2002).

The fact that the Chinese government began to sell parts of the largest and possibly also the most profitable companies on the international equity markets indicates that the overseas listing is seen by the government as one key component in its strategy for reform of troubled large-scale state-owned enterprises. Increasingly, overseas listing is justified on the grounds that diversified ownership helps improve management and governance structure and creates a responsive and globally oriented corporate leadership, rather than on the grounds of the necessity to raise investment funds. Overseas listing also creates a new platform and enables the pooling of necessary managerial expertise for the listed companies and their parents to mount cross-border mergers and acquisitions, which seem to be increasingly encouraged by the Chinese government. A new pathway for the transformation and transnationalisation of large Chinese state-owned companies has thus been instituted.

Outward investment from China since 1978: an overview

From our discussions above, it is clear that the picture of China's outward investment in 1978 and that in 2001 cannot be more different. A considerable number of China's aspiring global businesses have emerged as China becomes a significant Third World investor. The rest of this chapter attempts to provide an overall picture of China's overseas investment activities. This section offers a brief overview of China's outward investment since 1978, and the next section presents a profile of China's emerging multinational corporations. Following the conventional wisdom about a country's outward investment, we ask how much, why, where and in what industries such investment has been made. Accordingly, the accumulated total of overseas investment, the reasons and motivations behind it and its geographical spread as well as its industrial distribution are looked at in this section.

Size of outward investment

How much have Chinese firms invested beyond Chinese borders? What is the size of Chinese investment in other economies? The first question is related to China's total investment at its original cost, whereas the second question is concerned more with the total existing stocks of Chinese investment overseas. These seemingly simple questions, however, defy any definitive answer.[30] Trying to arrive at the accumulative total of both is near impossible. Quite apart from the problem of the lack of transparency in the Chinese economy, there is the problem of institutional arrangements. There is as yet no centralised and line-managed institution in China to register, not to speak of monitoring, all China's outward investment. Statistics provided by MOFTEC are probably the most systematic, but MOFTEC's registry only includes what it approves and what it could gather from other provincial and ministerial authorities about both trade-related and non-trade-related outflows.[31] MOFTEC's figures are therefore at best incomplete. Large investment projects by CITIC and Shougang, as will be examined in detail in Part III, are clearly beyond MOFTEC's authority to approve, even less to control. Further, the lion's share of CITIC's investment funds has been raised on the international capital markets. It is impossible to monitor systematically all such investment activity by Chinese firms. It is safe to assume that neither MOFTEC nor China's current balance of payment records this part of Chinese overseas investment.

Portfolio outflow, again, is totally out of the control of MOFTEC. Still more difficult is capital flight. As we have already discussed in Chapter 2, a huge amount of 'omissions and errors' have been entered in the *China Statistical Yearbook* throughout the 1990s, and are unaccounted for in China's capital account balance sheet. Further compounding the matter is the Hong Kong factor. As noted, the total of Chinese investment in Hong Kong is a big unknown, or maybe an unknowable. Rough estimates ran from $25 billion to $40 billion in the mid-1990s. But this was based on the total stocks of Chinese investment in Hong Kong rather than its original cost (Sung 1996).

With the above caveats, it is still possible, however, to suggest some rough data as indicators of the size of Chinese investment overseas.

In the first place, China's outward FDI in the 1990s reached an annual average of over $2 billion. This figure would be more meaningful if put into comparative perspective. As observed by both Zhan and Wall, China's FDI outflow in the early 1990s is as significant as that of Taiwan. Zhan's figures for 1990–95 are $2,429 million as an annual average for China, and $2,640 million for Taiwan. According to Wall, however, the annual average of Taiwan's FDI outflow was only $2,260 million in the period between 1992 and 94, much lower than China's $3,467 million. In China's boom years of 1992–94, China saw the second largest FDI outflow of all non-OECD economies, second only to Hong Kong (Zhan 1995: 71, Wall 1996: 50).[32] The IMF figures published in 2001 show that China continues to make substantial outward investment in the late 1990s. It only declines markedly in 2000.[33]

As a result, the ratio of outward investment in China's GDP and gross fixed capital formation (GFCF) also grows (see Table 4.4).

There is another comparison. In the 1990s, China is often ranked the fourth largest investor in developing Asia behind Hong Kong, Singapore and Taiwan (Dunning *et al.* 1998). The accumulated total of China's outward FDI stocks are estimated by UNCTAD to have been $22,079 million in 1998, a quantum leap from $2,489 million in 1990. In 1998, therefore, China's accumulative outward FDI stocks were larger than that of the following European Union members: Austria ($16,808 million), Portugal ($7,537 million), Ireland ($6,477 million) and Greece

Table 4.4 China's inward and outward investment, selected years

	Stock (in $ million)		% GDP		% GFCF*	
	Inward	Outward	Inward	Outward	Inward	Outward
1990	18,568	2,489	5.2	0.7	n/a	n/a
1995	131,241	15,802	18.8	2.3	14.7	0.8
1997	215,657	20,479	23.5	2.2	14.3	0.8
1999	305,900	24,900	30.9	2.5	11.3	n/a

* Gross fixed capital formation.
Sources: UNCTAD (2000) 491–2, 497, 509, 521, UNCTAD (2002).

Table 4.5 China's outward FDI stocks (selected years) in comparative perspective

	1980	1985	1990	1995	1997
China	40	131	2,489	15,802	20,416
Developing economies					
Korea	142	526	2,301	10,224	18,044
Malaysia	414	749	2,283	8,903	15,703
Singapore	652	9,675	9,675	32,695	43,400
Taiwan	97	204	12,894	18,854	34,178
Argentina	70	280	420	675	908
Brazil	652	1,361	2,397	7,238	8,730
Chile	42	102	178	2,769	5,797
Developed economies					
Austria	530	1,908	4,656	12,887	14,979
Denmark	2,065	1,801	7,342	19,934	25,684
Finland	743	1,829	11,227	15,177	20,332
Portugal	116	186	503	2,775	5,182
South Africa	5,722	6,504	7,827	9,492	11,898

Sources: UNCTAD (1999: 380–3), Dunning *et al.* (1998).

($850 million). It is even larger than that of South Korea ($21,505 million). Another equally interesting comparison is with other transitional economies. If we go by the UNCTAD statistics, in 1997, China's outward FDI stocks amounted to three times that of all transitional economies in Central and Eastern Europe put together, from Albania to Ukraine, including Russia (UNCTAD 1999: 379–84, UNCTAD 2000: 496–7). In 2000, China's outward FDI stocks increased further to $27,200 million (UNCTAD 2002, *Country Fact Sheet: China*).

The best estimate of China's investment in Hong Kong can also give us an indicator of the scale of China's outward FDI. Sung suggests that it is only possible to 'guestimate' the total of Chinese investment in Hong Kong over the years. The 'guestimation' is based on the stocks of investment, not on its original cost. Sung claimed that 'the most often quoted figures were $10 billion of Chinese investment in Hong Kong at the end of 1989, and $20 billion at the end of 1992'.[34] But he also observed that the conservative estimate was $15 billion in 1993 and $20 billion in 1994. China's investment is certainly 'well over $20 billion' (Sung 1996: 11–17). The Hang Seng Bank reported in October 1993, however, that in 1992 alone, China injected an estimated $20 billion into the Hong Kong economy. It suggested, however, that the bulk went through unlisted companies. Only $5 billion was invested by Chinese financial institutions and a further $1 billion through listed companies (*Financial Times*, 8 October 1993).[35]

In the year 2000, Hong Kong registerd an upsurge of inward FDI, which jumped to $63.4 billion from $24.4 billion in 1999. There is no breakdown of the origins of these investments. If the previous year can be used as a guide, however, 70 per cent are from China and tax havens (*Far Eastern Economic Review*, 13 June 2001). China's investment in Hong Kong continues to be shrouded in mystery and its exact size remains unknowable. As a scholar based in Hong Kong recently pointed out, the datasets from various authorities about China's investment stocks in Hong Kong are 'irreconcilable'. Beijing simply does not know the exact size of its investment in Hong Kong. He further cited an official document that candidly admitted that 'The obvious fact is that currently the state has no clear idea at all about the quantity of our country's firms and investments overseas' (Ding 2000: 123–4).

Geographical and sectoral distribution

Two characteristics stand out in terms of the geographical spread of China's outward investment. It is in general extremely wide. MOFTEC claimed in 1997 that China was conducting foreign economic cooper-ation (that is, aid and investment) with 178 countries and regions (MOFTEC 1997: 128). Dunning *et al.* find, however, that unlike most other developing economies in East Asia and elsewhere, China's out-ward investment has always been biased towards developed economies (Dunning *et al.* 1998). Research by Zhang and Van Den Bulcke based on the MOFTEC statistics comes to a similar conclusion. Of China's outward investment approved by MOFTEC from 1979 to 1992, over 68 per cent went to industrialised countries. The rest, around 32 per cent, went to developing countries, with only 9 per cent going to Hong Kong and Macao. They further note that 'Chinese firms tended to invest in countries with high technological and innovatory capaci-ties and abundant natural resources, such as the USA, Australia and Canada (Zhang and Van Den Bulcke 1996: 403, 410).

In value terms, it is further concentrated in the Asia-Pacific region. Most large-scale investment or acquisition projects – such as CITIC's investment in the Portland Aluminium Smelter and Anshan Iron and Steel Complex's investment in iron ore mining, both in Australia, Shougang's investment in Peru, Sinotrans's acquisition of forestry in 1990 and that of CITIC in 1996, both in New Zealand, CNOOC's most recent acquisition in Indonesia, not to mention CITIC Hong Kong's acquisitions of Cathay Pacific and Hong Kong Telecom – are all in this

Table 4.6 Geographical distribution of China's outward FDI stocks in comparative perspective, two periods

		Developing (%)	Developed (%)
China	1981	35.00	65.00
	1992	31.57	68.43
Brazil	1980	25.92	74.08
	1990	45.93	54.07
Colombia	1980	78.00	22.00
	1990	75.40	24.60
India	1980	91.05	8.95
	1993	77.53	22.47
Korea	1978	75.90	24.10
	1994	49.00	51.00
Taiwan	1978	79.00	21.00
	1994	77.20	22.80

Sources: Adapted from Dunning *et al.* (1998: 264), based an UNCTAD statistics.

broadly defined region. If we exclude China's investment in Hong Kong, it is possible to identify a further geographical concentration of Chinese investment in value terms: that is, in four resource-rich developed economies of the Asia-Pacific region, the United States, Canada, Australia and New Zealand.

Such a pattern of geographical concentration is closely related to the sectoral distribution of China's overseas investment. The bulk of investment, it has been observed, is *not* in the manufacturing industry. Zhan estimated in 1995 that only 15 per cent of China's total FDI outflow was in manufacturing (Zhan 1995: 76). Sung's estimate in 1996 of China's investment in Hong Kong's manufacturing is much lower. It is 'modest' and 'no more than four percent of China's total investment in Hong Kong', although 'China has an 11 per cent share of external investment in manufacturing in Hong Kong, third after Japan and the United States' (Sung 1996: 19). Zhang and Van Den Bulcke's survey of Chinese overseas subsidiaries established in Australia and New Zealand from 1985 to 1990 concludes that only 18 out of 64 of them were in manufacturing (Zhang and Van Den Bulcke 1996: 404). There is some indication recently that some Chinese manufacturing enterprises have made aggressive investments offshore. The Haier Group, for example, invested more than $30 million in 2000 to open a manufacturing plant in the United States to produce compact refrigerators, after it had opened more than ten manufacturing facilities around the world (*Wall*

Street Journal, 28 January 2002). The Chunlan Group, to give another example, has invested in a motor cycle factory in Spain and an air conditioner factory in Norway (www.news.sohu.com, 18 February 2002). This has not, however, changed significantly the low proportion of China's manufacturing investment.

The low ratio of China's overseas investment in the manufacturing industry is an indication that China has *not* followed the conventional pattern of outward investment from developing countries, that is, to invest mainly in the so-called 'downstream' industries. Wells once observed that 'Subsidiaries of developing country parent companies are almost all in other developing countries, in contrast to those of multinationals from the US, which have historically established their foreign manufacturing plants first and most frequently in other advanced countries' (Wells 1983: 4). This is clearly not the case for China. Such deviation from the conventional pattern is perhaps largely due to the fact that a large chunk of China's investment overseas has been put first into services, which Zhan estimated in 1995 at 61 per cent of the total.[36] The fact that the three Chinese companies listed in the Fortune Global 500 in 1995, as well as in 1998 – the Bank of China, Sinochem and COFCO – are all services companies supports this estimate.

It is, therefore, possible to identify two clusters geographically and sectorally in China's investment overseas. One is the Hong Kong cluster which concentrates heavily on the service sector, with large Chinese investment in, for example, the Bank of China Group, the China Resources Group and the China Travel Group. There are political, economic, social and cultural explanations for this clustering. The other is the resource cluster, which until very recently was primarily situated in four resource-rich developed economies: Australia, Canada, New Zealand and the United States.[37] The most recent investments made by China's oil giants in oil exploration and production in Sudan, Kazakhstan and Indonesia extends this cluster further into the resource-rich developing economies.

Motivations

Given China's relative shortage of investment capital and the lack of comparative advantage of Chinese firms, why then do these firms invest abroad? What are the motivations for them to do so? Preliminary surveys conducted by Chinese researchers in the early 1990s suggest that motivations vary greatly (Ye Gang 1993a, Kang *et al.* 1996). David Wall in his study, however, asserts that an analysis of the motivations of Chinese outward investment is still 'amenable' to Western economic theory (Wall 1996). This argument can be largely sustained. Similar to other developing countries, the transnational operations of Chinese firms can be broadly said to aim at promoting exports of Chinese machinery and technology, seeking market expansion and penetration of the tariff wall, circumscribing trade barriers, securing the supply of raw materials and acquiring advanced technology. These are not only among the declared purposes of Chinese investment abroad, they are also specified in government policies which constitute the regulatory framework for outward investment.

What distinguishes China from many other developing countries is the simple fact that in value terms, an exceptionally large amount has been channelled into the natural resource-seeking projects. Further, these projects are mostly found in the developed economies. Large overseas investment made by Chinese firms is concentrated on this sector. This has been guided obviously by government policies and reflects the concerns of the government about the shortage of resources within China. It overshadows China's technology-seeking investment in the developed economies, although such investment is important for upgrading China's industrial structure[38] and constitutes part of a strategy for China to circumvent the technology export restrictions and controls imposed in particular by the United States.

In sharp contrast, investment in manufacturing to expand the market for Chinese products in 'downstream' developing countries or to circumvent protectionism in developed nations accounts for only a small percentage of China's outward investment. Most market-seeking investment by China concerns trade-facilitating investment, although, increasingly, the so-called sunset industries in China and industries with excessive capacity have also to turn to the international market. As early as the mid-1980s, for example, the Northwest No. 5 Textile Mill had already made some investment overseas. *Dao guowai zhao fan chi* (go to foreign countries to find market for our products) was the inspiration behind the expansion of its international business (Interviews). As mentioned above, appliance manufacturers in China, such as the Haier Group and the Chunlan Group, and television manufacturers such as the Konka Group have also expanded into the international market through direct investment in manufacturing plants offshore. One of their key market expansion regions is Southeast Asia.

As China's multinational corporations are mostly state-owned enterprises, their overseas investment is not always commercially motivated. This is not unusual. As argued by many, sometimes the state guides or dictates the investment decisions of these state-owned enterprises to serve the interests of the state, even at the expense of the firms. Such politics behind investment decisions is also clear in the investment behaviour of Chinese firms. It is argued, for example, that at the beginning of economic reform, some Chinese enterprises were 'pushed' to engage in outward investment partly to boost the confidence of foreign investors in China's open door policy (Zhang and Van Den Bulcke 1996: 417). As noted by the *Far Eastern Economic Review*, to give another example, in the period leading to the handover of Hong Kong to China in July 1997, an extraordinarily large amount of Chinese capital entered Hong Kong (Gilley 1995). For still another example, in the 1990s, the Chinese government increasingly linked state-owned enterprises' investment projects with its reinvented foreign aid programme (MOFTEC 1997: 135–8). This is sometimes called 'politically induced investment behaviour' of Chinese multinationals (Zhang and Van Den Bulcke 1996: 405).

Finally, transfer of the property and assets of public ownership into private hands is said to be a distinctive motivation [with Chinese characteristics] for the rapid expansion of China's multinational businesses at all levels from the national to provincial and municipal, and throughout all sectors. This is dubbed as 'informal privatization through internationalization', which has often been cultivated by advantageously placed nomenklatura members of the Chinese elite and their kin to accumulate private wealth (Ding 2000). This does help explain why the loss of state assets has become a primary concern in the late 1990s for China's regulators of outward investment. It also contributes to a better understanding of the speed and scope of transnationalisation of Chinese firms, which often defies economic logic.

Entry mode

Finally, what about the preferred entry mode? In the earlier years when Chinese firms were making trade-related investments, particularly setting up representative offices and branches, the predominant entry mode was greenfield, such as MINMETAL'S offices in Tokyo and London. The establishment of the Bank of China International in the City of London in 1996 and of branches of the China Construction Bank in the USA are more recent examples of greenfield entry. But from the late 1980s, overwhelmingly the preferred entry mode seems to be through acquisitions. China's investments in the resource sector are good examples. In contrast to trade-related investments, where wholly owned subsidiaries are preferred, in non-trade-related investment, it is joint ventures, either with majority or minority equity, that are favoured by

Chinese investors. CITIC's investment in the Portland Aluminium Smelter in 1986, for example, acquired only 10 per cent of its total equity. In 1997, CITIC Australia's acquisition of an open-cut coal mine in Queensland amounted again to only 10 per cent of the total equity. The Chinese firms do not hesitate to mount a full takeover at the same time. In 1992, Shougang's acquisition of Hierro Peru bought 98 per cent of the target company at one stroke. More recently, both PetroChina and CNOOC's acquisitions in Indonesia took 100 per cent stakes of the gas and oil fields concerned (*Wall Street Journal*, 2 May 2002).

On some occasions, Chinese investors have also teamed up with local multinationals in a strategic alliance in their acquisition bid. CITIC's acquisitions in Hong Kong in the early 1990s are good examples (for a detailed discussion, see Chapter 5). In 1996, CITIFOR formed an international consortium with two New Zealand multinationals, Fletcher Challenge and Brierley's Investment, which mounted a successful bid to purchase the assets of the Forest Corporation of New Zealand with $1.34 billion.

China's multinational corporations today: a profile

The profile we offer here attempts to address four interesting and interrelated questions about the features of China's emerging transnational businesses and their identity. The four questions are: What is the scale of transnational operations by Chinese firms? How large are China's aspiring global businesses? To what extent are Chinese firms transnationalised? And which group of Chinese firms have a high propensity to transnationalise?

Scale

First, what is the scale of transnational operations of Chinese firms? In other words, how many Chinese firms are now engaging in foreign direct investment and own or control value-added activities in more than one economy? This seemingly simple question defies definitive answers. It is very likely that even the Chinese government does not know the exact figures. As discussed above, there are different levels of authority to approve different scales of overseas investment: the State Council, MOFTEC and the State Development Planning Commission, all line ministries, all provincial governments and the authorities of SEZs. The opening of China's border provinces and the flourishing border trade in the early 1990s saw further decentralisation of such authorities. It is impossible to monitor all outward investment by all

Chinese firms at all levels, either trade-related or non-trade-related. The easy access available to Chinese firms for investing in Hong Kong has already made it virtually impossible to know exactly how many official and unofficial 'window' companies these firms have opened in Hong Kong.

There are, however, some reported figures of subsidiaries of Chinese firms in foreign countries and in Hong Kong and Macao, although these figures are more indicative than definitive. The *Beijing Review* reported that by the end of 1993, MOFTEC had approved 4,497 overseas investment projects, of which 1,658 were non-trade-related and 2,839 were trade-related. Of this total, 1,789 were located in Hong Kong and Macao, and 1,268 of them were trade-related (*Beijing Review*, 21–27 March 1994). Chinese researchers estimated that by June 1994, Chinese firms had established 4,500 investment projects in more than 120 countries and economies, of which 1,704 were non-trade-related investments. The total assets of China's overseas subsidiaries and affiliates amounted to $20 billion (Wang and Wang 1994: 10, Lin Ye 1996: 13). *Renmin Ribao*, on the other hand, reported at about the same time that according to the State Administration for State-Owned Assets, China had by then established more than 10,000 enterprises and other entities in more than 120 regions and countries. China's overseas investment amounted to dozens of billions of US dollars. The state-owned assets overseas were close to 2,000 billion yuan (*Renmin Ribao*, 2 November 1994; see also Wall 1996: 41). Dick Wilson claimed in September 1996, quoting UNCTAD figures, that 'the overseas affiliates of Chinese corporations now number more than 5500 and hold total foreign assets of about US$200 billion' (Wilson 1996: 6–8).

Size

Second, how large are existing Chinese multinationals? Clearly, the size of Chinese multinationals varies greatly.[39] The smallest outward investment from a Chinese company on record is only $5,000. On the other end of the scale, based largely on UNCTAD data, Zhan observed that, 'Taking the list of "the largest TNCs [transnational corporations] based in developing countries ranked by foreign assets" as a bench mark, the top 10 Chinese TNCs can be ranked among the top 40 of the largest TNCs from developing countries, and 8 of them can be among the top 25' (Zhan 1995: 85). Of the fifty largest transnationals from developing economies listed in the UNCTAD *World Investment Report* of 2000, five are from China. Their ranking by foreign assets are the China State Construction and Engineering Corporation (12th); Sinochem (15th);

the China Shougang Group (24th); the China Harbour Engineering Company (36th); and MINMETAL (37th) (UNCTAD 2001: 48–9).[40]

Fortune Global 500 in 1995 and 1998 also has interesting stories to tell. In 1995, when *Fortune* decided to produce a 'new global scorecard' to list 500 of the world's largest corporations to replace the two lists previously knows as Global 500 Service and Global 500 Industrial,[41] three Chinese multinationals were among the 500. They are the Bank of China (ranked 207), Sinochem (ranked 209) and COFCO (ranked 342). The combined revenues and assets of the three were respectively $41.26 billion and $296.15 billion (*Fortune*, 7 August 1995).[42] In the 2002 list of Fortune Global 500, the number of companies from the Chinese Mainland has increased to ten. The Bank of China (ranked 251), Sinochem (ranked 276), and COFCO (ranked 414) are still there. The newcomers are Sinopec (ranked 68), State Power (ranked 77), CNPC (ranked 83), China Mobile (ranked 226), China Telecom (ranked 228), the China Construction Bank (ranked 411) and the Agricultural Bank of China (ranked 441) (www.fortune.com/lists/G500/index.html).

Engineering News Record provides a list of the 225 top international contractors in engineering and construction services which is updated annually. In 1994 and 1995, 23 and 19 Chinese companies were listed, respectively. The scale of the operations by China's engineering companies is also very large. As already mentioned earlier, in 1996 alone Chinese companies won the bid for four engineering and construction projects larger than $100 million each: a power station for Malaysia at $250 million, a textile plant in Syria for $180 million, a water gate project in Thailand for $110 million, and a railway construction in Nigeria for $530 million (MOFTEC 1997: 127–9).[43] In 2001, 31 Chinese companies were on the list, accounting for more than one-eighth of the total (www.enr.construction.com/dbase/2001tic.asp).

Transnationality

Third, how transnationalised are multinational corporations from China? To answer this question, we may take as an example four Chinese multinational corporations listed in the top 50 transnationals from developing economies in *World Investment Report 1998*. UNCTAD uses the composition of three quantitative data as the index to measure a firm's transnationality. The three data are foreign assets, foreign sales and foreign employment as a percentage of total assets, sales and employment. Table 4.7 lists the respective figures of all four Chinese transnationals in the list and puts them into comparative perspective. It is interesting to note that the average transnationality index of the

Table 4.7   Transnationality of the largest Chinese TNCs in 1996 and the national average in comparative perspective*

	State Construction	Sinochem	MINMETAL	Shougang	National average
China (*n* = 4)	40.2	36.4	25.7	16.1	30.0**
Malaysia (*n* = 4)					34.4
Taiwan (*n* = 7)					32.1
Philippines (*n* = 2)					16.1
Latin America (*n* = 17)					28.9

* Based on the UNCTAD list of top 50 TNCs from developing countries in *World Investment Report 1998* (UNCTAD 1999: 48). National calculations my own except otherwise indicated.
** This overall figure is given in UNCTAD (1999: 325). The discrepancy between this figure and the average of the four figures above is possibly due to round-up.

four firms from China in 1996 at 30 is close to that of Taiwan at 32.1 (*n* = 7) and of Malaysia at 34.4 (*n* = 4), but higher than that of Latin American countries at 28.9 (*n* = 17). In the *World Investment Report 2000*, though, the average transnationality index of PRC companies listed there falls to 22 (*n* = 5).

Propensity to transnationalise

Finally, which group of Chinese firms have a higher propensity to transnationalise? That is, what kind of Chinese firms have gone transnational? First and foremost, it is predominantly the state-owned enterprises that have become transnational, though there are non-state sector multinationals.[44] Of all state-owned enterprises, it is possible to identify five major groups of firms that make up the main body of Chinese multinationals. The first group is the trading companies, either the national ones or provincial and municipal ones. They are among the first group that the government mobilised as a major outward investment vehicle in 1979 and that has since transnationalised.[45]

The second group of companies that are now conducting transnational operations are what are called *guoji jingji jishu hezuo gongsi* (international economic and technical cooperation corporations) established with the sanction of the State Council or MOFTEC but managed by line ministries or by the provincial and municipal governments. They are offshoots of China's economic reform and are among what we call purposely built Chinese transnationals. The China State Construction and Engineering Corporation, the China Civil Engineering and Construction Corporation and the China Road and Bridge Engineering Co. Ltd are the oldest among this group. They differ from trade companies in that they are mainly designated to engage in engineering, construction and labour services on the international market. They have, nevertheless, quickly diversified into import and export and other areas of international business. By the end of 1996, there were around 700 such Chinese firms (MOFTEC 1997: 128). That number remained largely unchanged in 2000.

The third group is financial institutions, both banking and non-banking ones. Leading this group are the Bank of China and CITIC. The global presence of BOC is well-recognised. In addition to retail banking, the BOC has also established an investment bank, Bank of China International, in the City of London, and is one of the issuing banks of Hong Kong dollars. Other three state-owned commercial banks, that is the Industrial and Commercial Bank of China (ICBC), the China Construction Bank of China (CCB), and the Agricultural Bank of China (ABC), have also belatedly branched out overseas. ICBC, the largest commercial bank in China, is sanctioned by the PBOC to engage mainly in domestic operations. But in 1998, it extended into the securities market in Hong Kong by acquiring Natwest Securities Asia Ltd. Following its acquisition of the Union Bank of Hong Kong in 2000, ICBC (Asia) Ltd was established to be the flagship for ICBC's overseas expansion (www.icbcasia.com/html/eng/profile.html). ICBC, by the end of 2001, also established branches in Singapore, Frankfurt, Tokyo, Seoul and Luxembourg, in addition to its representative offices in London, Alma-Ata and Sydney. CCB at the same time opened branches in Singapore, Frankfurt, Hong Kong and Johannesburg and set up representative offices in London, New York, Tokyo and Seoul. Even the ABC, the least internationalised of the four, has branches in Hong Kong and Singapore and representative offices in London, New York and Tokyo. The importance of the presence of these state-owned banks overseas does not lie in the scale of their operation. Rather, it signals China's increasingly outward looking development strategy and its desire and willingness to engage and gain the access to the international capital markets.

Typical of non-banking financial institutions that have gone transnational are CITIC, the ill-fated Guangdong International Trust and Investment Corporation and many other ITICs. In the wake of the Asian financial crisis and the collapse of GITIC, however, Beijing has recently taken drastic and decisive measures to close down the most inefficient and loss-making ITICs as an important thrust of its financial sector reform.[46]

The fourth group consists of some large-scale manufacturing enterprises either state-owned or collectively and privately owned. These include Shougang and the China Ship Building Industrial Corporation mentioned earlier. The Shenzhen Electronics Group (SEG) is noted to have purchased in the early 1990s 46 per cent of a Canadian company to gain access to the American retail markets for electronic products (Tolentino 1993: 348). The People's Liberation Army (PLA) claimed to have set up its first transnational corporation in the late 1980s, the Sanjiu Enterprise Group, a pharmaceutical producer. In the early 1990s, its subsidiaries were found in Germany, Thailand, Russia and the United States (Bickford 1994: 466).[47] Outside state-ownership sectors, China's emerging home appliances manufacturing giants, the Haier Group and the Chunlan Group, have made significant overseas acquisitions and set up a number of manufacturing bases to capture the overseas markets.

Finally, there is the fifth group. These are latecomers to transnationalisation and include China's oil and telecom giants. These are traditionally inward-looking and domestically oriented large Chinese firms. Globalisation and enterprise reforms in China have changed their perspectives and perception of their role in the world economy. Recent listing of some of these firms on the international stock exchanges in Hong Kong and New York flushes these firms with cash and opens new pathways for their rapid transnationalisation. As discussed, China's reorganised oil giant CNPC and the petrochemical conglomerate Sinopec have already made large-scale acquisitions overseas.[48]

Summary

Transnational operations by China's state-owned enterprises started long before 1978. However, it was only after 1979 that the transnationalisation of Chinese firms began, with the active outward flow of China's FDI. Within just over twenty years, China became one of the most significant investors from the developing countries both in terms of its outward FDI flow and stocks and of the scale of transnational operations by Chinese firms. A number of Chinese companies have now been recognised and registered as among the world's largest multinational corporations. The rise and growth of China's multinational corporations is unmistakable.

The rise of Chinese multinationals is not only rapid but has also followed a pathway conspicuously different from that travelled by many other transnationals originating from developing countries. This is partly predetermined by two particular conditions in the political economy of China prior to 1978. One is the insulation of China from the world economy, particularly from international finance. The other is the ubiquitous state management of a centrally planned economy and the state-ownership of all large enterprises. Because of these conditions, policy innovations of the government assumed exceptional importance in initiating the early outward investment and internationalisation of firms. These policy innovations made it possible to bring in the locational and ownership advantages of Chinese firms, previously largely unknown or forgotten, into play. State-ownership only accentuates the importance of government policies. Throughout the twenty-year period of our discussion, therefore, the state becomes the most important explanatory variable in understanding the emergence of Chinese multinationals. Arguably, reform politics and government development strategy are more important variables than economics in explaining the transnationalisation of SOEs from this transition economy.

The speedy take-off of transnationalisation of Chinese firms in the 1980s owes, therefore, as much to the government push as to the firm-level initiatives. The near total absence of Chinese firms operating in other economies prior to 1978 presents inadvertently a large number of opportunities. The fast growth and marketisation of the Chinese economy, the unfolding of economic reforms in China and accelerated economic globalisation present challenges to Chinese firms. Many Chinese would-be multinational corporations have creatively responded to these challenges and opportunities offered by the changing policies of the government and the globalisation of the world economy. The rise as well as growth of China's multinationals is the result of that response, more often in defiance of domestic and international constraints.

Discussions of the rise of China's global businesses above only tell half of the story. Many interesting and serious questions about firm-level initiatives are left unexplored and unanswered. What are the incentives for state-owned enterprises to engage in transnational operations? Where does a state-owned enterprise derive its strength, advantage and competence to transnationalise? How does developing global businesses help revitalise and reinvent a state-owned enterprise? And has it done so? Why do different firms respond differently to the same policy environment? To seek answers to these questions, it is imperative that we conduct some institutional investigations at the firm level. It is to that task that we now turn in Part III.

Part III

The Transnationalisation of Chinese Firms: Institutional Investigations

In Part III, we undertake to conduct detailed empirical and institutional investigation of the process of transnationalisation of three Chinese firms, that is, CITIC, Sinochem and Shougang. This micro-level investigation is conducted to recapture the story and experiment of individual firms in their attempts to transform themselves into China's aspiring global businesses. It is meant to complement as well as supplement the broad discussions of political economy in the earlier part of the book to see how Chinese firms respond to and interact with the dynamics of political and economic changes in China as well as globally. In spite of the proliferation of economic analyses of China's state sector industrial reforms, there is a lack of 'detailed institutional investigation at the enterprise level' in the studies of Chinese economy (Nolan 1998: 1), which makes it imperative that this investigation is conducted to give a more complete picture of the emergence of China's aspiring global businesses.

The selection of our case studies is more than accidental. It has been made for obvious but important reasons. First, they are from different sectors of the Chinese economy. CITIC is China's flagship non-banking financial organisation designated to be the Chinese government's investment arm. Sinochem is the largest of China's trading companies, a major force in China's global reach in trade and services. And Shougang is a rare example of a large industrial enterprise engaged in extensive transnational commercial and business operations. Second, these three firms began in different periods in Chinese history. Shougang originated in China's early industrialisation attempts in the early years of the twentieth century, 1918 to be precise. Sinochem was set up as a state trading organ in 1950 shortly after the establishment of the PRC. CITIC, established in 1979, is the product of China's opening and economic reform. These three cases therefore offer a broad representation of industries and different categories of state-owned enterprises in transnationalisation. Third, all three have been at the forefront of China's economic reform. CITIC pioneered the internationalisation of Chinese firms. Sinochem piloted many experiments in China's trade reforms, whereas Shougang was once a much-trumpeted model in industrial reform in China. Fourth, because of their special status in the Chinese economic reform and controversies surrounding their practices, empirical data about the transnationalisation of these three firms turn out to be richer and more readily available than those of other Chinese multinationals, both in English and in Chinese. Last but certainly not least, as the unfolding stories in the following pages will tell, the trials and tribulations experienced by the three firms in transnationalising are critically instructive of the distinctive path that Chinese firms have to take in order to transnationalise.

In one other important aspect, the three firms selected also share common features. All three in their own fashion have secured particularistic policies from the Chinese government in their drive to become a global company. All three have exploited these privileges, sometimes unscrupulously, to their own advantage. The irony for particularistic policies, as mentioned earlier, becomes painfully clear here. They are deemed necessary and effective to overcome constraints embedded in the unreformed economy. Yet it is precisely the distortions in the Chinese economic system – the prominent role of the state in economic planning, the ubiquitous presence of administrative intervention in corporate decision-making, state-sponsored monopoly, among others – that permit and indeed perhaps encourage firms such as CITIC, Sinochem and Shougang to take the specific routes they have in transnationalising their economic activities. In other words, had China been a market economy, these firms would have conceivably taken entirely different routes to transnationalise, or they may well have been stopped from any transnational operations.

In the next three chapters, we undertake to write a 'contemporary business history' of the transnationalisation of these three prominent Chinese firms. As all three cases will show, the transnationalisation of Chinese firms in the first two decades after the launch of economic reforms is better explained by policy rationale than economic logic. The initial success of these companies' attempts at going transnational lies partially in their ability to exploit their positions in the unreformed economy of China. Entrepreneurship is directly related to how to cultivate the privileges accorded to these firms by the distortions in the existing domestic economy, such as the traditional monopoly of trade in the case of Sinochem and unprecedented high-level management autonomy of both CITIC and Shougang in financing their overseas expansion. In formulating and implementing the so-called particularistic policies discussed earlier, the government has not just acquiesced in, but also actively encouraged, such exploitation and cultivation. The question is: Will economic logic eventually prevail, and under what conditions?

China as a transitional developing economy may have made the analysis of China's emerging global businesses amenable to theoretical propositions about Third World transnationals. It is, however, such 'idiosyncratic' circumstances that make the study of the transnationalisation of individual Chinese firms interesting and challenging. To the extent that generalisations drawn from the study of these three firms are valid, 'idiosyncratic' differences in government and business relations are not only firm-specific, but also China-specific. This is exactly what renders the approach to and behaviour of outward investment by Chinese firms different from the situation for multinationals from other developing economies.

Two caveats are due here that set the limitations of the empirical focus of our institutional investigation. First, we are aware that there is an unfortunate bias towards large state-owned firms in our selection of cases. This is mostly determined by the access to available data and company information. This is also because these firms are pioneers of the transnationalisation of Chinese firms, and their experience is much more closely bound up with China's economic transformation and notably affected by the changing political economy of China's transition. They also have a much longer business history of internationalisation to examine. The new arrivals of China's emerging businesses from the non-state sector, such as the Haier Group and the Chunlan Group, are certainly fascinating cases to study. So will be China's oil giants, which have taken dramatic strides to transnationalise most recently. Their short history of transnationalisation, however, makes it infeasible to conduct detailed case studies.

Such bias, we believe, does not challenge in any significant way the validity of the generalisations derived from our empirical investigations. The stories of the three firms in transnationalisation inform us of the dynamic but also tortuous process of the emergence of China's global businesses in the changing political economy of the reform years.

Second, since in the institutional investigation conducted here we are undertaking to write a contemporary business history of how individual firms transnationalise, we have chosen purposely to concentrate on deliberations of the most dynamic and perhaps also controversial period of transnationalisation of each firm concerned. That means that our analytical focus will be on the 1980s and the 1990s, though wherever possible our discussions will also cover their most recent experience in transnationalising.

5
CITIC: A Pioneer Chinese Multinational

The China International Trust and Investment Corporation (CITIC) has occupied a unique place in the transnationalisation of Chinese firms. Established in July 1979 as a state-owned enterprise under the direct leadership of the State Council, CITIC has grown and expanded as China's economic reforms proceeded to unfold. Although just over twenty years old at the time of writing, CITIC is arguably the most reputable and successful global business in China today. In 1993, the *Far Eastern Economic Review* (*FEER*) called it 'China's most spectacular economic success story of the past decade' (21 January 1993: 50). The *Financial Times* hailed it as China's 'most prominent business conglomerate' and 'flagship of state-owned conglomerate' (16 March 1995, 5 June 1997). In 1996, Standard and Poor's Investor Services invoked CITIC's 'domestic and international expertise and *name recognition*' (italics my own), among others, as its basis for a BBB long-term foreign currency rating to three Samurai bonds issued by CITIC (Reuters, 4 November 1996).

One CITIC publication in 1995 boasted that CITIC was 'the largest non-banking financial organization in China', and that 'as China's pioneer multinational corporation, CITIC has developed into a global conglomerate of diversified interests in production, finance, trade, technology and services' (CITIC Australia Group 1995a: 1). The *Washington Post* called it 'China's leading "red chip" company' and 'the most sought-after partner for "blue chip" foreign firms seeking footholds in China'. CITIC's business partners, it continues, 'include Bechtel Group Inc., Coopers & Lybrand, Siemens AG, United Technologies Corp., Ciba-Geigy AG, Reynolds Metals Co. and Cable and Wireless PLC – to name a few' (26 March 1997). CITIC's own website boasts that 'CITIC has made explorations in many business

fields with remarkable successes', and 'After 20 years of development, CITIC has grown into a large transnational conglomerate'
(www.citic.com/english/about/index.html).

CITIC is not only the first among China's purposely built multinational corporations. More importantly, it has pioneered many aspects
of the transnational operations of Chinese firms. CITIC was the first corporation to venture into the international bond market in 1982 and the
first to issue bonds on the American market, in July 1993. It was also
the first to introduce international leasing operations into China in
the early 1980s. It blazed the trail of Chinese firms making large-
scale investments in resource sectors overseas in the mid-1980s. One
estimate puts CITIC's overseas investment by 1990 at over $570 million
(UNTCMD 1993: 52). Although the exact total of CITIC's overseas
investment as it currently stands is not available, its past and present
investments include the steel industry in the USA, telecommunications,
aviation, a satellite launch company and real estate in Hong Kong,
cement manufacturing in Macao, forestry in the USA, Canada and New
Zealand, an aluminium smelter and a coal mine in Australia, as well
as numerous industrial and infrastructure projects in China. It holds
controlling stocks in publicly listed companies on the Hong Kong and
Australian stock exchanges as well as in China. It owns two banks:
CITIC Ka Wah Bank in Hong Kong and CITIC Industrial Bank (CIB) in
China, and has a joint venture with the British insurance giant
Prudential Holdings, CITIC Prudential Life Insurance Co. Ltd. Its sub-
sidiaries operate all over the world. Two subsidiaries, CITIC Pacific and
CITIC Australia, have become multinationals in their own right.

As the one and only firm in 1979 to receive a special blessing from
the State Council to set itself up as a ministerial-level organisation for
the specific purpose of engaging in financial services and investment at
home and abroad, CITIC has often been called 'the Chinese government's investment arm' in the international media. CITIC has always
seen itself, on the other hand, as an important window on China's
opening up to the outside world. As such, this investment vehicle of
the State Council is an equally important window through which to
gain a glimpse of the evolution of the Chinese government's policy on
outward investment and transnational operations by Chinese firms.
This chapter traces the origins of CITIC, looks at its growth and expansion from a modest beginning, and provides a sketch of this pioneering
Chinese multinational and aspiring global business. Profiles are also
drawn of two of CITIC's overseas subsidiaries, CITIC Pacific and CITIC
Australia.

CITIC today

CITIC today is a multinational investment-holding company, which boasts a vast business empire with its tentacles extending all over the world. As is proudly claimed at its well-designed website, 'After 20 years of development, CITIC has grown into a large transnational conglomerate. It now owns 38 subsidiaries (banks) including those in Hong Kong, the United States, Canada, Australia, New Zealand and the Netherlands'. Although principally an investment company engaged in financial services, CITIC also has considerable strength in industry. In 2000, CITIC's industrial investment at home and abroad still accounted for 18 per cent of its total assets (www.citic.com/english/about/index.html). A major corporate restructuring was underway in 2001.

The corporate headquarters of CITIC are now located in the Capital Mansion in the famous 'Silver Triangle' of Beijing's eastern suburbs. In Hong Kong, the CITIC Tower, erected on a former Royal Navy dockyard in Tamar Basin, and standing next to the former British garrison headquarters overlooking Victoria Harbour, is rich in symbolism. Looking at these CITIC skyscrapers today, it is hard to imagine that this now world-renowned business empire, with total assets at the end of 2000 valued at 358.61 billion yuan and after-tax profit at 2.54 billion yuan, began very modestly in the first half of 1979, when a dozen people were cramped into a few rooms in the old Peace (Heping) Hotel near Beijing's shopping precinct of Wangfujing, with little capital injection from the government.

Two indicators help us to appreciate CITIC's phenomenal growth and rapid transformation into China's leading global business. One is the rapid growth of its assets and profits from 1983 to 2000 (see Table 5.1 and Figure 5.1). The allocation of CITIC's assets in 2000 is indicative of CITIC's transformation into an investment holding company in finance (see Figure 5.2).

The other is the transnationality of the CITIC. This can be illustrated by looking at the earnings of its overseas operations and assets. It is reported that some 80 per cent of CITIC's 3.3 billion yuan profit in 1993 came from its overseas operations (Ji Honggeng 1995: 259).[1] In 1995, it was estimated that CITIC's foreign assets amounted to $15 billion (Zhan 1995: 84). The annual report of the CITIC identified that in 1997 and 1998 respectively, 43.06 per cent and 45.14 per cent of its total revenues were still 'derived from overseas operations' and that around 31.07 per cent and 38.15 per cent of its consolidated assets were located overseas

Table 5.1   Assets, net assets and profit of CITIC, 1991–2000 (in billion yuan)

	Assets	Net assets	Profit
1991	45.26	4.95	0.37
1992	50.71	5.02	0.38
1993	82.80	9.51	3.60
1994	135.50	12.79	2.11
1995	166.70	17.0	2.43
1996	191.50	21.33	2.47
1997	220.80	32.60	2.84
1998	244.57	34.73	2.278
1999	268.18	36.74	2.287
2000	358.61	39.60	2.535

Sources: CITIC *Annual Report* (various years), www.citic.com/about/data/html.

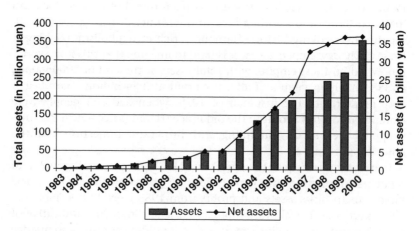

Figure 5.1   Growth of CITIC's assets and net assets, 1983–2000
Sources: As for Table 5.1.

(CITIC 1997: 25, 1998: 19). Indeed, one senior executive of CITIC publicly blamed the parent company's dependence on 'contribution' from CITIC Pacific in Hong Kong for the drop of its profit from 2.7 billion yuan in 1997 to 2 billion yuan in 1998 (*Reuters*, 15 March 1999).[2]

A glimpse of CITIC's global interests can be graphically seen in the

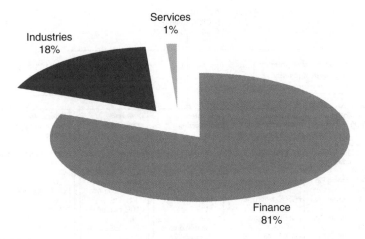

Figure 5.2 Allocation of CITIC's assets, 2000

Sources: www.citic.com/english/about/index.html.

organisation chart shown in Figure 5.3. In terms of CITIC's trans-nationality, this chart is, at the very least, an understatement. It conceals more than it reveals. Both CITIC Hong Kong and CITIC Australia, for example, have developed into multinationals in their own right, with sizeable transnational operations, as will be discussed in some detail later in this chapter. Even CITIC Development Co. Ltd can claim to be a multi-national: according to the information provided on its website, this company has outward investments in real estate in Phoenix, Arizona and Seattle, Washington in the United States. It has also invested in seven joint ventures in Morocco, Japan, France, the United States and New Zealand (www.chinabusiness.net/citicdev/projects.html).[3]

Rong Yiren and the establishment of CITIC

The establishment of CITIC in 1979 has now become almost a legend. Behind this legend is a legendary person, the first Chairman and General Manager of CITIC, Rong Yiren, who was to become the Vice-President of the People's Republic of China in 1993. The first official announcement of the State Council's decision to establish CITIC was made on 8 July 1979 (*RMRB*, 9 July 1979). Less than three months later, on 4 October 1979, the establishment of CITIC was officially announced at a press conference in the Great Hall of the People. In a brief state-ment, the *People's Daily* managed to include all important information

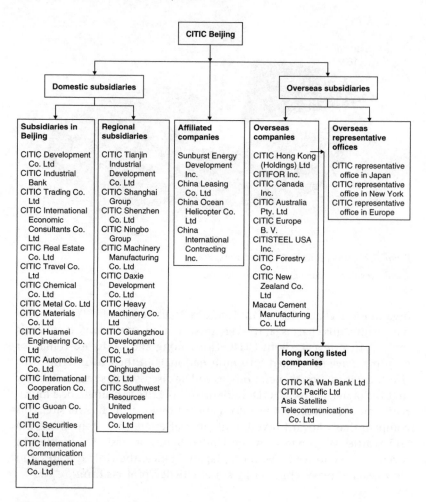

Figure 5.3   CITIC's corporate structure, 2000

Source: CITIC *Annual Report* (2000, 2001).

about this pioneering entity: the purpose of CITIC was to attract foreign investment, the registered capital for CITIC was 200 million yuan,[4] the temporary address of the new company was the Peace Hotel, and Rong Yiren was appointed by the State Council as General Manager of the new entity (*RMRB*, 5 October 1979). Behind these headlines lies an intriguing story of personalities and politics of the early stages of China's opening up and reform.[5]

Meeting with Deng

On 17 January 1979, less than one month after the conclusion of the epic Third Plenum of the Eleventh CCP Party Congress, the then Vice-Premier, Deng Xiaoping, met with five 'patriotic' industrialists and financiers, the so-called 'red capitalists', at the Great Hall of the People: Hu Zi'ang, Gu Gengyu, Hu Juewen, Zhou Shuyuan and Rong Yiren.[6] Rong was the youngest of the invited group. Deng briefed the group about the CCP's new policy of economic reform and encouraged them to contribute to the reform process, in particular China's opening up to the outside world. It is at this meeting that 'Deng made it clear that China could *make use of some capitalistic practices*' in its opening up and economic reform (*Beijing Review*, 29 August–4 September 1994: 22).[7] Deng also expressed his hope that Rong would be able to play his part in promoting this process and to help China earn foreign currency. Rong was encouraged to submit a proposal to Deng and to the CCP leadership for that purpose.

As Rong himself recalled in an interview with *Euromoney* in 1991, 'In February [*sic*] 1979, Deng arranged a meeting attended by some former industrialists and entrepreneurs. He hoped that we could play a role in the opening of the nation to the outside world in revitalising the national economy, and that I contribute my share to this endeavour' (Rafferty 1991: 27).

Rong was already 62 in 1979 and had a chequered history as an entrepreneur prior to 1949 and as a 'red capitalist' in the post-1949 period. Before 1949, the Rong family had presided over one of the four largest indigenous industrial empires in pre-1949 China, with vast business interests in textiles and food processing, mostly in Wuxi and Shanghai.[8] In 1949, when the Chinese Communists took over Shanghai, Rong Yiren was managing the business interests of the Rong family there. Despite his doubts and misgivings about the Communists, Rong stayed in Shanghai after 1949.[9] As a 'red capitalist', he had been made Deputy Mayor of Shanghai in 1957 and Vice-Minister of the Textile Industry Ministry in 1959. Like all other industrialists, Rong suffered humiliation and personal abuse during the Cultural Revolution, but survived the political turbulence. In 1978, he was appointed Vice-Chairman of the Chinese People's Political Consultative Conference (CPPCC).

After his meeting with Deng, Rong discussed his ideas with a coterie of friends in Shanghai, mostly former industrialists and financiers. Not all of them were in favour of Rong's ideas. The Cultural Revolution was still fresh enough in their minds for Rong's adventurous proposition to evoke fear and scepticism.

Rong's two submissions

Between February and May 1979, however, Rong made two submissions. The first was to Deng himself and the Party leadership, proposing to establish an investment company to introduce foreign investment and advanced technology to facilitate the four modernisations. Deng quickly approved the proposal, as did Chen Yun and Li Xiannian, both vice-premiers at the time. It was Chen Yun who proposed that this investment company should be a state-owned enterprise directly under the State Council. Once this proposal was endorsed, the special status of CITIC was established.

The endorsement of Rong's proposal by the CCP leadership was out of both political and practical considerations. At the January meeting mentioned above, Deng had already clearly indicated that the Chinese government was keen to solicit investment from the overseas Chinese community. In his words, 'Some Hong Kong entrepreneurs wrote to me and asked me why they could not open factories in Guangdong. In my view, our expatriates, overseas Chinese, and even foreign citizens of the Chinese origin should all be allowed to open factories back in China' (Deng 1987: 156–7). Even more revealing is a comment made by Marshal Ye Jianying at the end of 1978, which is worth quoting in full:

> Now we are talking about opening up [China] and attract foreign investment. But we are communists. The others may not necessarily believe you. They will wait and see what our policies are like. Rong Yiren is well-known internationally, and many members of his family are resident overseas. We can make good use of his influence, and take advantage of his family network overseas to attract foreign investment in his name. More foreign investment will then follow. No one can take Rong Yiren's place, not even a communist. But we also need to consider carefully what organisation is the best for him to operate. It is better to be non-governmental because the fear of communists is widespread.
>
> (Ji Honggeng 1999: 198–9)

The second submission, made to the State Council, consisted of a detailed proposal for establishing CITIC. With the approval of the CCP leadership, the State Council simply rubber-stamped this proposal in June 1979, with one minor change. In Rong's original proposal, the company was called the China International Investment and Trust Corporation. In the State Council's document approving Rong's proposal, it became the China International Trust and Investment Corporation, hence CITIC today, rather than CIITC.

The birth of CITIC

Preparations for establishing CITIC had started in late May at Rong's home in Beijing, after Rong's consultations with a number of friends, industrialists and financiers, largely from Shanghai, staying in the Beijing Hotel.[10] In July, the preparatory group moved into the old Peace Hotel, renting twelve rooms as offices and accommodation for those invited by Rong to join him in Beijing. Preparations began in earnest, leading to the formal establishment of CITIC in October.

The timing of the official announcement of the State Council's approval to establish CITIC is intriguingly significant. It was made on the same day that China's first Foreign Joint Venture Law was promulgated, on 8 July 1979. Both appeared in the front page of the *People's Daily* on 9 July. In the short announcement, it was stated that the State Council had approved the establishment of CITIC, with Rong Yiren in charge of the new entity.[11] Further, the major task of CITIC was to attract foreign investment, introduce advanced technology and equipment, and set up joint ventures with foreign capital in China in accordance with relevant laws and regulations of the PRC (*RMRB*, 9 July 1979).

Deng met Rong again shortly after the State Council's official approval of Rong's submission. Placing full responsibility for managing the soon-to-be-established CITIC into Rong's hands, Deng is credited with having said to Rong, '*ren you ni zhao* [you find the right people (for CITIC)]; *shi you ni guan* [you manage (CITIC) as you see fit]; [and] *you ni fu quan ze* [you are fully in charge (of CITIC)]'. In the early stages of China's economic reform, this would prove to be much more easily said than done.

The first board meeting of CITIC was held on 4 October 1979 at the Great Hall of the People. All 44 board members were present, many of whom were prominent industrialists and financiers from Hong Kong and Macao as well as Mainland China. One interesting fact is that CITIC's first Board of Directors actually outnumbered its employees, officially only 36 in total at the time. At the first board meeting, Vice-Premier Gu Mu officially announced that Rong had been appointed by the State Council as the Chairman and General Manager of CITIC, and that CITIC would be directly under the leadership of the State Council (*RMRB*, 5 October 1979, Ji Honggeng 1987). At 3 p.m., in the capacity of Chairman and General Manager of CITIC, Rong Yiren announced to the world at a press conference the establishment of CITIC, and answered a myriad of questions by the Chinese and foreign press. In 1979, to use a press conference to announce the establishment of a company in China was not only novel but extremely rare (Ji Honggeng 1999: 223–4).

What was not clearly reported in the *People's Daily* nor announced at the press conference was the unusual decision by the State Council that CITIC would enjoy the equivalent privilege and status of a ministry in the Chinese bureaucracy. As the first ministerial-level corporation, the special status of CITIC in China's opening up and economic reform was thus institutionally guaranteed. The power delegated by the State Council to CITIC at the early stage of reform was, if anything, exceptional.

The presence of two groups of personalities on 4 October at the inauguration of CITIC had significant implications for the future of CITIC. One group consisted of senior Chinese leaders: Marshall Ye Jianying, then Vice-Chairman of the CCP and the President of the National People's Congress, and Vice-Premier Wang Zhen, among others, greeted the board members and offered their blessings to the new corporation. From its inception, therefore, CITIC's special status was not only guaranteed institutionally, but was further secured by the personal endorsement of CCP leaders, although Deng himself was not present.

The other group present was a number of overseas industrialists and financiers who had been invited to sit on the first CITIC Board of Directors. Most important among them were George C. Tso, Li Ka-shing, Wang Foon-shing and Fok Yingtung.[12] Their presence already foreshadowed the outward orientation of CITIC and would prove pivotal in CITIC's expansion into Hong Kong and other parts of the world, as CITIC's strategic alliance with Li Ka-shing would eventually prove. It was a clear signal of the Chinese government's willingness and desire to cultivate the resources of the overseas Chinese community for China's economic reform.[13]

Early transnational operations, 1979 to 1986

Although the registered capital of CITIC was reported to be 200 million yuan, CITIC's real starting capital was only 20 million yuan allocated by the People's Bank of China, and 10 million yuan borrowed from Rong privately. From 1981 to 1984, the PBOC again allocated, each year, 20 million yuan to CITIC. The total capital allocated to CITIC by the government was therefore only 100 million yuan, half of the publicised registered capital for CITIC (Ji Honggeng 1999: 218). In the first year of its operation, CITIC was already flooded with visits by interested foreign partners and engaged in hundreds of negotiations. However, only a very small number of joint venture projects materialised (Ji Honggeng 1999: 231).

Blazing the path on the world bond market

CITIC as a transnational player first came to prominence through its private issuing of bonds in the Japanese market in January 1982 and controversies surrounding the proposed offering in China. It was the first-ever offering of bonds after 1949 by a Chinese entity on the international capital market. In 1980, Yizheng Chemical Fibre, one of 22 key national projects under construction, encountered severe funding problems. The Ministry of the Textile Industry came to CITIC and asked Rong Yiren for help. Rong proposed issuing 10 billion Yen bonds on the Japanese market to raise funds for Yizheng Chemical Fibre. In the political climate of 1981, it was courageous of Rong to make such a daring proposal. The opposition was strong. Some argued that 'It is disgraceful [for China] to issue bonds in a capitalist country.' Others said that the interests of bond issuing were higher than that of intergovernmental loans and also higher than those for loans from import and export banks. Even with Rong's special connections with the top leadership, and his personal influence and efforts, it took CITIC more than a year to get final approval to go ahead and issue 10 billion Yen bonds in Japan (Ji Honggeng 1987).

It was an instant success. Yizheng was saved, and began operating in 1985. It is now the largest polyester producer in China. Not only did it repay its debt years ago, it is also one of the first nine state-owned enterprises that the Chinese government floated on the Hong Kong Stock Exchange in 1993. As reported in the *Financial Times* (7 March 1994), in 1994, ICI and Amoco, the two largest multinationals producing and trading chemicals, each took a 2.5 per cent stake in Yizheng.[14]

Encouraged by CITIC's successful foray into the international bond market, the Bank of China and other ITICs also began to issue bonds on the global capital market. For CITIC, issuing bonds to raise funds for its domestic investment activities has since become one of its major overseas operations. In 1985 alone, CITIC made its appearance in bond markets in Hong Kong, Japan and West Germany, with four issues respectively in four different currencies: the Japanese yen, the Hong Kong dollar, the Deutschmark and the US dollar (see Table 5.2).

Table 5.2   CITIC's foreign and Eurobond issues, 1982–85

	Borrower	Market	Currency	Amount
Jan. 1982	CITIC	Japan	Yen	10 billion
Jan. 1985	CITIC	Japan	Yen	30 billion
Aug. 1985	CITIC	Hong Kong	HK dollar	300 million
Sep. 1985	CITIC	W. Germany	Deutschmark	150 million
Dec. 1985	CITIC	Japan	US dollar	100 million

Sources: Li Cheng (1986: 20), *Beijing Review* (10–16 March 1986: 29), *Beijing Review* (15–21 June 1987: 29).

In the 1990s, CITIC, as one of the officially designated vehicles for borrowing on the international bond market, was a 'regular and significant issuer for China'. By the end of 1999, it had raised altogether $6 billion by issuing bonds on the global capital market (www.citic.com). At the beginning of the twenty-first century China is a significant borrower on the global capital market, and China's regular engagement with the international bond market has become a significant part of the internationalisation of the Chinese economy. Such regular and intensive engagement by China with the international bond market owes much to the pioneering work of CITIC in 1982.

Early overseas investment

CITIC is reported to have started its overseas investments in 1981, initially in Hong Kong, although it was not until the second half of 1984 that it established its Overseas Investment Department. It should be noted that the Chinese government's original and primary purpose of establishing CITIC in 1979 was to use it to solicit foreign capital and to provide financial services for the purposes of domestic investment. In early 1984, however, the State Council instructed CITIC to explore overseas investment in resource sectors in which China was suffering acute shortages. Initially it also provided a sizeable venture capital for CITIC's new endeavours (Interviews).[15]

Soon after setting up its Overseas Investment Department, CITIC ventured into the United States, establishing CITIFOR Inc. as a joint venture in Seattle. CITIC invested 40 million yuan and acquired 50 per cent of equity in shares (Interviews). CITIFOR was to engage in forestry and timber processing. In 1986, CITIC bought the remaining 50 per cent of shares in the joint venture company and CITIFOR became a wholly owned subsidiary of CITIC. In 1985, the first shipment of timber from

CITIFOR had already been sent to China. By 1989, CITIFOR had shipped back to China more than one million cubic metres of timber (Shi Lin *et al.* 1989: 465). Over the years, CITIFOR has become CITIC's main investment arm in forestry and related industries. To date, it has made significant investments in the United States and Canada, and more recently in Russia, Chile and New Zealand. Between 1984 and 1986, the Overseas Investment Department also investigated investment opportunities in minerals around the world, including iron ore mines in Brazil and Australia and copper mines in Tanzania (Interviews).[16]

It was not until 1986 that CITIC became a notable transnational investor, two years after the establishment of its Overseas Investment Department, through two significant investments in Canada and Australia respectively. In May 1986, CITIC bought 50 per cent of the Celgar Pulp Mill in British Columbia, Canada. This mill had the capacity to produce 180,000 tons of bleached long-staple kraft pulp. CITIC invested $40 million and entered into a joint venture agreement with the Power Corporation of Canada, which held the other 50 per cent of shares in the pulp mill. In June of the same year, CITIC invested over A$120 million and obtained 10 per cent of the shares in the Portland Aluminium Smelter in Victoria, Australia.

With these two large overseas investments, CITIC embarked on its transnational operations in earnest. These investments are significant as well as revealing. They are significant because of the huge amount of investment involved, but more importantly because of the way in which the funds were raised for the two investments. The purchase of the Celgar Pulp Mill was financed by a syndicated loan of C$62 million from the Royal Bank of Canada.[17] The funds for investing in the Portland Aluminium Smelter were also raised by a syndicated loan through lease-leverage financing. In both cases, investments were made with no actual capital outflow from China. The investment capital was raised on the international capital markets locally. Both investments have proved extremely successful. In the case of the Celgar Pulp Mill, for example, CITIC repaid its loan within three years (Interviews).[18] Not surprisingly, both are often regarded as successful examples of Chinese firms cultivating the international capital market for project financing (Zhang Jijing 1998).

These two cases are also revealing. First, in both cases, CITIC entered the local market through direct acquisition and formed joint ventures with local partners. Since then, this has been the preferred mode of entry in CITIC's strategy to make overseas investments.[19] Second, both investments are in the resource sector. This was guided as much by government policy as by shrewd business decisions. It is worth emphasising that investment by state-owned enterprises in China, like that by public sector companies in other developing nations, is invariably shaped by government policy. Third, both investments were made in developed economies. CITIC did not appear to be deterred either by its lack of comparative advantage or its shortage of funds.

CITIC's venture into Hong Kong is an indispensable part of its early transnational operations. As early as October 1979, at the first Board meeting, Rong Yiren reported that CITIC was already actively preparing to set up its subsidiary in Hong Kong (*RMRB*, 5 October 1979). In fact, earlier in August, Rong had already been to Hong Kong and talked with Xinhua News Agency (Hong Kong) and the Bank of China Hong Kong Branch about setting up a branch of CITIC in Hong Kong (Ji Honggeng 1999: 296). CITIC Hong Kong, however, was first registered only in May 1985 (Ye Gang 1993a: 306, Ma Kefeng 1997: 284–5). Soon after, CITIC Hong Kong acquired the Ka Wah Bank, purchasing initially 74 per cent and later 95 per cent of its equity shares with an injection of HK$300 million.[20] As discussed in Chapter 4, this acquisition was, however, a passive one. CITIC came to the rescue at the request of the bank, which was on the brink of bankruptcy. Unwittingly, CITIC acquired a listed company on the Hong Kong Stock Exchange as early as the mid-1980s. The acquisition also gained CITIC Hong Kong's banking licence, said to be worth around HK$150 million at the time (*Euromoney*, February 1986: 15). With Ka Wah Bank's branches in Los Angles and New York, and its representative office in London, CITIC Hong Kong also extended its presence beyond China and Hong Kong. In 1998, Ka Wah Bank was renamed CITIC Ka Wah Bank.[21]

With the establishment of CITIC Australia Pty Ltd and CITIC Canada Ltd, both in 1986, in addition to its active investment activities in Hong Kong, CITIC was poised to take on the world. CITIC's aggressive expansion overseas did not escape the notice of the global business community. In early 1987 *Fortune* named Rong as one of the '50 most fascinating business people' in 1986 (Kraar 1987: 109). In Hong Kong and Southeast Asia, Rong came to be known as Mr CITIC (*Beijing Review*, 29 August 1994: 22–3, Ji Honggeng 1999: 228–9).

Controversies and policy support

The early years of CITIC's transnational operations were by no means plain sailing, however. The pioneering issue of bonds in Japan in 1982, as mentioned earlier, was highly controversial. As recalled later by some

CITIC veterans, the first four years of its operation (1979 to 1983) were rife with uncertainty and contention even within CITIC itself about the direction in which the company should seek to develop (Interviews).[22] Operations were also hindered by bureaucratic constraints. China's economic reform had, to all intents and purposes, just started. Rong Yiren was reported to have complained to government leaders that 'I simply cannot go personally to all the departments and ministries concerned to sort out problems. Please appoint one person who is directly in charge of us' (Ji Honggeng 1987: 184). In 1985, when the first shipment of timber from CITIC's joint venture CITIFOR arrived in China from the United States, it could not be cleared through customs simply because the shipment had not been authorised beforehand in the import plan and did not have an import licence. The matter was eventually referred to Premier Zhao Ziyang, who supported a proposal by Zhang Jifu, the State Councillor, that CITIC be given the autonomous right to import timber produced by its overseas venture (Ji Honggeng 1987, 1999: 313).[23] Some argued that CITIC could only operate within what was called the 'cage' of overall government policies, hence the 'cage theory'.[24] Not surprisingly, in the early 1990s Wei Minyi, who succeeded Rong Yiren as Chairman of CITIC, maintained that CITIC had managed to survive and thrive in the clashes between China's two incompatible economic systems, the old and the new (Wei 1995).

Political as well as policy support for CITIC was therefore vital. Rong was candid when he claimed that for further development and growth of CITIC in the environment of China's existing economic system, he needed 'particularistic and preferential policies [applied to CITIC]' (Ji Honggeng 1999: 245). In September 1986, Rong Yiren submitted an important proposal that CITIC be organised as a socialist group company (*shehui zhuyi qiye jituan*) with greater autonomy. On 9 September 1986, Zhao Ziyang, the then Chinese Premier, met with Rong and personally endorsed Rong's proposal in principle. He also suggested that Rong formally submit his proposal to the State Council's executive meeting. On 10 February 1987, the State Council's executive meeting approved Rong's detailed proposal after listening to his report (Interviews).

Two State Council decisions were important in promoting the transnationalisation of CITIC. First, the State Council expanded the authority of CITIC in approving overseas investment projects. For example, CITIC was granted the authority to approve projects in energy, transportation and raw materials, and proposals no longer needed to be submitted to the government or ministries concerned for screening and authorisation as long as they did not require government financing or the export of capital. Second, the State Council gave the green light to Rong's plan to restructure CITIC into a group company with its own bank (Ji Honggeng 1989: 185–6). In structural terms, 1987 therefore marked an important milestone in CITIC's history. It was the first among the Chinese state-owned enterprises to experiment with enterprise grouping, which was to become widely practised in the 1990s (Zhan 1995: 83). Rong's plan to restructure CITIC attracted great interest among international business circles. *Fortune* noted that 'borrowing an idea from Western multinationals, Rong is spinning off CITIC's many divisions into largely autonomous subsidiaries' (Kraar 1987: 109).

Restructuring and expansion, 1987 and after

Restructuring in 1987

The expansion and growth of CITIC in the decade following 1987 started with the restructuring of CITIC into a holding company to decentralise management. Many divisions and departments were reorganised and restructured into subsidiary companies. In April 1987, CITIC Industrial Bank (CIB) was established out of the finance department as a wholesale commercial bank to act as the financing arm of the CITIC Group. Today, CIB is one of the top six commercial banks in China. This restructuring also led to the establishment of a number of other subsidiaries, including CITIC Real Estate Co. Ltd, CITIC Development Co. Ltd, and CITIC Trading Co. Ltd in 1987. The Overseas Investment Department was scaled down, however, and eventually dismantled. CITIC's overseas investments have since largely been carried out by its overseas subsidiaries (Interviews).

The restructuring of CITIC in 1987, combined with the State Council's new authorisation, facilitated the expansion and growth of the corporation's transnational operations. In June 1988, for example, CITIC bought the bankrupted Phoenix Steel in Delaware, for $13.50 million, and established CITISTEEL, a wholly-owned subsidiary of CITIC. CITIC appointed 31-year-old Lu Ming, a recent MBA graduate from Belgium, as CITISTEEL's first Chairman (*Fortune*, 18 July 1988: 11–12; Kang *et al.* 1996: 43–6). CITISTEEL has proved to be a headache for CITIC for many years, however, only becoming profitable in 1993, 1997 being the fifth consecutive year that it made a profit (CITIC 1997: 17).

Expansion in Hong Kong

Nowhere is the rapid expansion of CITIC's overseas investments more clearly visible, however, than in Hong Kong. In February 1987, as part of the restructuring of CITIC, CITIC Hong Kong was reorganised into CITIC Hong Kong (Holdings) Ltd, with a capital injection of HK$300 million from CITIC Beijing.[25] Larry Chi Kin Yung, son of Rong Yiren, was appointed as its General Manager and Deputy Chairman.[26] The restructuring brought to an end uncertainties about the general orientation of CITIC Hong Kong which had bedevilled its operations since 1985.[27] The restructured CITIC Hong Kong (Holdings) immediately embarked on aggressive acquisitions and investments in Hong Kong.[28]

In February 1987, CITIC Hong Kong purchased 12.5 per cent of Cathay Pacific, Hong Kong's *de facto* flagship carrier, with an investment of HK$2.3 billion. Larry Yung later recalled that 'We had done our analysis for six months [before our acquisition] . . . We then sent our report [of the proposed acquisition] to CITIC Beijing and to the State Council. Within five days, it was approved. The State Council also allocated HK$800 million as CITIC Hong Kong's assets in support of our acquisition' (Ma Kefeng 1997: 288). In 1988, CITIC became one of the founding shareholders of the Asia Satellite Corporation (AsiaSat), a joint venture with Cable & Wireless and Hutchinson Whampoa.[29] In early 1989, it acquired 20 per cent of Macao Telecom, with HK$250 million.

In December 1989, CITIC Hong Kong embarked on two other significant acquisitions. One was its acquisition of 38.3 per cent of Dragonair, with HK$390 million. The other was 20 per cent of Hong Kong Telecom, the company with the largest capitalisation on the Hong Kong Stock Exchange at the time. With an investment of HK$10.01 billion,[30] CITIC Hong Kong became Hong Kong Telecom's second largest shareholder. In less than three years after its restructuring, CITIC Hong Kong became a significant investment holding company, with substantial strategic stakes in key companies in Hong Kong, particularly in telecommunications and aviation.

The early years of the 1990s saw another 'great leap forward' by CITIC Hong Kong in its aggressive expansion. If the purchase of 20 per cent of Hong Kong Telecom towards the end of 1989 shocked the local market, two acquisitions in the early 1990s established CITIC Hong Kong as a formidable player in the Hong Kong economy. In 1990 it acquired Tyfull, a small listed property company, as a shell company. In the words of Larry Yung, 'We want Tyfull to become a CITIC vehicle and convert it into a diversified investment company' (*Euromoney*, June 1991: 32). Yung was true to his word. In 1991, CITIC Tyfull was renamed CITIC Pacific. By 1993, with an injection of assets from CITIC HK, CITIC Pacific became one of the top ten companies by market capitalisation on the Hong Kong Stock Exchange. In 1991, in a strategic alliance with Li Ka-shing and Robert Kwok, among others, CITIC Hong Kong launched its acquisition bid for one of the largest unlisted companies in Hong Kong, Dah Chong Hong (Chan 1996: 195–6). CITIC Pacific quickly gained a reputation as one of the most dynamic players in M&A in Hong Kong.

CITIC's aggressive expansion in Hong Kong perhaps has its own natural logic. Economically, its expansion can be explained both by CITIC's location and its ownership advantage. The location advantage is not only related to Hong Kong's geographical proximity to the Mainland. By the late 1980s, CITIC had already been operating in Hong Kong for a number of years and had accumulated a fair amount of knowledge about the local market. Of more significance was CITIC's business networking in Hong Kong and Macao. As mentioned earlier, at least four prominent business leaders in Hong Kong and Macao were present at CITIC's first Board of Directors. Some of CITIC's early strategic acquisitions in Hong Kong, such as its purchase of 12.5 per cent of Cathay Pacific in 1987, were said to have taken place on the advice of Li Ka-shing (Chan 1996: 6). CITIC's takeover of Hang Chong Investment in 1991 was mounted in a strategic alliance with local blue chips, among which was Li Ka-shing's Cheung Kong (Chan 1996: 195–6).[31] All this substantially reduced the risks and costs for CITIC's entry, as well as its expansion.

CITIC's ownership advantage obviously relates to the vast potential market in China. The ability of CITIC Hong Kong, and later CITIC Pacific, to raise funds in the Hong Kong capital market, and the success of their reverse investment in China's infrastructure and energy projects, stand as testimony to CITIC's ownership advantage.

As a state-owned enterprise, directly under the State Council, CITIC cannot totally avoid having to consider the politics surrounding investment in Hong Kong, particularly in the wake of June 1989 and in the years before the British handover of Hong Kong to China in 1997. This has been acknowledged by Rong Yiren himself in an interview with the *China Business Review* in late 1991. When asked about CITIC's investment in Hong Kong, Rong was candid:

Hong Kong is a unique case, as China will resume sovereignty over the area in 1997. In Hong Kong, we must invest with the idea of maintaining the area's stability and prosperity. In the last few years we invested extensively in Hong Kong, and will continue to invest in the future.

(Bodinger 1991: 42–3)[32]

Post-1992 growth and diversification

The intensification of economic reform in China in 1992 offered new opportunities for the expansion of CITIC's transnationalisation. As early as 1991, Li Peng, then Premier, had already told Rong Yiren that the State Council would continue to give policy support to CITIC's business operations at home and abroad. Rong was encouraged to make a submission to solicit further preferential policies. On 30 October 1991, Rong sent a personal submission to Li Peng, in which he asked for greater autonomy for CITIC as a legal person (*faren*) in commercial operations and for CITIC to go 'one step ahead' in the reform and liberalisation of the Chinese economy. It was, however, not until July 1992 that a new package of particularistic policies towards CITIC was formally endorsed by the State Council (Ji Honggeng 1999: 303–4).

The new package gave CITIC greater autonomy to borrow and invest.[33] As the *Financial Times* reported, 'CITIC can now borrow overseas without obtaining prior approval, as long as it keeps within a ceiling set for the five years ending in 1995. CITIC now also has complete autonomy to decide on investment projects under Yn200m at home and $30m abroad.' This new policy package for CITIC prompted Wei Minyi, the Chairman of CITIC, to claim that 'CITIC now has complete freedom to decide the amount of loans, their tenure, the market, the lead managing bank and the currency and that CITIC hopes to diversify its investments around the world with its shares listed and traded on exchanges world-wide within a decade' (*Financial Times*, 12 August 1992; see also Ji Honggeng 1999: 315).

The record of CITIC's acquisitions after 1992 is testimony to the diversification of CITIC's overseas investment. In Australia, CITIC Australia acquired Metro Meat in January 1994 with A$100 million and in 1995 it purchased the Naracoorte Slaughterhouse from the Smorgan family. With these two acquisitions, CITIC Australia became almost overnight the second largest company in Australia's meat processing industry (CITIC 1995). In January 1997, CITIC Australia obtained a 10 per cent interest in the Coppabella Open-cut Coal Mine in Queensland (CITIC 1997: 11). CITIC Australia also engaged in investing from Australia.

In 1994, it bought 10 per cent of the Yaohan International Co. Ltd with 'less than A$50 million', becoming the second largest shareholder of Yaohan. It also had two industrial investments back in China (Interviews, Wall 1996: 34).[34]

In Hong Kong, CITIC Hong Kong and CITIC Pacific acquired a former Royal Navy dockyard in Tamar Basin with a bid of HK$3.351 billion in 1995. Also in 1995, a consortium including CITIC Pacific with a 20 per cent interest acquired the right of land development over the Tsing Yi MTR Station on the line to the new Hong Kong airport with the right to construct commercial and residential buildings totalling 3.14 million square feet. Towards the end of 1996, CITIC Pacific's acquisition of 20 per cent of China Light and Power (China L & P) again shocked the market.

CITIC's investment in forestry has also been diversified in terms of its locations. Previously CITIC's forestry investment was concentrated in North America. Although this region continues to be an important location, as seen for example in its acquisition in Alaska in 1997, CITIC also extended its forestry investments into Chile and New Zealand.[35] In 1996, CITIFOR formed an international consortium with Brierley's Investment and Fletcher Challenge of New Zealand, which successfully won a bid to purchase the state-owned New Zealand Forest Corporation with $1.34 billion (*Beijing Review*, 23–29 September 1996: 26). CITIC held a 37.5 per cent interest in the 188,000 hectares of forest land purchased, Fletcher Challenge 37.5 per cent and Brierley's 25 per cent. In 1997, CITIC New Zealand was established on the basis of CITIFOR New Zealand Ltd to manage the single largest investment project of CITIC overseas (Interviews). In 1998, the beleaguered Brierley's sold its 25 per cent interest to the other two partners of the consortium, CITIC and Fletcher Challenge Forest, each owned 50 per cent of the joint venture until 2001 when it was put into receivership. CITIC's investment in this project amounted to $700 million, the largest single overseas investment by a Chinese company.

The diversification and expansion of CITIC's investment can also be seen in the reverse investment mounted by CITIC Hong Kong through CITIC Pacific in China, particularly in infrastructure and in the energy sector.[36] All of its thirteen principal cooperative joint ventures listed in CITIC Pacific's 1998 annual report are located in China, ranging from power stations in Jiangsu and Zhengzhou to tunnel and bridge development in Shanghai and infrastructure development in Chongqing (CITIC Pacific 1998: 108–9).[37] CITIC Pacific is in a unique position to cultivate the China market. As a listed company, it can take advantage of its standing in the Hong Kong Stock Exchange to raise funds in Hong Kong for investment projects in China.[38] As a company incorporated in Hong Kong, its investment in China enjoys every privilege granted to foreign direct investment. At the same time, its unparalleled connections with CITIC and its expertise in the China market afford considerable advantages. As Larry Yung put it as early as 1993, 'CITIC Hong Kong is different from CITIC Beijing. The main difference is independence. I can invest in China: I have the power, the money and the people' (*Financial Times*, 13 January 1993).

In addition to active transnational acquisitions, CITIC has also expanded its cross-border financial services. It continues to be an important player on the international capital market. In 1993, it issued $250 million worth of non-callable, ten-year Yankee bonds in the United States, becoming the first Chinese entity to issue bonds on the American market after 1949 (*Financial Times*, 21 August 1993).[39] By 1994, CITIC had made nineteen bond issues and raised a total of $3.6 billion (Hong 1995: 10). As one World Bank report claims, CITIC is 'most active [on the international bond market] with a strong balancing sheet, accounting for some 30 percent of China's external bond issues and more than half of non-government bond issues' (World Bank 1997a: 25). By 1995, it had also arranged and obtained 60 commercial loans totalling $2 billion.

Examples of CITIC's expansion of its financial services overseas also include the following. In 1995, CITIC Industrial Bank, together with Lehman Brothers, acted as the chief underwriter for the US$200 million Dragon bond issued by the Ford Motor Company, the first Chinese bank to underwrite bonds for a foreign company. Also in 1995, CITIC expanded its operations in short-term foreign currency financing by establishing a European commercial paper programme of $100 million as a multi-currency facility, the first Chinese financial entity to have done so (*Financial Times*, 7 May 1996, CITIC 1995). CITIC Australia entered into a joint venture with Hambros Australia in 1993 to form CH China Investments Ltd, which offers investment services for equity to flow into China's securities markets (*Financial Times*, 28 April 1993). It remains the only pure China fund listed on the Australian Stock Exchange (Interviews). The overseas branches of Ka Wah Bank in New York and Los Angeles have also expanded their services.

CITIC has also expanded into the international engineering and construction markets. In 1995, CITIC International Cooperation Co. Ltd signed a $300 million contract with the Tehran Urban and Suburban Railway Company on the construction of the Tehran subway, serving as the general contractor of the project (CITIC 1995: 12). By August 2001, the first phase and the first section of the second phase of this project was completed (CITIC press release, 17 December 2001). In 2001, CITIC International Cooperation Co. Ltd was ranked 165th on the list of the 225 top international contraction compiled by *Engineering New Record*.

Growing pains

The phenomenal growth and aggressive expansion of CITIC over the 1990s has not been painless. Like many other aspiring global businesses in the early stages of transnationalisation, CITIC has paid a heavy price for its experience in overseas investment. In the words of a *Financial Times* report, CITIC has 'a far from unblemished record of investing overseas', but is 'undaunted by past blemishes'. In an interview with the *Financial Times* in May 1993, the newly appointed Chairman of CITIC, Wei Mingyi, put on a brave face. He was quoted as saying, 'Business is always aggressive: maybe sometimes you win, sometimes you fail, but you must be aggressive' (*Financial Times*, 1 May 1993). Being aggressive, however, has incurred its price. In its domestic operations, for example, CITIC was publicly criticised by Xinhua News Agency in July 1989 for illegally exporting 100 tons of electrolysed nickel worth $1.26 million. In September of the same year, CITIC was fined 18.81 million yuan ($5.05 million) for foreign exchange speculation (*Far Eastern Economic Review*, 5 October 1989: 86).

There are examples of CITIC's stumbling in its transnational operations, too. In 1990, riding on the success of its initial investment in the Celgar Pulp Mill, CITIFOR and its joint venture partner Power Corporation decided to upgrade the Celgar Pulp Mill to bring its production capacity to 420,000 tons, with a C$700 million loan from the Royal Canadian Bank. Although the renovation and upgrading was largely completed as planned by 1993, the changing market conditions, especially the continuous slump in the price of pulp and rising price of timber,[40] forced CITIFOR to dispose of its 50 per cent interest in the pulp mill in 1997 (Interviews).[41] CITIC Australia has also exited from its ventures into the meat processing industry in Australia. The liquidation of Yaohan International Co. Ltd in 1998 in the wake of the Asian financial crisis, also forced the debt and equity restructuring of CITIC Australia (Interviews).[42]

CITIC Shanghai's debacle on the London Metals Exchange (LME) in 1994 caused a major stir in the business world. A series of unauthorised copper futures deals on the LME carried out by a young 'rogue' trader,

Chen Tongsheng, from CITIC Shanghai incurred CITIC a staggering $40 million worth of debt to Lehman Brothers and Merrill Lynch, among others. Four officials from CITIC Shanghai were subsequently arrested in December 1994 on corruption charges (*Wall Street Journal*, 19 December 1994). CITIC (Beijing) stepped in quickly to protect CITIC Shanghai from bankruptcy and eventually settled with all fifteen creditors in March 1995, while at the same time arguing that CITIC (Beijing) as the parent company was not legally responsible for those debts. After its LME debacle, CITIC quickly tightened up its internal control and centralised its trading in shares, bonds, futures and other derivatives on the international market (*Financial Times*, 16 March 1995). The debacle may also have caused CITIC's Chairman, Wei Mingyi, who had been appointed only about two years before, to tender his resignation (*New York Times*, 18 March 1995).

CITIC's largest overseas investment project, its investment in forestry in New Zealand, is also now in tatters, after CITIC New Zealand fell out with its partner Fletcher Challenge Forest. The joint venture, the Central North Island Forestry Partnership (CNIFP) is now in receivership, although talks continue between CITIC (Beijing) and Fletcher Challenge Forest to buy back the assets of the CNIFP (*New Zealand Herald*, 18 June and 22 June 2002).

As a state-owned enterprise, CITIC is obliged to implement mergers, albeit reluctantly, directed by the State Council.[43] In 1988 and 1993 respectively, two large loss-making manufacturing state-owned enterprises were merged into CITIC.[44] They still form two subsidiaries of CITIC, namely, CITIC Heavy Machinery Co. Ltd and CITIC Machinery Manufacturing Co. Ltd. In April 1995, the newly appointed Chairman of CITIC, Wang Jun, commented, not without complaint, that 'CITIC is burdened by responsibility for several large loss-making state enterprises' and called for the rationalisation of CITIC's loss-making activities (*Financial Times*, 5 April 1995).[45] Even more difficult, such mergers reduce CITIC's focus as a finance and service company.

To the corporation's further frustration, for unspoken policy reasons CITIC's application to engage in insurance business in China's domestic market was stalled for a number of years. It is stated in its 1995 annual report that it was about to break into China's domestic insurance markets. In November 1996 it made public that it had submitted a new application to the PBOC, China's central bank, to set up a general insurance company with a registered capital of 500 million yuan (*South China Morning Post*, 18 November 1996). It was only in late 1999 that it was able to set up its own insurance subsidiary, CITIC Prudential Life

Insurance Co. Ltd, a joint venture with the British insurance company Prudential Holdings.

In 1999 CITIC celebrated its twentieth year. As it matures, CITIC faces daunting challenges. Its direct reporting line has been changed from the State Council to the PBOC.[46] In June, Moody cited this change as one reason for its downgrading of CITIC's credit rating (*Financial Times*, 6 June 1999). Earlier in March, it was reported that CITIC's profits in 1998 were only 2 billion yuan, down from 2.8 billion yuan in 1997, largely due to the substantially reduced contribution from CITIC Pacific in Hong Kong, which was severely hit by the Asian financial crisis. Zhang Xiao, Vice-Chairman of CITIC, reportedly said:

> CITIC Beijing relied very much on the contribution from CITIC Pacific in the past and a drop in earnings of CITIC Pacific affected earnings of CITIC Beijing . . . However, our reliance on CITIC Pacific is being reduced as CITIC Beijing is continuously expanding its other businesses such as in the field of finance and telecommunications.
>
> (*Reuters*, 15 March 1999)

Towards a financial investment holdings conglomerate

Towards the end of the 1990s, CITIC as a financial investment holdings company was taking shape. Its financial assets include the ownership of two commercial banks, CIB and the Kah Wah Bank in Hong Kong. Its subsidiaries are significant players in China's securities markets. It has a joint venture with the Prudential Holdings to operate on China's life insurance market. It has also sizeable engagement in trust, leasing and futures activities. By 2002, CITIC's financial assets accounted for more than 90 per cent of its total assets. As early as 1997, CITIC's top executives began to think of setting up a financial investment holdings company within the CITIC Group to manage its financial interests. Consultation went on at the same time with the central government departments concerned. In 1998, at the height of the Asian financial crisis, CITIC formally submitted to the State Council its establishment proposal. It took three years for the central government to approve CITIC's proposal, in December 2001. A radical restructuring of CITIC was under way in 2002. Central to this restructuring is the aim to establish the CITIC Investment Holdings to manage all its financial assets. At the same time, it has disengaged itself from investment in small and medium-sized industrial enterprises. Its construction and engineering companies and its trading interests are also being reorganised. With the prospect of floating both CIB and CITIC Securities Co. Ltd in domestic stock exchanges, a new and leaner CITIC is to emerge as a financial conglomerate (Hu *et al.* 2002).

CITIC Pacific

The following discussion briefly profiles two subsidiaries of CITIC that have evolved into multinationals in their own right: CITIC Pacific Group and CITIC Australia Group. They represent two of the most aggressive thrusts of CITIC's transnational operations, particularly in the 1990s.

CITIC Pacific is a subsidiary of CITIC Hong Kong (Holdings), an investment holding company that is 100 per cent owned by CITIC Beijing. The 'king of red chips', as it is now popularly known in Hong Kong and beyond, started as CITIC Tyfull, when in 1990, CITIC Hong Kong acquired Tyfull, a small property investment company listed on the Hong Kong Stock Exchange as a shell company. CITIC Tyfull changed to its present English name in 1991 when the first large injection of assets from its parent company CITIC Hong Kong, 12 per cent of Cathay Pacific and 20 per cent of Macao Telecom, was completed (*Financial Times*, 29 June 1991, CITIC Pacific 1991).[47] Larry Yung, Deputy Chairman and General Manager of CITIC Hong Kong, was appointed Chairman of CITIC Pacific. In 1991 and 1992, CITIC Pacific completed its acquisition of one of the largest unlisted companies in Hong Kong, Hang Chong Investment, in two stages: first, by leading a consortium with 36 per cent interest, and then by acquiring additional interests from its consortium partners. By January 1992, CITIC Pacific took full control of Hang Chong Investment and Hang Chong's major trading arm, Dah Chong Hong, became a wholly owned subsidiary of CITIC Pacific (*Financial Times*, 14 January 1992; *Far Eastern Economic Review*, 23 January 1992: 62).

The acquisition transformed CITIC Pacific in two senses. First, after taking full control of Hang Chong Investment, CITIC Pacific's market capitalisation was estimated to have risen from HK$8.5 billion to HK$11 billion, making it one of the 25 largest listed companies on the Hong Kong Stock Exchange. CITIC Pacific became a constituent of the Hang Seng Index in 1992 (*Financial Times*, 14 January 1992). Second, it began to shed its image as a passive investment holding company. Through the acquisition of Dah Chong Hong, a diversified trading company, CITIC Pacific extended its operations overnight beyond Hong Kong to Canada, Singapore, Japan and China, trading and distributing a wide range of products, including electronic appliances, cosmetics, food products and motor vehicles. As the *Financial Times* reported in 1993, 'CITIC Pacific, which a year ago acquired Hang Chong, a trading company, has been keen to throw off its image as an investment company and present itself as a manager of businesses' (8 January 1993). The acquisition of Hang Chong, therefore, began to transform CITIC Pacific into a multinational with diversified interests. Such transformation is acknowledged in the *World Investment Report* compiled by UNCTAD. Ranking CITIC Pacific as one of the fifty largest transnational conglomerates from developing countries, *World Investment Report 1997* specified CITIC Pacific's business activities as diversified/trading/automotive, whereas *World Investment Report 1998* defined its activities as trading/distribution/motor vehicles/supplies (UNCTAD 1998: 32, 1999: 48).

In 1993 and 1994, a series of asset injections into CITIC Pacific were carried out by CITIC Hong Kong. These included 12 per cent of Hong Kong Telecom, 20 per cent of a chemical waste treatment plant on Tsing Yi Island, 25 per cent interest in the Western Harbour Tunnel Company, 28.48 per cent interest in a road tunnel on the Eastern Harbour Crossing, 56.3 per cent of a power station in Jiangsu, 50 per cent of a power station in Henan and 50 per cent interest in the Shanghai Yanan East Road Tunnel (CITIC Pacific 1994, 1995). As Henry Fan, Managing Director of CITIC Pacific, candidly admitted in 1995, CITIC Hong Kong played the role of a 'nursery', 'nurturing projects that need longer lead times or carry more risk prior to injecting them into CITIC Pacific. The Cathay Pacific shares owned by the group, and its Dragonair holding started life in CITIC HK, as did the entire stake in Hong Kong Telecom' (*Financial Times*, 15 June 1995). According to CITIC's annual report, the market value of CITIC Pacific rose from HK$38 billion at the beginning of 1995 to HK$53 billion at the end of the year (CITIC 1995: 10). Through aggressive mergers and acquisitions, and with the injection of assets from CITIC Hong Kong, by June 1996 CITIC Pacific was ranked seventh by market capitalisation on the Hong Kong Stock Exchange (*Financial Times*, 13 June 1996).

It is not surprising that in Hong Kong, CITIC Pacific is regarded as one of the most aggressive companies, if not the most aggressive, in M&A operations in the last decade. CITIC Pacific's Chairman, Larry Yung, was known as 'China's best-known capitalist', and as 'an *arriviste* who has shaken up the corporate scene by taking strategic stakes in Hong Kong Telecom and Cathay Pacific' (*Financial Times*, 29 January

1997). *Fortune*'s cover story of January 1997 called Yung 'the man to know in Hong Kong' (Kraar 1997). CITIC Pacific's purchase of 20 per cent of China Light and Power with HK$16.25 billion in 1996, and its disposal of 15 per cent of the same in 1999, further reinforced this image.[48]

As mentioned above, CITIC Pacific has been listed as one of the fifty largest transnational conglomerates from developing countries since 1994 in UNCTAD's *World Investment Report*. In 1995, CITIC Pacific was ranked 20th by foreign assets and 11th by the transnationality index. In terms of foreign assets, CITIC Pacific is larger than the Acer Group (ranked 26th) and smaller than Hyundai (ranked 16th). Its transnationality index at 49.5 is close to Daewoo at 54.5 (ranked 9th) and LG Electronics (ranked 13th) (UNCTAD 1998: 32). In 1996, it was ranked twentieth in foreign assets and thirteenth (at 49.5) in the index of transnationality respectively (UNCTAD 1999: 48).[49]

One interesting phenomenon merits closer attention. As CITIC Pacific grows, subtle changes in its relationship with its parent company in Beijing have taken place. In 1996, Qin Xiao, CITIC's President, went out of his way to say that CITIC Pacific was not under any special instructions and did not have to consult Beijing on every occasion (*Financial Times*, 13 June 1996). Also in 1996, CITIC's annual report stopped listing CITIC Pacific as one of its direct subsidiaries. The parent company has also progressively reduced its stakes in CITIC Pacific, from 42 per cent in 1996 to 16 per cent in 1999. As mentioned earlier, concerns have been expressed by the parent company through its Vice-Chairman, Zhang Xiao, about CITIC's dependence for its earnings on contributions from CITIC Pacific. At the same time, CITIC Pacific has been increasingly assertive in its bid for independence. Larry Yung, for example, has repeatedly reassured his investors that he has complete freedom from Beijing to make business decisions.[50] In a rare, in-depth interview with *Fortune* in 1996, he said bluntly, 'I don't ask Beijing what to do and how to do it' (Kraar 1997: 34). The Managing Director of CITIC Pacific, Henry Fan, also claimed that 'All our [CITIC Pacific] financing activities are quite independent of our parent. So even if they [CITIC] are put on the watch list or are downgraded it should have no impact on the listed company in Hong Kong' (*Financial Times*, 6 June 1998).

CITIC Australia

CITIC Australia is a wholly owned subsidiary of CITIC. It started in 1986 as a project management company established in the wake of CITIC's purchase of a 10 per cent stake in the Portland Aluminium Smelter for A$120 million (Zhang Jijing 1998). In contrast to CITIC Pacific, CITIC Australia does not enjoy either geographical proximity or a pre-existing business network, both of which CITIC Hong Kong has carefully cultivated for the purposes of expansion. The simple reason why CITIC expanded into Australia in the first place was to exploit the factor-endowment of the host country, in this case, natural resources. As David Wall observed, in the late 1980s, four out of China's five largest outward investments were in Australia, and all were involved in mining activities (Wall 1996: 33, 56). For this reason, Australia remains one of the major destinations of China's outward investment. One paper on CITIC Australia's corporate strategy makes it clear that its operations in Australia aim at 'achieving optimal resources disposition' by cultivating the complementary nature of the Chinese and Australian economies (CITIC Australia 1995b: 238).

CITIC Australia's growth and expansion since 1986 has to date gone through three phases. The first phase was 1986–90 when CITIC Australia existed as a pure project management company, managing CITIC's investment in the Portland Aluminium Smelter in Victoria, Australia. The second phase, which lasted from 1990 to 1997, was a period of rapid expansion and diversification of the company, through which CITIC Australia grew quickly into a diversified group company. In the third phase, that is, from 1997 onwards, CITIC Australia carried out a process of restructuring and rationalisation to refocus its investment on minerals and raw materials (Interviews). As the company states recently, 'During the last 14 years, the company has been developed and expanded into a diversified corporate group covering a wide range of business areas including direct investments, international trading, property development and funds management. It is now one of the top 200 companies in Australia' (www.citic.com.au/about/index.html).

CITIC Australia's expansion in the period from 1990 to 1997 largely took the form of diversifying in two main directions. In other words, there are two thrusts of the company's expansion and diversification. One thrust was to diversify into other sectors within Australia. Already in 1993, 42 per cent of its total operating revenue of A$116.68 million came from food processing and other trading activities. In comparison, its operation in the Portland Aluminium Smelter accounted for 56 per cent of the total revenue (Wall 1996: 34).[51] The acquisition of Metro Meat, the third largest meat exporter in Australia, in January 1994, with A$100 million was a significant step that the company took in diversifying into the food processing industry. The acquisition also established

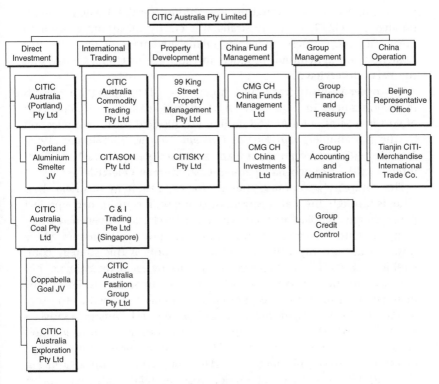

Figure 5.4 CITIC Australia's corporate structure, 2000

CITIC Australia's presence in the US market through Metro Meat's American subsidiary, renamed Metro Meat USA (International) Ltd, located in New Jersey. In 1994, CITIC Australia's total turnover jumped to A$420 million, and its total assets to A$350 million (*Far Eastern Economic Review*, 23 February 1995: 60).[52] As a follow-up, in 1995, the company acquired further interests in the Australian meat processing industry by purchasing the Smorgon Meat Group's works in Naracoorte in South Australia (*Australian Financial Review*, 21 December 1995).[53]

CITIC Australia's aggressive diversification into Australia's meat processing industry in 1994–95 may seem baffling at first glance. However, it must be remembered that in 1994 and 1995, as China's negotiations for its membership of the World Trade Organisation entered into a critical period, many Chinese confidently and over-optimistically expected

that China would be granted membership of the WTO when it incorporated the GATT. CITIC Australia was clearly 'positioning' itself to
break into the Chinese market by taking advantage of possible tariff
reductions on agricultural products in the wake of China's entry into
the WTO (Interviews).

Two other acquisition attempts mounted by CITIC Australia are worth
mentioning here. In 1995, CITIC Australia's bid to acquire 52.5 per cent
of Portman Mining for A\$37.8 million was blocked because of rejection
by the shareholders (*Far Eastern Economic Review*, 23 February 1995:
59).[54] In 1997, however, the company successfully acquired a 10 per cent
interest in the Coppabella Open-cut Coal Mine in Queensland.[55]

The company's corporate strategy for expansion in Australia, it is
clear, is through direct acquisition. By doing so, it transformed a project
management company in a relative short period into a diversified group
company with an emphasis on resource and primary industries where
Australia has a competitive advantage. Not only is this strategy compatible with CITIC's overall strategy for its overseas investment, but
it is also an indispensable part of it: that is, to secure access to raw
materials vital for China's economic development, as well as to other
markets in the Asia-Pacific region. In explaining CITIC Australia's investment in Metro Meat, David Wall argued that 'In addition to location
advantages (grazing land) and the diversification motive for FDI, this
investment also complements the CITIC group's ownership advantages,
allowing it to internalise transaction costs by taking advantage of its
links in the growing Asia-Pacific market for meat' (Wall 1996: 35).
However, reflecting at the end of the 1990s on the company's aggressive acquisitions of meat processors in 1994–95, top executives of the
company did admit that it may not be the optimal investment strategy
for the company at the time (Interviews).

Other expansion and diversification activities of the company within
Australia which merit our attention are related to trade and financial
services. The establishment of CITIFashion Pty Ltd in 1992 was aimed
at taking advantage of new opportunities in Australia's garment market,
as Australia began to liberalise its textile import regime. In 1993, the
turnover of CITIFashion reached over A\$10 million, and in 1999 A\$50
million (CITIC Australia 1995b: 243 and Interviews). Other trading
activities carried out by subsidiaries of the company include exporting
minerals, fertiliser and agricultural products from Australia, and importing a range of industrial products from China ranging from car batteries
(said to amount to 20 per cent of the imported car battery market of
Australia) to tyres and alloy wheels (Interviews).

In late 1992, CITIC Australia formed an equal joint venture with Hambros Australia, CH China Financial Services Ltd, to tap China's embryonic securities markets. Its wholly owned subsidiary, CH China Securities Ltd, is an authorised foreign broker on the Chinese stock markets in both Shanghai and Shenzhen, with Australian dealers' licences. In 1993, CITIC Australia and Hambros Australia jointly launched CH China Investment Ltd, a fully subscribed investment company with total funds of A$35 million, which was listed on the Australian Stock Exchange in December 1993 (CITIC Australia 1995a: 23). In 1996, CH China Investment Ltd was ranked as the top Chinese equity fund in a worldwide survey. It remains one of the few pure China funds listed on the Australian Stock Exchange (Interviews).

The other thrust of CITIC Australia's expansion and diversification has been its investment activities beyond Australia. It is principally this thrust that has made CITIC Australia a multinational in its own right. One major overseas acquisition was that of 10 per cent of Yaohan International Co. Ltd in March 1993, which was later converted to 7.5 per cent of Yaohan International Holdings when the latter was listed on the Hong Kong Stock Exchange in October 1993. One of the main reasons for this acquisition was to form a partnership with Yaohan, which would help CITIC Australia to expand its trading network and its exports to Southeast Asia and Hong Kong, and even Japan (Interviews). With this one stroke, CITIC Australia became the second largest shareholder of Yaohan, until Yaohan's ill-fated collapse in Hong Kong in 1998.

Even before the acquisition of Yaohan, CITIC Australia had already entered into a joint venture, in January 1993, with the Singapore-based International Merchandise Mart Pte Ltd, an associated company of Yaohan. C & I Trading Pte Ltd, in which CITIC Australia had a controlling interest of 55 per cent, became the major vehicle for the company to explore markets and opportunities for trading between Australia, China and Southeast Asia (CITIC Australia 1995a: 21).[56] The establishment of CITIFashion as mentioned earlier also led to CITIC Australia's equity investment in two manufacturers in China: Terri Hua Fashions Corp. Ltd in Beijing and Suzhou CIWA Clothing Corp. Ltd in Suzhou. CITIC Australia also has other investments in China, for example, through its joint venture Symbol Australia Geo-services Pty Ltd, of which it holds a 50 per cent interest (CITIC Australia 1995a: 25).[57]

Through such expansion and diversification, CITIC Australia has grown into a group company. As CITIC Australia's own brochure published in 1995 states:

Since 1986 CITIC Australia's assets have grown 81-fold from initial A$4.3 million to A$350 million in 1994, while the annual turnover has jumped from A$1.1 million to A$420 million during the same period, putting it among the top 300 Australian companies by the end of 1994.

(CITIC Australia 1995a: 3)

CITIC Australia's rapid expansion in 1990–97 created its own problems. In 1997, the company started a process of debt and equity restructuring and rationalisation. The most difficult and also most urgent restructuring is to exit the meat processing industry. China's long-awaited entry into the WTO did not materialise until the beginning of the twenty-first century. The already depressed meat market in the Asia-Pacific region was further battered by the Asian financial crisis in 1997. Increasingly the company's investment in Australia's meat-processing industry cannot be justified by its economic return. It took almost two years for the company to sell off its meat-processing interests, slaughterhouse by slaughterhouse and factory by factory. Only in June 1999 did the company completely exit from the Australian meat-processing industry (Interviews). The collapse of Yaohan International Holdings Ltd in 1998 also forced the company's exit from retailing industries in the Asia-Pacific region.

At the same time, the company increased its stake in the Portland Aluminium Smelter in 1998 from the original 10 per cent to 22.5 per cent (CITIC 1998: 12). The capital to finance the acquisition, a total of A$170 million, was secured in two weeks. As mentioned earlier, the company also acquired a 10 per cent interest in an open-cut coal mine in Queensland in 1997 (Interviews). Such restructuring and rationalisation enabled CITIC Australia to refocus its investment strategy on natural resources for industrial use and to remain at the same time a diversified group company. In 1999, its gross profit was A$16 million, and in 2000 was projected to reach A$29 million (Interviews). The operation revenue of CITIC Australia reached A$700 million in 2000. And in June 2002, CITIC Australia Trading Limited was listed on the Australian Stock Exchange.

Summary

In just over twenty years, CITIC has grown from infancy to be the most prominent and best-known Chinese global business. Established in 1979 by the Chinese government as a purpose built investment company, CITIC was intended to be the central government investment vehicle, fostering a particular kind of linkage between the Chinese economy and the global economy. For that very purpose, the government granted CITIC an unusual and special status as a ministerial-level organisation when established. That was followed by a set of particularistic and preferential policies afforded specifically to CITIC. The special status of CITIC, it is important to note, has not only been guaranteed institutionally, but also endorsed, and therefore protected, by the personal patronage of the Chinese leadership up to Deng Xiaoping. The special status of CITIC, combined with particularistic policies, enabled CITIC, particularly at the early stage of its evolution, to retain and exercise a high level of autonomy in its business decision-making. These are the necessary conditions for the first unfolding of the success story of CITIC.

The sufficient condition for the success of CITIC is the entrepreneurship demonstrated first and foremost by Rong Yiren, which in 1979 was a rare and valuable asset. Even in the midst of controversies in the early years of CITIC, Rong was determined to run it as a commercial firm, rather than a government bureaucracy. Rong did not only demonstrate by personal example, but also conscientiously fostered such entrepreneurship throughout CITIC. After all, even though state-owned, CITIC has to operate on the internal and the international market as a firm. The combination of CITIC's special status with particularistic policies granted by the government and the entrepreneurial spirit of the firm seems to be the winning formula for CITIC in its expansion and reinvention. The restructuring of CITIC in 1987, its large investment in resource sectors overseas and its phenomenal growth in Hong Kong are testimony to this. The professionalism demonstrated among the personnel of CITIC and its operations has become an important asset of the company and part and parcel of its reputation. If CITIC's case is unique, it is neither because of the special status that it enjoys nor simply as a result of Rong's entrepreneurship. It is the combination of the two that ensures the success of CITIC.

One important ingredient in the CITIC success story, which may not have stood out as clearly as it deserves in the analytical account above, should be emphasised here. Rong Yiren's reputation and his networking among the overseas Chinese community is an important asset clearly recognised by Deng Xiaoping and the CCP leadership. From the very beginning, Rong was encouraged to cultivate this important asset in engaging in international business. CITIFOR, the first substantial joint venture that CITIC entered into in North America, was initially with an overseas Chinese entrepreneur. More importantly, the most significant thrusts of CITIC's transnationalisation, that is, CITIC's entry and expansion in Hong Kong, have all been mounted either with the advice of local Chinese entrepreneurs or in strategic alliance with the local blue chips controlled by overseas Chinese entrepreneurs, as in the case of Li Ka-shing and Robert Kwok. This is just a reflection of the important role that the overseas Chinese community has played in the internationalisation of the Chinese economy, and in the transnationalisation of the Chinese firms.

The enviable achievement of CITIC illustrates not just the importance but also the limits of particularistic policies. In so doing, it also highlights the constraints within which a state-owned enterprise has to operate in transnationalising: among which are non-market economic conditions, limited liberalisation of most if not all sectors, administrative interference, state intervention and, finally, ambiguous public ownership of the company. It is a paradox that while particularistic policies are indispensable and helpful in circumventing political and economic constraints and in fostering the initial transnationalisation of Chinese firms, they alone are not sufficient to overcome the systemic constraints inherent in the Chinese economy and may indeed even prove to be hampering the further transnationalisation of Chinese firms, as is clearly demonstrated in the cases of Sinochem and Shougang examined in the next two chapters.

6
Sinochem: Global Reach

China's trading companies, as discussed in Chapter 4, are one of the major forces among Chinese firms engaging in transnational operations and outward investment. The original twelve national trading corporations were among the very first to internationalise. When China started opening up in 1978, these twelve firms were of comparatively large size in terms of their annual turnover. They also possessed undeniable advantages (in comparison with other Chinese firms) in engaging the international markets. They were clearly among a very small number of Chinese firms that had expertise in importing and exporting, and knowledge of the international market with existing contacts and a client base. Their monopolist position in respective lines of trade, though geared to fulfil government import and export plans, put them in an advantageous position to exploit the opportunities offered by China's changing development strategy increasingly oriented towards export-led growth. In subsequent years, all these trading corporations have been transnationalised and engaged in global operations.

This chapter examines the transnationalisation of Sinochem, China's largest multinational trader to date. In the 1980s and the 1990s, Sinochem has been at the forefront of the Chinese government's effort to foster the internationalisation, and then transnationalisation, of Chinese firms. For that purpose, a set of particularistic policies has been applied by the government to the Sinochem experiment. The transformation of Sinochem into a corporation with global reach is a dual process. One is Sinochem's responses to the transformations of the Chinese economy brought about by opening up and economic reform and its capitalisation on the particularistic policies applied to its experiment. The other is that of reinventing and reengineering Sinochem as a commercial firm in response to the globalisation of the world economy. A study of Sinochem, therefore, illustrates the evolution and competencies of China's state-owned trading companies in reinventing themselves in a radically different economic and policy environment, and through transnationalisation into a global company.

The evolution of Sinochem into a multinational conglomerate is dramatic, and sometimes traumatic. The speed with which this transformation has taken place is extraordinary. Sinochem made its debut in the *Fortune* Global 500 Service Companies in 1988, only ten years after China's economic reform began. From 1989 to 1994, Sinochem's appearance in the Global 500 Service Companies list was erratic. But whenever it did appear, it consistently ranked among the top thirty in terms of annual turnover. In 1994, it was ranked 26th. In 1995, when *Fortune* for the first time produced a combined list (of industrial and services companies) of the Global 500, Sinochem was ranked 209th, with a total revenue of $14.98 billion.[1]

Sinochem attracts attention not only because of its large annual turnover and its ranking in the Global 500. More importantly, Sinochem was chosen by the central government as a pilot experiment first for the internationalisation of Chinese firms and later for transforming large-scale state-owned enterprises through transnationalisation. In 1987, the State Council chose Sinochem to experiment in internationalising the business operations of Chinese enterprises. In 1995, with the approval of the State Council, Sinochem started a conglomeration pilot project, 'with the purpose of establishing a comprehensive trading company consolidating trade with industry, technology, financing, information and other major functions' (*RMRB*, 11 April 1995). Like the other two cases examined in this study, the state has played a special role in the transformation of Sinochem.

The institutional story of how Sinochem has evolved into a global business is worth investigating for a variety of additional reasons. First, it occupies a special position in China's experimentation with transnational operations of state-owned enterprises, especially trading firms. Second, the apparent achievements of, and the lessons learned from, Sinochem's transnationalisation is also part of Sinochem's reinvention of itself in the ever-changing domestic and international economic environment. An in-depth analysis of the Sinochem experiment shows how Chinese firms respond to the incentives and constraints of the policy environment and how the politics of reform affects their transnationalisation. Third, in generic terms, the transnationalisation of Sinochem is not atypical of the transformation of many other Chinese trading companies. The rapid emergence of China's multinational traders is therefore illustrated by an examination of Sinochem's trans-nationalisation. Finally, Sinochem is chosen as a 'middle-aged' firm established immediately after the founding of the PRC. It is in a different sector from both CITIC, a financial service company (investigated in the last chapter), and Shougang, an industrial giant (to be discussed in the next chapter). The examination of the transformation and transnationalisation of Sinochem can then be compared to that of 'young' CITIC (just over twenty years old) and of 'old' Shougang (more than eighty years old). This comparison should shed some light on the capacity of China's large state-owned enterprises of different age and in different sectors to transform and to reinvent themselves.

In the broader international and theoretical perspective, there is one more reason for undertaking a detailed examination of the story of Sinochem's transnationalisation. Trading companies, Geoffrey Jones noted, 'represent different types of international business than the much more intensely studied manufacturing multinationals'. A study of Sinochem's transnationalisation can help alleviate what Jones most recently called 'the paucity of literature on trading companies' in the study of multinational corporations (Jones 1998: 1).[2]

Sinochem at its prime

In comparison to the other two firms examined in this study, CITIC and Shougang, Sinochem had just reached its prime in the mid-1990s. In 1995, it celebrated its forty-fifth anniversary with the publication of *Zhonghua Sishiwu Nian, 1950–1995* [Forty-five years of Sinochem, 1950–1995]. As Zheng Dunxun, the President and CEO of Sinochem, stated in his opening message:

> For the past 45 years, Sinochem has experienced different historical periods – from a planned economy to the transition to a socialist market economy ... It has made remarkable achievements in its management and fulfilled import-export tasks assigned by the government with a total trade volume worth US$ 150 billion.
>
> (Sinochem 1995a: 13)

In 1995, Sinochem was one of three Chinese companies that were listed among the Global 500 largest companies by *Fortune* and was ranked 209th by total revenues.[3] It was ranked 8th by foreign assets among the top 50 TNCs from developing countries (UNCTAD 1999: 48). It had been for six years in a row the largest trader among China's 500 largest import and export enterprises (*International Business*, 18 April

1995).[4] Figure 6.1 shows the growth of Sinochem's revenues in the first half of the 1990s.[5]

In 1996, more than 40 per cent of Sinochem's revenues came from its overseas operations, which amounted to $7.966 billion out of the total of $17.955 billion. Sinochem's annual report proudly records that 'overseas operations [in 1996] accounted for 40% of the whole company in terms of business turnover, and 50% in terms of profit' (Sinochem 1997: 9). The breakdown of Sinochem's total turnover in 1996 is shown in Figure 6.2.

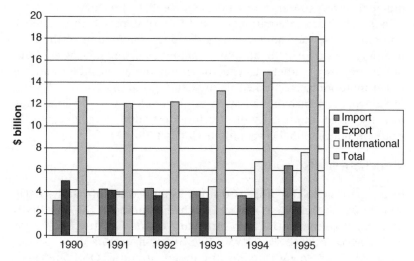

Figure 6.1   Sinochem's turnover, 1990–95

Sources: Sinochem (1995a: 79–82), Sinochem *Annual Report* (1996: 4–5).

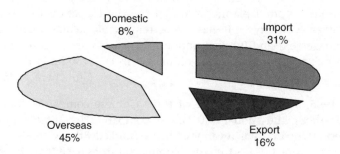

Figure 6.2   Breakdown of Sinochem's turnover, 1996

Sources: Sinochem *Annual Report* (1997).

As is clear from the above statistics, Sinochem's growth in the 1990s came mostly from its international operations rather than its traditional import and export business.[6] While the overall value of its import and export on a year-to-year basis in the early 1990s did not decline markedly, their percentage in the total of Sinochem's turnover dropped steadily from about two-thirds in 1990 to less than a half in 1996. The rapid increase in the volume of Sinochem's international operations is testimony to Sinochem's rapid transnationalisation. This is clearly recognised in the *World Investment Report*. In 1996, Sinochem's transnationality index is 36.4 per cent, ranked 21st among the top 50 TNCs from developing countries (UNCTAD 1999: 48).[7]

There is another aspect of Sinochem's growth that is worth mentioning. Sinochem's assets grew rapidly in the 1990s. Total assets increased from \$4.67 billion in 1994 to \$6.6 billion in 1996, and net assets from \$679 million to \$1 billion in the same period. Extensive consolidation and rationalisation from 1997 to 1999 have reduced its total assets to \$4.736 billion but increased its net assets to \$1.159 billion (Sinochem 1996, 1997, 1998, 1999, 2000). Sinochem's growth has been accompanied by, and achieved at the same time as, rapid diversification both in terms of the geographical distribution of its business and the scope of its operations. Geographical diversification means that Sinochem has a presence all over the world, from Johannesburg to Sydney, from Port Moresby to Dubai and from New York to London. Trade diversification saw Sinochem's non-petrochemical imports and exports reach a total value of \$536 million in 1994 (Sinochem 1995: 48). That went up to \$818 million in 1997 (Sinochem 1998: 4). Diversification also means that Sinochem has increased its involvement in warehousing and transportation, manufacturing, finance, insurance, leasing, consultancy, real estate and other non-trade service sectors, such as engineering and labour, on both the domestic and international markets (Sinochem 1995a: 32).[8]

At its prime, Sinochem had undoubtedly become a multinational trading conglomerate with diversified operations on the global scene. In 1996, Sinochem's foreign assets had already reached \$3.2016 billion (UNCTAD 1999: 48).[9] The transformation of Sinochem from a little-known state trading company to one of the largest transnationals in the world was achieved in little more than fifteen years.

It is perhaps more than coincidental that on the eve of Sinochem's forty-fifth anniversary the State Council approved, on 31 December 1994, Sinochem's proposal that it be a pilot project for the conglomeration of Chinese enterprises following the example of Japanese *sogo shosha* (general trading company). The State Council Document No. 144, 1994, laid down clearly that Sinochem was to carry out the conglomeration pilot project pursuant to building a modern enterprise system. With trade as its core business, Sinochem was to diversify into, and integrate its trade with, industry, technology, finance and information services so as to create a truly internationalised multifunctional trading conglomerate (*Economic Daily*, 11 April 1995).

A new set of particularistic policies for Sinochem's conglomeration was granted by the State Council. The most important was to allow Sinochem to conduct a variety of financial services. Although not able to own a bank, as Shougang was allowed to do (discussed in the next chapter), Sinochem incorporated the China Investment and Trust Corporation for Foreign Economic Cooperation and Trade (FOTIC), formerly the financial arm of MOFTEC, as its core subsidiary company.[10] Sinochem's pilot project for conglomeration was approved, it must be noted, at a time when the government was beginning to tackle in earnest the reform of China's large state-owned enterprises. Sinochem's conglomeration is therefore not just a step towards further transnationalisation of Sinochem; it is also part of the government attempt to reform state-owned enterprises through corporatisation and transnationalisation.

One of Sinochem's first steps towards conglomeration was to reorganise its corporate structure. After restructuring, Sinochem's corporate structure in 1996 is as shown in Figure 6.3.

Sinochem's 52 major overseas subsidiaries were organised into five group holding companies. The five group companies are the Sinochem American Holdings Incorporation, Sinochem Asia Holdings Co. Ltd, Sinochem Europe Holding PLC, Sinochem Hong Kong (Holdings) Co. Ltd and Lief International Pty Ltd, headquartered in New York, Singapore, London, Hong Kong and Sydney respectively. This corporate structure proved to be short-lived, however.[11]

The second half of the 1990s, witnessed what could be regarded as a mid-life crisis for Sinochem. By 1997, Sinochem's conglomeration pilot project was stalled, as the Asian financial crisis exposed the malaise of Japan's *sogo shosha* and Korea's *chaebol* on which Sinochem's conglomeration project was supposed to be modelled. The two models have now been shelved, if not ditched, by the Chinese leadership in their reform of state-owned enterprises. In 1998, the long-serving President and CEO of Sinochem, Zheng Dunxun, retired, and a new management team was appointed by MOFTEC. But even before Zheng's retirement, Sinochem had already carried out what it called the 'rationalization, restructuring

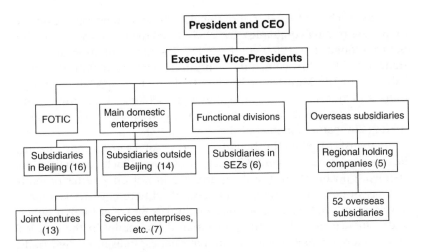

Figure 6.3   Corporate structure of Sinochem, 1996
Sources: Adapted from Sinochem *Annual Report* (1996, 1997).

and consolidation' of its investment projects. As revealed in its 1998 annual report, 'By June 1997, more than 70 projects which were either not closely related to Sinochem's main businesses or improperly managed were terminated by means of share transfer, expiration of contract and reporting loss' (Sinochem 1998: 11). In 1999, the new management initiated a comprehensive risk management system which has now been integrated into Sinochem's operational system. The radical restructuring of China's petroleum industry in 1997–98 also presents an uncompromising challenge to Sinochem's future development.

Trading with a difference, 1979 to 1987

Sinochem and state trading before 1978

Sinochem has indeed 'come a long way' to reach its prime as a multinational conglomerate, as claimed by Zheng Dunxun in 1995 (Sinochem 1995a: 14). It was first of all a product of China's planned economy. The predecessor of Sinochem, the China National Import Corporation, was established in February 1950, shortly after the establishment of the People's Republic of China. From 1950 to 1955, a system of state trading to handle China's imports and exports was founded with the gradual establishment of a dozen national trading corporations. In

1950, as much as 31.6 per cent of the PRC's foreign trade was conducted by private trading companies. By 1955, it had dwindled to as little as 8 per cent (Shen *et al.* 1992: vol. I, 10–11). The nationalisation of foreign trade in the PRC first gained momentum in 1952 when, with the establishment of the Ministry of Foreign Trade, sixteen specialised foreign trade and transportation companies were set up. At the same time, the central government tightened foreign currency control for private trading companies (Shen *et al.* 1992: vol. I, 93).

In August 1958, at the height of the Great Leap Forward, Beijing further centralised foreign trade authorities. Such centralisation, claimed a document of the Politburo, would not only better promote China's imports and exports and serve the interests of its economic development, but would also support China's 'peaceful foreign policy' and 'enhance the role of the proletarian dictatorship' in the political and economic struggle against international capitalism. Foreign trade, in line with this logic, had a dual function to fulfil, political and economic. It was therefore clearly stated in the Politburo document that all foreign trade must now be conducted by national trade corporations under the Ministry of Foreign Trade and their subsidiaries and that no local authorities or other institutions were allowed to engage in foreign trade.[12] National trade corporations were also to determine prices for exports (Shen *et al.* 1992: vol. I, 24–5, 64–5). A trade system of state monopoly and centralisation was thus established by 1958. This system remained largely intact until 1978.

The state monopoly of trade and the centralisation of trade authorities were partially supported and partially complemented by the annual foreign trade plan, which was, in Lardy's words, 'an integral part of the economic planning process' in China (Lardy 1992: 17). The function of national trading corporations was, understandably, to implement state import and export plans. China's trade regimes established in the 1950s, on the other hand, were typically biased towards import substitution. As Zhang Huadong, vice trade minister of China, claimed in 1955:

> The purpose of importing more industrial equipment from the Soviet Union is to lay the foundation of China's industrial independence, so that in the future China can make all of the producer goods it needs and will not have to rely on imports from the outside.
>
> (Quoted in Ross 1995: 438)

Foreign trade, therefore, was used principally to supplement shortfalls in China's domestic production, particularly essential raw materials and capital goods. The main purpose of exports was to earn sufficient foreign currency to finance necessary imports so as to avoid foreign borrowing.[13] A quick glimpse at China's trade statistics from 1956 to 1975 reveals that a healthy surplus was maintained between China's annual exports and imports, except in 1960, 1974 and 1975 (MOFERT 1990: 299).

As an offshoot of China's trade system nestled in a command economy, Sinochem, like all other trading corporations, conducted its import and export business according to the national foreign trade plan each year. It was responsible for implementing the plan, but not for losses and profits. Like all other trading corporations, Sinochem was run not as a commercial entity but as a government organ. Nevertheless, in the late 1950s, Sinochem already occupied an important position in China's foreign trade. Take 1957 as an example. The trade volume of Sinochem reached $394.04 million, 12.7 per cent of the national total of $3.103 billion (Sinochem 1995a: 8). By Sinochem's own account, it was 'officially transformed into a specialized trading company in the 1960s' in petroleum and chemical products. In 1973, Sinochem pioneered the export of China's crude oil to Japan (Sinochem 1995a: 22).[14] The significance of Sinochem in China's overall foreign trade from the 1950s to the 1970s can be seen in a simple set of statistics. From 1952 to 1978, China's foreign trade total was, according to MOFTEC, $166.23 billion (MOFERT 1990: 299). The total trade conducted by Sinochem in the same period was $21.45 billion (Sinochem 1995a: 82). That is 12.9 per cent of the national total.

On the eve of China's economic reform and opening up, Sinochem was undoubtedly an established and significant player that enjoyed a rather comfortable monopolising position in China's foreign trade. The lines of products monopolised by Sinochem were vital to China's industrialisation and modernisation projects, which included petroleum, petrochemical products, rubber, chemical fertiliser, plastic products and chemicals. It was, further, a firm of considerable size with wide business scope.

There is a curious anomaly, however. Sinochem, in spite of a relatively significant trade volume in the pre-1978 years, did not have any transnational operations. In its first thirty years, Sinochem, like all other national trading companies in China, conducted its trade largely behind closed doors. The official account of the development of China's foreign trade from 1949 to 1988 confirms two interesting facts. One is that apart from an office in East Berlin and some subsidiaries in Hong Kong and Macao, China's foreign trade institutions did not have any overseas presence until 1979.[15] The other is that trade and other related activities were carried out, where appropriate, by commercial sections of Chinese embassies in resident countries (Shen *et al.* 1992: vol. I, 107–9).

Responding to trade reform

The importance of foreign trade reform for the internationalisation of China's national trading firms like Sinochem, therefore, can hardly be overemphasised.[16] Foreign trade reform in the following three areas carried out from 1979 to 1983 radically transformed the trading environment in China and presented challenges as well as opportunities that Sinochem had to respond to.

One important component of China's earliest trade reform was to create the possibility for Chinese trading companies to set up offices abroad. This important policy liberalisation was to have a profound impact on the internationalisation of China's trading firms: establishing a foreign presence was to become the first thrust of Chinese traders' international business operations. In September 1979, a memorandum from the Japanese Embassy in China, which clarified the legal status, taxation and other related matters concerning representative offices of Chinese trading companies in Japan, opened the way for Chinese companies to get a foothold in that country. In 1980, the Ministry of Foreign Trade set up in Tokyo, London, Paris and Hamburg representative offices of the China National Import and Export Corporation. At the same time, China's trading companies also began to make both trade-related and non-trade-related ventures overseas. By the end of 1981, seventeen ventures with investment from China's trading companies were established (Shen *et al.* 1992: vol. I, 109–11).[17] As is often argued in conventional theory, the setting up of trade offices overseas was an important step towards the internationalisation of firms. By making it possible for China's trading firms to establish a presence in foreign countries, this changing policy opened immense possibilities for the transnationalisation of China's trading firms.

Sinochem responded to this policy liberalisation by opening its first overseas representative office in Tokyo in April 1980. It was followed by the opening of Deutsche Sinochem GMBH in 1982, and by that of Sinochem HK and Sinochem UK, also in the early 1980s. By the beginning of 1987, Sinochem had set up over thirty offices and subsidiaries worldwide, and established its presence in its major markets, including Japan, the United Kingdom, the United States and Southeast Asia. Sinochem made its initial outward investments, mostly trade-related, in those countries. In what could be regarded as the first stage of

Sinochem's overseas expansion, its presence and investment overseas were mostly motivated by trade promotion and market-seeking. Such geographical diversification as the first step in a trading company's transnationalisation is consistent with findings in a recent study edited by Geoffrey Jones (1998).[18]

The second transformation of the trading environment came about as a result of the decentralisation of foreign trade authorities, a decision initiated in 1979. With decentralisation, the state virtually renounced its monopoly of foreign trade. From 1979 to 1981, the Ministry of Foreign Trade approved the creation of hundreds of foreign trade companies in provinces, in newly created special economic zones and under the ministries of national production. Some large-scale state-owned enterprises were also granted limited foreign trade authority. Furthermore, Sino-foreign joint ventures were normally allowed to trade their own products, thus further reinforcing decentralisation. Such decentralisation led quickly to, and was followed by, what could be regarded as the 'demonopolising' of foreign trade. Newly established trading companies began to trade those products traditionally monopolised by national trading companies. The MOFERT was to eventually legitimise in 1984 such cross-trading of products as part of the reform to introduce competition and to encourage diversification.[19]

In the case of Sinochem, even its monopoly of the petroleum and petrochemicals market was slowly but steadily eroded. For example, the Chinese National Petrochemical Corporation (Sinopec), a subsidiary of the Ministry of Petroleum responsible for both refining crude oil and the domestic distribution of petroleum products, began to export petroleum products in the early 1980s (Lardy 1992: 95 and 164, Christoffersen 1998: 16).

The liberalisation policies were a double-edged sword. While they led to a gradual erosion of the traditional monopolies of the specialised trading firms, they also opened up new opportunities for expansion of their trading activities into non-traditional fields. For Sinochem, information and knowledge of both domestic demands and foreign markets in its non-core businesses were cultivated for diversification. Eventually, Sinochem would engage in, for example, trading of consumer goods and even food and electronic devices. It would also find a niche in exporting engineering and construction services.

The decentralisation and demonopolising of foreign trade authorities did not seem to have immediately threatened the monopoly of Sinochem in China's foreign trade, at least throughout most of the 1980s, even with a spectacular rise in the number of trading companies.

This was probably largely due to the fact that the main commodities monopolised by Sinochem in trading, rubber, chemicals, chemical fertiliser and petroleum belonged to the so-called category one commodities, which were 'mass commodities of vital strategic importance to the national economy and people's livelihood'. For that reason, the state remained in total control of trade in these commodities. Another reason might be that trading chemicals and petrochemicals requires special expertise, as well as considerable capital, neither of which the newcomers to China's trading system could afford. Either by design or by default, Sinochem's traditional monopoly was protected and remained largely intact. Nevertheless, the senior management of Sinochem already felt the looming threat of the double whammy of decentralisation and demonopolisation, even though the actual monopoly of Sinochem had been little dented (Interviews).

The third area in the transformation of the trading environment was related to the changing macro-economic policies concerned. The early 1980s saw a progressive shrinkage in the traditional foreign trade plan, particularly after 1984. The introduction of mandatory and guidance plans for both imports and exports effectively diluted the role of the traditional plan. Lardy's study indicates that whereas the mandatory plan for exports covered around 70 per cent of China's total in 1986, by 1988 it had fallen to only 45 per cent (Lardy 1992: 163 and 40–1). Imports under the command plan, according to the World Bank estimate in 1988, covered 'only the seven key raw materials which are under "unified management"' comprising about 40 per cent of total imports (World Bank 1988: 22). That would fall to just 20 per cent in 1991 (Zhang Xiaoguang 1993: 9). The introduction of an import and export licensing system in the early 1980s, the promotion of an agency system, particularly in imports, and an increasing use of customs tariffs as an economic lever further dented the role and function of the foreign trade plan.

One area of macro-economic reform, that is, the relaxation of exchange controls, was vital for Sinochem's international operations. Starting from 1979, as a measure to encourage export growth, a system of foreign exchange retention was introduced, which allowed exports-producing firms, among others, to retain and use a portion of their export earnings. A series of steps was taken in the 1980s to further rationalise and expand the system. At the same time, China's exchange rate policies underwent some reform. In the mid-1980s, China began to practise what the World Bank called 'a managed floating exchange system', with the US dollar as the intervention currency (World Bank

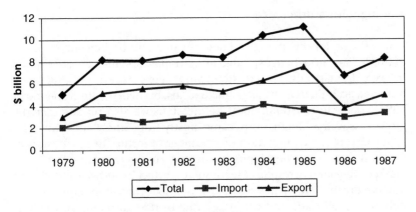

Figure 6.4   Sinochem's trade volume, 1979–87

Source: Sinochem (1995a: 82).

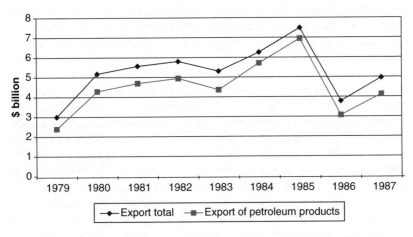

Figure 6.5   Sinochem's export of petroleum products, 1979–87

Source: As for Figure 6.4.

1988: 72). In July 1986, RMB, the Chinese currency, was devalued by 15.8 per cent. Relaxation of foreign exchange controls and reform of exchange rate policies afforded Sinochem, with a large turnover in exports annually, crucial and ready access to funds for its eventual engagement in international operations and its own outward investment.

Trading with a difference

Under the rapidly changing and radically different trading environment of this period, Sinochem exploited its monopoly and managed to expand its trade dramatically. The growth in Sinochem's trade in the 1980s was, however, accompanied by large fluctuations, particularly in the period of 1984–87. A closer examination of the statistics also reveals that the growth, as well as fluctuations, came mostly from Sinochem's exports.

In the 1980s, a conjunction of a number of fortuitous circumstances for China's domestic development strategy, and on the international oil market, were largely responsible for such spectacular growth and violent fluctuations in Sinochem's trade. Given Sinochem's monopoly particularly in the oil trade and the state's role in trade promotion, this was expected. To finance its ambitious modernisation plan, China exported a large quantity of crude oil. Sinochem's export of crude oil and petroleum products increased dramatically from $2.38 billion in 1979 to $6.95 billion in 1985, which accounted for the lion's share of Sinochem's total exports (Sinochem 1995a: 82). On the other hand, the sharp fall in oil prices on the international market in 1986, and China's cutback of exports of crude oil in 1987, inevitably affected Sinochem's trade.[20] The fluctuations in Sinochem's trade in value terms were almost synchronic with those changes (see Figures 6.4 and 6.5). Sinochem's vulnerability to such ups and downs would prove to be one of the major stimuli for its drive to internationalise and to diversify its business operations. It is perhaps not surprising that after 1987, and throughout the 1990s, Sinochem's import and export total hovered between $7 billion and $8.5 billion per annum.[21] The record of Sinochem's 1985 trade total of $11.13 billion still stands in 2002. Growth since 1987 has come almost exclusively from sectors other than imports and exports.

From 1979 to 1987, therefore, Sinochem, like all other Chinese foreign trade firms, operated in a constantly changing trading environment, which provided incentives and exerted pressures, as well as afforded opportunities, for their expansion as well as transformation. How to adapt to this changing environment and to grasp the opportunities offered for growth was the challenge faced by all firms. As Sinochem's senior management admitted later, the decentralisation of foreign trade authorities, together with other liberalisation policies, introduced 'keen and fierce' market competition and had a 'great impact on Sinochem'. It also led to an anomaly in China's foreign trade competition, which is often described as 'raising procurement prices at home, slashing prices abroad, letting an outflow of profits'.[22] At the same time, the 1986 slump in oil prices seriously challenged Sinochem's traditional lines of trade. Because of this collapse, Sinochem's total earnings from crude oil exports were $3 billion less than originally expected.

Sinochem's strategic decision to go transnational in 1987 can be viewed as a creative response to these changes. The decision was also based on a careful evaluation of its advantage and relative strength in comparison with other Chinese companies in cultivating international markets including, in particular, Sinochem's reputation, its extensive contacts and networking, and its expertise in trading petroleum and petrochemicals and chemicals. As Fu Yong, executive Vice-President of Sinochem, claimed, 'Faced with changes brought about by foreign trade reform, we seriously studied the external environment and international conditions of our enterprise and formulated accordingly a strategy for transnational operations' (Fu Yong 1994a: 1–5). The strategic choice that Sinochem made in 1987, as he recalled, was to 'move our main operation from within the country to the world, to utilize the international resources, funds, technology and labour force to actively explore the international market to conduct international operations and to strive for a breakthrough in our corporation's operation model' (Fu Yong 1994a: 4).

Sinochem thus embarked on the rocky road to reinventing itself.

Experimenting with transnational operations, 1988 to 1990

Internationalisation experiment

In early 1987, Sinochem began to rethink its corporate strategy in the domestic and international markets. Internationalising Sinochem's business operations was on the agenda as Sinochem groped for a response to the changing trading environment. President Zheng Dunxun personally oversaw the feasibility studies of the project (Interviews). It was on 17 October 1987 that Sinochem made its submission, *A Programme for Experimenting with Internationalised Operations and Comprehensive Contract Responsibility*, to the MOFERT for approval. On 4 December, MOFERT and the State Commission for Restructuring the Economic System jointly submitted Sinochem's proposal to the State Council. In the submission, MOFERT and SCRES reassured the State Council that 'Sinochem is one of our foreign trade companies with a long history and extensive channels. It has good management and quality personnel', and, further, that Sinochem's strategic initiative to internationalise its business operations 'is compatible with the general orientation of the reform of the foreign trade system. Its programme is feasible. The successful implementation of this programme could pioneer a new way for the development of our country's foreign trade and economic co-operation' (Sinochem Corporate Strategy Study Group 1991: 273–5).

The submission called for a threefold transition of Sinochem; that is, from a single import–export business to an international trader, from commodity trader to a diversified and multifunctional operation, from a Chinese foreign trade company to a transnational corporation – thus making Sinochem 'a socialist enterprise marked by internationalisation of operations, modernization of management, conglomeration of organization[s]'. This is the so-called *san zhuan san hua* (literally three transitions and three '-isations'). The submission clearly envisaged the internationalisation of Sinochem as the key to these three transitions and '-isations', and embodied the first explicit call for the building of Sinochem into a transnational corporation. It also marked the beginning of the conglomeration of Sinochem. In 1989, Sinochem was to become one of the first 55 Chinese companies to experiment with enterprise grouping.

It is important to note that in its submission, Sinochem asked specifically for more enterprise autonomy (*qiye zizhuquan*) and emphasised that this was the key to the success of the proposed experiment. Although the progressive expansion of decision-making power for enterprises started as early as 1979, by 1987 control and constraints from government and bureaucracies were still severe and widespread. As recalled by Gao Shangquan, Vice-Minister of the SCRES, the State Council promulgated from 1979 to 1987 'thirteen documents and ninety-seven provisions on the expansion of the enterprises' decision making power . . . the effect of which has been to remove their subordinate relation to government' (Gao 1996: 70). The simple fact that the State Council had to issue so many documents to give enterprises the elementary power to make commercial decisions is an indication of the difficulties. As Naughton noted, only 'a small minority of enterprises enjoyed most of these privileges [of enterprise autonomy] at the end of 1985' (Naughton 1995: 205).[23]

Even such a firm as Sinochem, which enjoyed a comfortable monopolising position, cannot escape from these constraints entrenched in the existing economic system. In retrospect, Sinochem's senior management complained that 'the lack of decision-making power and state monopolised revenues and expenditure at that time [in 1987] restrained the self perfection and development of enterprises' (Interviews). Sinochem's proposed experiment in transnational operations could therefore be seen in part as its struggle to free itself from the constraints of the existing political and economic system, as well as from bureaucratic control. Particularistic policies granted would enable Sinochem to get around those constraints and controls, or at least to find some room for manoeuvre. The irony is that those particularistic policies afford Sinochem rare privileges which are also open to abuse and may impede, even though rather unwittingly, the development of Sinochem's market-oriented behaviour by shielding Sinochem from market competition through prolonging its monopoly.

The importance of special and particularistic policies for the success of Sinochem's experiment was explicitly emphasised by Zhang Jinfu, China's erstwhile Finance Minister and a member of the powerful Central Leadership Small Group of Finance and Economy. In a personal memo to Li Tieying, Minister of SCRES on 29 October 1987, Zhang emphatically stated that

> Sinochem has the expertise and resources and is determined to experiment with a new strategy of diversification and internationalization. If we *apply similar policies to Sinochem as applied to CITIC* now, and give Sinochem the same autonomy [as CITIC has], they are confident that they can make a breakthrough [in the internationalisation of its operations].
>
> (Sinochem Corporate Strategy Study Group 1991: 274)[24]

Such patronage from Zhang undoubtedly helped Sinochem's application. The momentum of economic reform in 1987 also created favourable conditions for Sinochem's submission. The decision of the Thirteenth Party Congress in October 1987 called for speeding up and deepening economic reform. The foreign trade contract system began to be applied to national trading corporations also in 1987, and was to be introduced to provincial-level trading companies in 1988. The first devaluation of RMB took place in 1986, the first step in an inexorable move towards a realistic exchange rate. The successes of CITIC in pioneering China's transnational operations, as discussed in the last chapter, may have also served as an inspiration for the State Council's approval.

On 19 December 1987, the State Council approved the submission by the MOFERT and SCRES that Sinochem start a pilot scheme for internationalising its business operations. In the atmosphere of optimism pervasive in 1987, the State Council document stated that Sinochem should try with all its endeavour to ensure the success of this experiment in order to 'blaze a new path for the development of China's foreign trade'. Sinochem was given a three-year period from 1 January 1988 to the end of 1990 to implement the programme. Particularistic policies accompanying State Council approval gave more decision-making power to the management of Sinochem with regard to its outward investment and its international operations (Sinochem Corporate Strategy Study Group 1991).

Overseas expansion

Sinochem took immediate action in internationalising its operations, especially in the following ways. First, the company made two large overseas acquisitions in the manufacturing sector. In 1988, it bought 50 per cent of the Pacific Refinery of West Coast Corporation in the United States, which purported to be a technology-seeking investment (Zhan 1995: 88). On the basis of this acquisition, it established the Pacific Oil Refinery Company. In March 1989, the company obtained foreign financing to purchase a phosphorus mine and a phosphate fertiliser factory, both in Florida, on the basis of which Sinochem's US Agri-Chemical Co. Ltd (USAC) in Florida, a wholly owned subsidiary of Sinochem, was established. These two overseas investments were to succumb to different destinies. While Sinochem had to dispose of its interest in the Pacific Oil Refinery eventually in the 1990s,[25] USAC remained one of the largest Chinese investments overseas in the manufacturing sector for many years (Zheng 1991a: 9; Fu Yong 1994b: 5). In both 1995 and 1996, USAC was one of three Sinochem subsidiaries with an annual turnover of over $1 billion, producing more than two million tons of phosphate fertiliser each year.[26]

Second, it quickly expanded its international trading activities and dramatically increased its overseas turnover. It broke into the international futures market in crude oil to engage in position trade, option dealing and hedging. By 1988, over 10 per cent of Sinochem's total turnover came from its operations in oil futures. In 1989, Sinochem's turnover on the oil futures market was $3 billion, or 24 per cent of its total turnover in that year (Zheng 1991a: 9).[27] Also in 1988, Sinochem's spot trade in crude oil as part of its transit trading on the international market reached millions of tons. Other diversified trading activities in this period included transporting Middle Eastern crude oil to Singapore

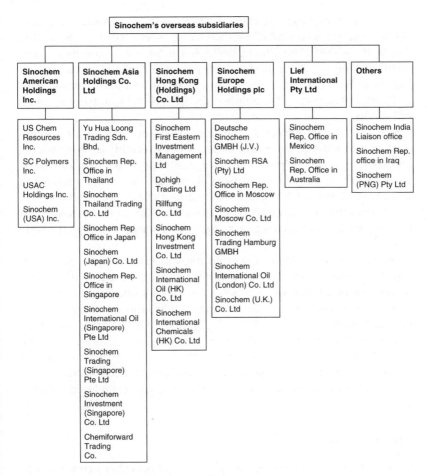

Figure 6.6 Sinochem's overseas subsidiaries, 2000

Source: Sinochem *Annual Report* (2000).

and Japan for processing and sale, and shipping Morocco's phosphate to Finland to produce fertiliser and then sell it to third countries (Sinochem Corporate Strategy Study Group 1991: 276).

Third, Sinochem diversified into a wide range of economic activities, other than trading, in internationalising its operations. It invested in oil refuelling facilities in Singapore, Hong Kong, the Netherlands and New Zealand in the form of joint ventures. It also established several joint venture or wholly owned shipping companies abroad. The ships controlled by these companies exceeded one million dwt by the end of 1990 (Zheng 1991a: 9–10). Sinochem also had investments in hotels in Hong Kong, rubber plants in Thailand and a garment factory in Belize. The company also entered into a joint venture with C. Heath in London and established the Sino-Heath Company in financial services.

It is only to be expected, therefore, that the bulk of Sinochem's growth in 1988–90 was found almost exclusively in its international operations. While traditional imports and exports stagnated in those years, the total turnover of overseas operations increased by leaps and bounds. By 1989, a triumvirate was taking shape, with import, export and international operations each accounting for around one-third of total annual turnover. Such a pattern was largely maintained in the early 1990s.[28]

The crucial beginning of the rapid transnationalisation of Sinochem thus took place between 1988 and 1990. By Sinochem's own account, by the end of 1990 its overseas assets, its foreign sales and the number of its overseas employees each accounted for around 25 per cent of their total respectively (Zheng 1991b: 22). By UNCTAD standards, therefore, a high level of transnationalisation of Sinochem had been achieved. Towards the end of 1990, when Sinochem's three-year experimental period came to an end, Zheng Dunxun proclaimed that by international standards, Sinochem was 'now a transnational corporation' (Zheng 1991a: 10).

Global reach

In the 1990s, the transnational operations of Sinochem continued to expand. Based on Sinochem's apparent success in internationalisation in 1988–90, the State Council gave its approval in 1991 for the Sinochem experiment to continue during the Eighth Five-Year-Plan period, that is, from 1991 to 1995. With the end of the Cold War and the improvement of bilateral relations between China and a number of countries, in particular Russia, Vietnam and South Africa, Sinochem was able to extend its foothold into these previously barely accessible territories and markets. Sinochem's presence in Moscow in the early 1990s was followed by the establishment of Sinochem South Africa Co. Ltd in Johannesburg in 1994. In 1996, a Sinochem subsidiary became operative in Vietnam. With this geographical extension, Sinochem had truly become a trader with global reach. In phrases that certainly have 'Sinochem characteristics', the geographical reach of Sinochem was summarised by Vice-President Fu Yong as 'emphatically orienting towards European, North American, Japanese and Southeast Asian and Hong Kong markets and taking West Asia, South Africa, East Europe and the Former Soviet Union, and Latin America as two wings' (Fu Yong 1994b: 6).

At the end of 1994, when Sinochem was about to launch its conglomeration project, it had 46 secondary subsidiaries overseas. Its affiliated subsidiary companies outside Beijing also boasted 39 overseas offices and enterprises. They were scattered in more than thirty countries and economies. Sinochem dispatched 266 of its employees to work overseas. Its overseas subsidiaries had more than 800 foreign employees (Zheng 1995: 4). In 1996, eleven Sinochem overseas subsidiaries achieved an annual turnover of more than $100 million. Of the eleven, Sinochem International Oil (London) Co. Ltd, US Agri-Chemicals Co. Ltd[29] and Sinochem International Oil (Hong Kong) Co. Ltd had a turnover of over $1 billion (Sinochem 1997: 29).

Sinochem's global reach is best illustrated by Figure 6.6.

Two aspects of Sinochem's growth in the 1990s are worth further discussion. One is that it was envisaged in 1990 that by 1995, its international operations should reach $3 to $4.5 billion (Sinochem Corporate Strategy Study Group 1991: 281). That target was easily surpassed as early as 1993. In 1995, the total turnover of Sinochem's international business was $7.633 billion. It was $7.966 billion and $11.24 billion respectively in 1996 and 1997. Accordingly, the transnationality index of Sinochem increased from 36.4 per cent in 1996 to 43.1 per cent in 1997 (UNCTAD 1999: 48, and 2000: 86).

The other aspect is that in the 1990s, Sinochem made no large-scale overseas acquisitions such as those of 1988 and 1989. In fact, the Pacific Oil Refinery, of which Sinochem owned 50 per cent, had to be sold, as mentioned earlier, largely because of Sinochem's lack of expertise in managing such manufacturing facilities (Interviews). There seems to be a conscious decision to divest from large manufacturing facilities overseas, while at the same time to intensify investment in domestic projects from an oil refinery in Dalian and oil storage in Zhoushan to Jingmao Tower in Pudong, Shanghai, which boasts of being the tallest building in China today. The inspiration for such a strategy seems to have come from what Sinochem's management regarded as the successful strategy of *chaebol*.[30]

Sinochem's global reach in the 1990s had other manifestations. In 1996, Sinochem American Holdings Incorporation successfully issued

$200 million worth of commercial paper in the United States (Interviews). In both 1997 and 1998, Sinochem sought to list its Asian interests first on the Singapore Stock Exchange and later on the Hong Kong Stock Exchange, but with no success (Interviews).[31]

Towards a multinational trading conglomerate?

The conglomeration project

The latest boost to Sinochem's transformation and reinvention is the State Council's approval at the end of 1994 of Sinochem as a pilot project for conglomeration to build a Chinese model of *sogo shosha*, which are firms, in Yoshihara's words, that 'trade all kinds of goods with all nations of the world' (Yoshihara 1982: 1) The first proposal to model Sinochem's future development on Japanese *sogo shosha* was made by Zheng Dunxun in November 1992 at a board meeting of Sinochem (Interviews). The inspiration for such a proposal obviously came from what were regarded as successful examples of Japanese *sogo shosha* and Korean *chaebol*. In the next two years, Sinochem spearheaded debate and discussion in China about the feasibility and desirability of fostering China's *sogo shosha*. By late 1993, MOFTEC was brought on board. In a report by the MOFTEC Research Group, establishing China's *sogo shosha* was regarded as an important strategic choice in deepening reform and the internationalisation of trading firms. It was also looked upon as a possible way to bring some order out of the chaotic situation in China's foreign trade competition (MOFTEC Research Group 1993: 4–8). By late 1994, SCRES also publicly endorsed the *sogo shosha* model for reorganising China's trading firms. In August 1994, SCRES organised a seminar in Beijing on experimenting with the *sogo shosha* model at which Ma Kai, Vice-Minister of SCRES, gave a keynote speech entitled 'Develop China's Sogo Shosha Actively and Steadily' (Ma Kai 1994).

Interestingly, for Sinochem, the move towards conglomeration represented its latest bid not so much to enhance the firm's international competitiveness and profitability as to seek further expansion and growth, this time by trying to escape from, or to break the straitjacket of, the existing economic system. In early 1994, Sinochem's Corporate Strategy Study Group listed five major reasons why Sinochem should seek to form itself into a *sogo shosha*. First, increasing decentralisation had accelerated the fragmentation of foreign trade and substantially reduced its economy of scale. This was said to be one major reason why there had not been a substantial increase in Sinochem's total turnover in import and export in much of the 1990s. Second, the decentralisation of foreign trade had been implemented when macro-economic policies were yet to be made to work and when fundamental changes in the enterprise management system were yet to take place. Under such circumstances, while decentralisation stimulated the growth of exports, it also led to 'cut-throat' competition among trading firms, an anomaly in China's export trade. The deterioration in the export trade environment was blamed for the slow growth of Sinochem's exports in the 1990s. Third, decentralisation could not solve the problem of the compartmentalisation of the Chinese economy, particularly the separation of foreign trade from industry and from domestic trade embedded in the Chinese economic system, which had long constrained the expansion of China's foreign trade. Further, the monopoly of domestic trade, transportation and finance, among others, was still largely intact. Without integration with industries, it would be problematic, if not impossible, for trading firms to realise group conglomeration and internationalisation. Fourth, faced with the regionalisation of the world economy and rising protectionism, Chinese trading firms found it more and more difficult to compete with transnationals from the West which were expanding in size. Finally, the different organisational structure of foreign trade firms made it difficult for the government to exercise macro-economic coordination and control, and was not conducive to establishing a rational competition in the market. It was argued that Sinochem's attempt to transform itself into a Chinese *sogo shosha* aimed at finding a feasible way of reforming and reinventing China's trading firms (Sinochem Corporate Strategy Study Group 1994: 1–5). It also amounted to a frontal assault on the compartmentalisation of China's existing economic system (Interviews).

Project implementation

In the wake of the State Council's approval for the Sinochem experiment, three attempts were made towards achieving Sinochem's goal. First, to enhance the financial strength of Sinochem and to encourage Sinochem to diversify into financial services, the State Council directed the transfer of FOTIC, previously the financial arm of the MOFTEC, to the Sinochem Group. After restructuring, FOTIC became a core subsidiary of Sinochem.[32] Sinochem, therefore, now has its own 'internal bank' (Sinochem 1995: 59). This is a typical example of what Nolan called 'administrative merger' (for further discussion, see Chapter 7).

Sinochem was also given the privilege of establishing a joint venture with a subsidiary of Manulife of Canada, Zhonghong Life Insurance Co. Ltd, in November 1996, to offer life insurance products and services on China's lucrative domestic market. The venture has a registered capital of 200 million yuan, with Sinochem holding a 49 per cent and Manulife a 51 per cent equity share. This is the first joint venture ever approved by the government to operate in China's life insurance market. The venture was opened in Shanghai by the Chinese Premier Li Peng and the Canadian Prime Minister Jean Chretien (Sinochem 1997: 22).

Second, as an indispensable part of its conglomeration efforts, Sinochem began an aggressive restructuring of its corporate organisation. The purpose of this restructuring was to integrate its import and export sections with its international operations as well as with its domestic trade, and to integrate trade with industry and finance. From 1995 to 1997, five interrelated operating systems were nurtured within the corporate structure: namely, 'an operating system of global trade, a modern management system focusing on financial management, an asset management system specifically designed for the Company's development, a personnel allocation system which is fair and full of incentives, and a corporate culture system with Sinochem's characteristics'. Also, five operating centres were being set up for its core businesses of trading in petroleum, fertiliser, rubber and plastic as well as for transportation (Interviews).

Third, Sinochem was encouraged to conduct aggressive domestic mergers and acquisitions as this was considered essential for conglomeration and, to a lesser extent, for the reform of China's loss-making state-owned enterprises. From the perspective of Sinochem's corporate strategy, mergers and acquisitions were also seen as a fast track for trading firms to diversify into industries, as well as to achieve vertical integration. FOTIC, as mentioned earlier, is an example of an administrative merger which immediately led Sinochem into financial services. Sinochem's acquisition of shares in the Dalian West Pacific Petro-Chemical Co. Ltd is an example of its attempt at the vertical integration of its business. Here, Sinochem's strategy seems to have been strongly influenced by the successful experience of the Korean *chaebol*, Daewoo. In particular, it emphasised domestic rather than overseas acquisitions of, and investments in, industrial enterprises. It also seems to have been inspired by Shougang's experience in the 1980s (Sinochem Corporate Strategy Study Group 1994: 5).[33]

Sinochem's mid-life crisis

In June 1995, six months after the launch of Sinochem's ambitious conglomeration project, Zheng Dunxun was reported in the *Asian Wall Street Journal Weekly* to have said 'We [Sinochem] can't overtake Mitsubishi right away, but that is our direction' (26 June 1995). This euphoria did not, however, last long. Even before Zheng's elated claim, the *South China Morning Post* was reporting that Sinochem was scrambling to diversify into oil refining and storage, facing a dwindling market share as more and more competitors jumped into oil trading (14 March 1995). The limits of the State Council's particularistic policies to foster Sinochem's conglomeration were soon to be severely tested. Sinochem's new attempts at conglomeration were blocked before long by exactly what the Sinochem experiment had set out to overcome, a deeply entrenched structural problem: the compartmentalisation of the Chinese economy and the vested interests in such compartmentalisation. Looming large was a mid-life crisis for Sinochem.

Take the oil industry as an example. While the exploration, production and refining of crude oil, as well as the domestic distribution of petroleum products and petrochemical products, were the responsibility of the Ministry of Petroleum Industry and later the Ministry of Energy, the import and export of crude oil, petroleum products and petrochemical products were long monopolised by the MOFTEC. The irony of China's economic reform is that the legacy of such compartmentalisation has actually been strengthened rather than weakened in the reform process. The creation of Sinopec in 1983 and the China National Petroleum Corporation (CNPC) in 1988 out of the Ministry of Petroleum Industry was a process both of administrative reform and of marketisation of the petroleum industry. It nevertheless maintained a rigid division between upstream exploration and production and downstream refining and distribution. With Sinochem deeply involved in oil imports and exports, a three-way division of labour, instead of being transformed by economic reform, has simply been transferred to the commercial operations of China's oil industry with CNPC together with the China National Offshore Oil Corporation and the China National Star Petroleum Corporation (CNSPC)[34] in upstream exploration and production, Sinopec in refining and distribution of oil and petrochemical products and Sinochem in import and export of the same products and of crude oil (see Christoffersen 1998 and Lin Ye 1997d).

Until 1997–98, vertical integration both downstream and upstream in China's oil industry was largely sought within each compartment. Sinopec started to lobby for the rights to trade oil products on the international markets as early as 1983. Sinochem, on the other hand, invested heavily both at home and abroad in oil refineries,[35] whereas CNPC was noted to have 'signed an agreement with the Japanese corporation Marubeni for downstream joint ventures in third countries such as Uzbekistan' (Christoffersen 1998: 12). As late as June 1997, CNPC entered into an agreement with Agip of Italy also in a downstream joint venture (*Financial Times*, 6 June 1997).

Some upstream and downstream integration has been attempted by Sinochem with both Sinopec and CNPC, but with only limited success. Two joint ventures provide examples. The China United Petroleum Corporation (Unipec) was formed between Sinochem and Sinopec for joint downstream production and for the import and export of oil products and petrochemicals. At the same time, Sinoil (also called Chinaoil) was established between Sinochem and CNPC to import and export crude oil. Neither seemed to get very far (Lin Ye 1995: 3–4, Christoffersen 1998: 16).

It is small wonder that in 1997, one of Sinochem's chief strategists complained bitterly and openly in *International Economic Cooperation* that '[A]lthough Sinochem has taken great efforts to restructure its internal management system, its pilot conglomeration project has made only slow and difficult progress because of problems it has encountered in its *external* environment' (Lin Ye 1997b: 39). He further listed four areas of what he called the 'external environment' which he argued presented impediments to the progress of Sinochem's conglomeration. Two of these systemic constraints are related to the compartmentalisation of the Chinese economy. First, two decades of economic reform have not changed the compartmentalised nature of the Chinese economic system. This compartmentalisation divides the market and blocks market access, but is unyieldingly maintained by vested interests. And second, and by the same token, the separation of downstream and upstream production in most industries still prevails, most conspicuously in the oil industry. The separation in the oil industry of production, refinery and trade is contrary to normal international practice in the petroleum industry. Further, such separation not only creates unnecessary conflict of interest, but also makes each entity uncompetitive in the international market. Coupled with the fragmentation of the domestic market, this blocks Sinochem's efforts to integrate domestic trade with international trade (Lin Ye 1997b).[36] At the same time, Lin argued in another forum, *Intertrade*, that only an oil company integrating upstream production with downstream distribution and operations can hope to compete on the international market. Understandably, he was ambivalent as to how this integration in China's oil industry should happen: that is, whether it should be CNPC and Sinopec that incorporate Sinochem, or vice versa (Lin Ye 1997d).

Sinochem's mid-life crisis seems to have been further aggravated by at least three events at three different levels: the international, the domestic and the firm. Internationally, the Asian financial crisis in 1997 prompted rethinking among the Chinese leadership about the developmental model, especially corporate conglomeration, followed by Korea and Japan. Domestically, the radical shake-up of the oil industry further marginalised Sinochem's position in China's oil trade. At the firm level, the retirement of the long-serving president and chief executive officer, Zheng Dunxun, in 1998 helped to expose the firmly embedded problems of corporate management within Sinochem.

The Asian financial crisis in 1997–98 affected Sinochem's conglomeration project in at least two important ways. First, it cast severe doubt on the apparent success of Japan's *sogo shosha* and Korea's *chaebol*. Korea's *chaebols*, in particular, were seen rather as a malaise in the Korean economy, which needed to be urgently, and in some cases surgically, reformed. Though the *sogo shosha* model was not publicly disavowed by the Chinese leadership, there was little enthusiasm to continue experimenting with it in China's SOE reforms. For Sinochem, which proudly claimed to be building itself into China's first *sogo shosha*, there was an added urgency in seeking an alternative path to conglomeration. Second, like many *sogo shoshas* and *chaebols*, Sinochem has single-mindedly pursued its extraordinary growth since the mid-1980s. Such growth, however, has been pursued sometimes at the expense of sound management and profitability, and consequently has exposed the vulnerability of Sinochem to risky business transactions. Sinochem seems to be growing too big.

At the domestic level, Sinochem was conspicuously excluded from the radical restructuring of China's oil industry carried out in 1997 and 1998 by the State Council. The revamped CNPC and Sinopec have become two giants and competitors in China's oil industry, each with integrated upstream production fields and downstream refining and manufacturing facilities and with undisputed trading rights in petroleum and petrochemical products on the domestic, as well as international, markets. As far as petrol and petrochemical products are concerned, Sinochem's position as a trader has been severely compromised (Interviews). In late 1998, it was reported that Sinochem had accumulated a debt of $300 million to CNPC, and the latter had even threatened to cut supply to Sinochem's exports if that debt were not settled soon (*South China Morning Post*, 14 November 1998). The allocation of an import quota on petroleum in 1999 favoured CNPC and Sinopec, not Sinochem. In 1999, the total of Sinochem's export of crude oil and oil products came to only $410 million, in comparison to $1.768 billion in 1996. In percentage terms, then, this line of export by Sinochem has dropped sharply from about 62 per cent of its total export in 1996 to a little more than 26 per cent in 1999. The total volume of Sinochem's ex-port has dropped accordingly from $2.881 billion to $1.563 billion (www.sinochem.com/en/achievement/annals.asp, and Sinochem 1997: 4).[37] Sinochem's attempts at conglomeration and at 'integrating trade with production and integrating the domestic market with the international market', at least in the oil industry, have been undermined, perhaps inadvertently, by the structural reform of China's oil industry. This poses perhaps the most difficult challenge that Sinochem faces in its mid-life crisis.

Finally, at the firm level, amidst the uncertainties as to Sinochem's future direction in conglomeration and transnationalisation, Zheng Dunxun, the long-serving president and CEO of Sinochem who presided over the transformation of Sinochem for more than a decade, retired in 1998. Zheng's retirement at this crucial juncture has a number of implications for Sinochem's future direction. On the one hand, it heightened the uncertainties faced by Sinochem in the future at a time when both the growth of its international business and its conglomeration seem to have been stalled, and when there was a big question mark over the model it has followed. On the other hand, it may have helped Sinochem's search for a new corporate strategy. The new executives appointed by MOFTEC, and headed by Liu Deshu, have little attachment to the *sogo shosha* model. With no historical baggage, the new leadership envisaged, and has carried out, a radical restructuring plan of Sinochem's senior management, including recentralising its control over its overseas regional group companies. MacKenzie has been enlisted to design and implement a comprehensive risk management system in the structure of Sinochem. The enlisting of MacKenzie indicates both the seriousness of the problem embedded in Sinochem's internal management and the future model that Sinochem is likely to follow in its corporate rebuilding (Interviews).

Radical internal management restructuring started in 1998. In 1999 the Management Improvement Project began to be implemented, and Enterprise Resource Planning was introduced. Investment decision was re-centralised with the set-up of an investment committee at the company headquarters in Beijing, which is authorised to approve and rationalise all investment projects. In 2000, to rationalise its assets structure and maximise the profitability of its current assets, Sinochem made a strategic move to spin off assets irrelevant to its long-term development strategies and at the same time acquire companies that enhance the core competitiveness of the company. Sinochem's 2001 annual report states that as a result of implementing such restructuring and rationalisation, 'the debt structure of the company has been improved remarkably'. A new investment strategy was laid out, targeting high-tech industries such as bio-technology, fine-chemicals and information technology, as well as financial services. Also in 2000, a New Performance Evaluation system was introduced and a risk control system was put in place. As a result, the company reported a good recovery of its annual turnover from $13.8 billion in 1998 to $18.04 billion in 2000, with a net profit of $92.3 million compared with $67.6 million in 1998 (www.sinochem.com/en/achievement/annals.asp).

It is perhaps still too early, though, to pass firm judgement on the impact of this change of guard on the corporate development of Sinochem. If, as Jones has suggested, continuous family ownership constitutes one strength of trading firms and resourcefulness in reinventing themselves (Jones 1998), the interesting question for China's state-owned trading firms would be: whether and how does a relatively stable (or frequent change of) top management affect the competencies of Chinese trading firms in reinventing themselves?

Summary

By its own description in 2002, Sinochem has become 'a multinational trading conglomerate that enjoys high prestige in the world. It is well known by the name of "Sinochem" in the international petroleum and petrochemical area'. 'A new Sinochem in a new century' is the image that the company now strives to build (www.sinochem.com/en/about-us/index.asp). What does Sinochem's experience in transnationalisation then tell us? At least three lessons can be learned from that experience. First, initiatives at the firm level are particularly important. For both its internationalisation experiment in the 1980s and for its conglomeration project started in 1995, the proposal and push came initially from Sinochem, not from the government. These innovative drives are directly related to a firm's capacity to reinvent itself. Without those innovative drives, the scale and speed of Sinochem's transnationalisation would have been much less notable. Second, the Sinochem experience has been conditioned and shaped by the peculiar nature of China's transitional economy. Particularistic policies are used again here by the government as an instrument to promote a show case of transnationalisation. These policies have, however, played a significant and also intriguing role. On the one hand, the particularistic policies are crucial in empowering the Sinochem management with more autonomy in business decision-making, indispensable for the management in overcoming some systemic constraints in China's transitional economy. On the other, it may have also enabled Sinochem to retain its monopolist position in China's foreign trade, a position which it has unscrupulously exploited. Moreover, the privileges afforded by these policies do not foster market-oriented behaviour of the firm. They have proved to be a stumbling block to developing Sinochem's competitiveness in a market environment.

Third, there are severe limits to what particularistic policies can do in a transitional economy. As the difficulties encountered by Sinochem in the late 1990s show, the compartmentalisation of the Chinese economy is not a hurdle that any simple administrative measures or policy pronouncements can overcome. Further, transnationalisation of Chinese firms is not likely to be reliant on simple government policies promoting transnationalisation, but to be determined by overall economic reform that will decide how far and how fast the Chinese economy moves towards marketisation. As the most recent restructuring of China's oil industry illustrates, however, radical reforms of the Chinese economy such as the rationalisation of the oil industry could generate uncompromising and even threatening challenges that firms have to face in reinventing themselves.

All the above helps explain why Sinochem has taken what can be called an 'idiosyncratic' route to transnationalisation. An additional factor is that Sinochem is a trader. The Sinochem experience seems to support the hypothesis that the transnationalisation of trading firms tends to follow a route that is different from that of classic industrial enterprises (Jones 1998). It also raises some important questions that have broader theoretical implications for the study of multinational traders. Sinochem's efforts in the 1990s, particularly after 1995, sought to build Sinochem not just into a multinational trader, but into more of a diversified conglomerate with trade at its core. What then are the advantages and disadvantages for a trading firm in engaging with such a diversification strategy? What are the competencies of such firms in doing so? Is it the best way for trading firms to reinvent themselves? Put in a different way, what are the limitations of a multinational trader in transnationalising? Are there any boundaries for multinational traders seeking transnationalisation? If there are, what are they?

7
Shougang: Going Transnational

The third institutional story to tell in this study is about Shougang (the Capital Iron and Steel Corporation Ltd), which differs from CITIC and Sinochem in some important ways. First, it is one of the oldest industrial enterprises in China, and one that epitomises China's early attempts at industrialisation. It was established in 1919 just outside the city of Beijing in the Shijingshan area. At the time of writing, it is more than eighty years old, sixty years older than CITIC and thirty years older than Sinochem. Second, unlike either CITIC or Sinochem, which are in the service sectors, Shougang is a manufacturing giant in one of the most traditional industries, iron and steel. These two characteristics have predetermined that Shougang's pathway to transnationalisation would have to be appreciably different from that of either CITIC or Sinochem.

Yet, like CITIC and Sinochem, throughout the reform years until recently, Shougang enjoyed a kind of special status among state-owned industrial enterprises. As early as 1979, it obtained a high degree of autonomy in management decisions. It was later boasted of as the 'model' for China's state-owned enterprises reform, though controversy has always been rife about the 'successes' of Shougang. As in the case of CITIC and Sinochem, a set of particularistic policies was applied by the central government to Shougang, particularly after 1992, to facilitate Shougang's transnational operations. These policies were first embedded in the so-called Shougang experiment in China's economic reform, and later ensured by the political patronage of Shougang by the Chinese leadership, particularly Deng Xiaoping himself, which would ironically prove to be the undoing of the Shougang model.

The case of Shougang is interesting and instructive for two additional reasons. Shougang falls into the category of what is often called 'classic', that is, manufacturing, multinationals (Jones 1998: 6). The process by which Shougang has gone transnational is perhaps also 'classical'. Once political hindrances were lifted in 1978, Shougang increased its international involvement progressively, and sometimes dramatically, throughout the 1980s and early 1990s. Much more than the two firms previously examined, Shougang's transnationalisation approximates the models discussed in the existing literature on the internationalisation of firms in terms of its 'stages' and sequence (Buckley and Ghauri 1993: particularly chapters 11, 12, 14, 15; Dicken 1992: 137–8). At each stage, Shougang had to make the organisational and structural changes in order to adapt itself to its progressive engagement in transnational operations. The Shougang case therefore informs us of how well the traditional model of the internationalisation of firms works to explain the cases of Chinese state-owned manufacturing enterprises in transnationalisation.

Shougang is a rare example of a state-owned manufacturing firm that started to engage in transnational operations on a large scale in the early 1990s. China's outward investment in manufacturing, as discussed in Chapter 3, is comparatively small at around 15 per cent of the total. It is mostly either in labour-intensive industries, or in low-technology-content industries such as bicycles, textiles and simple electronics. Outward investment by Chinese manufacturing firms on a per project basis tends to be small. That seems natural given where the comparative advantage of Chinese firms is. Although some large manufacturing firms did make substantial outward investment in the resource sector, for example An'gang's (Anshan Iron and Steel Complex Corporation) investment in Australia, as mentioned in Chapter 5, none of them have so systematically blasted into transnational operations and on such a scale as Shougang did in the early 1990s through its diversified investment overseas.[1]

A concise description of Shougang below encapsulates strikingly the profile of this industrial giant of China in the mid-1990s:

> Shougang Corporation is one of the largest enterprises in China, with 9 major subsidiary groups in iron and steel, mining, electronics, machinery, construction, ocean-shipping, trade and finance (including banking), stretching over 16 industries and possessing 105 large and medium-sized plants and mines, 41 Sino-foreign joint ventures, more than 200,000 employees and domestic fixed assets of more than 30 billion Chinese Yuan.
>
> (Zhan 1995: 85)

Shougang and economic reforms in China[2]

When China's opening up and economic reform started at the end of 1978, Shougang was a sixty-year-old industrial enterprise with a chequered history.[3] Its predecessor, the Shijingshan Iron Factory, Longyan Mining Administration, was built in 1919 by the warlord government in Beijing with equipment mostly purchased from the United States. By 1922, the construction work of the original pig iron plant had been completed. The first casting of iron was not made in the factory, however, until November 1938.[4] Before 1945, the factory produced 250,000 tons of pig iron and from 1945 to 1948 another 36,000 tons. Before the establishment of the PRC in 1949, therefore, the total accumulated output of the factory was 286,000 tons. It produced no steel.

From 1949 to the 1960s, the Shijingshan Iron and Steel Factory developed rapidly into an integrated iron and steel producer, which incorporated such subsidiaries as iron ore mines, iron factories and steel rolling mills. In 1967, the Shijingshan Iron and Steel Factory was renamed the Shoudu (Capital) Iron and Steel Corporation (Shougang). In 1978, Shougang produced 2.45 million tons of pig iron, 1.79 million tons of crude steel and 1.16 million tons of steel products. In terms of its output, however, Shougang was the smallest of the eight iron and steel producers in China at the time. Its crude steel output was only one-quarter of that of An'gang in 1978. Further, as Steinfeld observed, '[l]ike An'gang [Anshan Iron and Steel Complex], Shougang at the time was also a "living museum of steel technology," still using steam turbines and Bessemer converters from the days of the Empress Dowager, Ford-style boilers from the turn of the century, and waste-heat coke ovens from the 1920s' (Steinfeld 1998: 171).[5] This was so in spite of some Soviet assistance in the 1950s. Prior to 1979, Shougang had no international business to speak of (Kang *et al.* 1996: 115–17, Nolan 1998: 20–2).

Shougang and the contract system in industrial reform

Shougang occupied an exceptional position in China's industrial enterprise reform from the very beginning. On 25 May 1979, Shougang was selected as one of the first eight enterprises from three municipalities, Beijing, Shanghai and Tianjin, to experiment with the profit retention system for enterprise reforms in China. From 1979 to 1981, profit retention was implemented on an annual basis, with the retention rate subject to negotiations. In 1981, Shougang was authorised by the State Council, through the State Economic Commission, to experiment with a profit-responsibility system, called the 'progressively increasing profit remission contract system' (Shirk 1993: 232–4, 242–3). After some hard bargaining, Shougang secured a fifteen-year contract with the State Council, with an annual increase of first 6 per cent and later 7.2 per cent of profit remission to the government (Interviews). The progressive profit-contracting system constituted the core of the 'Shougang experiment', as it was commonly known later, until its spectacular collapse in 1995.

Before we discuss the features of this contract, which proved to be critical to the start of Shougang's international business, it is necessary to point out first that in the early stage of China's industrial reform, progressive profit-contracting was experimental and was fraught with controversies. The contentions between the progressive profit-contracting and the tax-for-profit approaches to the enterprise reforms in the 1980s reflected policy conflicts at the very top of the CCP leadership, to be more precise, between Premier Zhao Ziyang and the General Secretary of the CCP, Hu Yaobang (Shirk 1993). For that simple reason, Shougang was, perhaps rather unwittingly and unfortunately, already deeply involved in China's reform politics in the early 1980s. Second, similar profit-responsibility contracts were offered, prior to 1982, to other steel producers in China such as Magang (Maanshan Iron and Steel Complex), at the time a more efficient firm than Shougang with newer technology. It was nevertheless not taken up by the management of those firms (Steinfeld 1998: 179). This set of policies is then particularistic to Shougang only because Shougang had accepted the challenge of progressive profit-contracting and managed to keep it in spite of later attempts by various authorities to subvert its continued application to Shougang.[6]

The profit contract, among other things, established the special status of Shougang, and gave the company a high degree of what is commonly called 'enterprise autonomy' (*qiye zizhuquan*) in its management issues. This 'autonomy' does not mean, however, that the government, both central and local, did not interfere in Shougang's production plan or distribution of profits. But since the contract cut Shougang off completely from state subsidies, both central and local government would have only limited leverage *vis-à-vis* Shougang's business decisions. As the 1980s marched on, friction was to arise between Shougang and various central government authorities and the Beijing government agencies over such autonomy (Interviews).[7]

The contract stipulated not only that Shougang could retain all profits after its profit remission under the contract to the government, but also that 60 per cent of the retained profits must be used for the purpose of reinvestment to modernise and expand the existing production facilities of Shougang.[8] Under the contract, Shougang was also allowed to sell 15 per cent of its products within the state economic plan and all products above the state plan at the market price. One could argue that both stipulations were *quid pro quo* to make sure that Shougang could meet the target of an annual increase of 7.2 per cent profit remission to the central government (for further details of the main features of the contract, see Zhou Guanwu 1992, Nolan 1998: 26–30).[9]

Such a high degree of autonomy afforded to an industrial firm was unprecedented in China in the early 1980s. However, it carried with it risks as well as opportunities, particularly when the direction and the prospect of economic reform in China remained uncertain and unclear. With the contract, Shougang would no longer have access to the government investment fund either for technical renovation or for capital construction. From 1982, 'state investment in Shougang was reduced to zero' (Nolan 1998: 49). Wages and other benefits and welfare for Shougang employees also depend exclusively on the sales and profits of the company. These were to be met only after Shougang's fulfilment of the set profit quota. To all intents and purposes, it was a courageous choice that Shougang's top management made at the time in exchange for its autonomy, as a majority of state-owned enterprises, then as now, were showing huge losses, particularly the large-scale ones in traditional industries. As profitability is the key, the contract encouraged Shougang's market-oriented behaviour and compelled the management to come up with innovative ways of efficiency-seeking in both its investment decisions and in marketing. The fifteen-year duration of the contract ensured a longer-term strategic planning for renovation, expansion and restructuring. But as Shougang's own chronology records, in the early years, Shougang had to make concessions and to plead with the authorities to allow its profit-contract responsibility system to operate as it had been originally conceived without switching to the tax-for-profit system widely practised in the mid-1980s among state-owned enterprises (Zhou Guanwu 1992, Hao Zhen *et al.* 1992: vol. 1, 273–89).

Chinese leadership and the Shougang experiment

From the very beginning, the Shougang experiment was shrouded by a political myth. Shougang's special status at the early stage of China's industrial reform, it is sometimes claimed, was owing to the political patronage of the Chinese leadership, particularly the personal patronage of Deng Xiaoping, China's paramount leader. There is still no evidence, however, that Deng was interested in Shougang at all in the early 1980s (Steinfeld 1998).[10] Wan Li, Vice-Premier at the time, did go to Shougang several times in 1980 (Interviews).[11] But such patronage is of very limited significance. As far as granting Shougang its profit contract is concerned, any political patronage is certainly not the determining factor. The set of particularistic policies applied to Shougang in the profit contract owes much to the government's early efforts to search for a viable approach to enterprise reforms rather than to the alleged personal connections of Zhou Guanwu, Shougang's Party Secretary.[12] Nolan's recent research reveals that in the early stages of industrial reform in China, ceding autonomy to large enterprises such as Shougang was in fact part of the government's attempt to shift 'the financial burden to the enterprise itself'. This is certainly supported by Shirk's earlier research findings (Shirk 1993). Commenting on granting Shougang such autonomy, the Beijing government officials impishly admitted that 'this is the only way out when there is no way out' (*meiyou banfa de banfa*) (Nolan 1996: 7). Shougang was later groomed by the Chinese leadership as a model of revitalised state-owned enterprises, not so much because of Zhou Guanwu's connections with Deng as because of the apparent success of the Shougang experiment.

Shougang, as a special experiment in China's industrial reforms, did have direct attention from the top leadership in the early and mid-1980s, which few other firms had. In April 1982, Premier Zhao Ziyang personally approved the proposed experiment, in spite of his qualms about the so-called progressive contracting. Later in August, Zhao suggested that the annual increase in Shougang's profit remission be increased from 5 per cent to 6 per cent (Hao Zhen *et al.* 1992: vol. 1, 281; Shirk 1993: 234). In June 1984, Hu Yaobang, then the General Secretary of the CCP, personally endorsed a proposed plan for Shougang's expansion. On 24 August of the same year, Hu visited Qian'an, the proposed site for Shougang's new iron and steel plant. In November 1985, Deng Xiaoping, Hu Yaobang and Zhao Ziyang all officially and publicly endorsed the Shougang experiment (Hao Zhen *et al.* 1992: vol. 1, 289–92).[13]

Such political patronage certainly helped ensure that Shougang's profit contract was not discontinued or derailed at the will of lower-level officials when China's industrial reform was groping for an answer to the revitalisation of state-owned enterprises. Shougang's special status was then preserved. For example, it was after Hu Yaobang's endorsement of Shougang's proposed expansion plan of 1984 that the State Planning Commission and the State Economic Commission reconfirmed that 'after consultation with the Ministry of Finance, it is decided that the duration of Shougang's profit contract *could* extend to 1995' (Interviews).[14] That is probably why 'even when most other enterprises went for the tax-for-profit system in the mid-1980s, Shougang was able to continue its profit-contract system' (Shirk 1994).

Growing big through M&A

The rapid expansion of Shougang and its equally rapid diversification may also be partly attributed to the attention paid by the top leadership to the Shougang experiment. As Nolan noted, short of privatisation and in the absence of a developed stock market, state-mediated merger operations played an important role in Shougang's expansion. He further identified three main processes through which such merger operations take place. The top-down process refers to initiatives taken by the state to require profit-making and well-managed state-owned enterprises to take over loss-making enterprises so as to restructure management and make it profitable. For a number of years, this was seen as an important way to solve the problem of state-owned enterprise reform.[15] Bottom-up pressure refers to the initiatives taken by a firm, Shougang in this case, to take over firms, no matter whether they are profit-making or loss-making, to increase overall business capabilities, or to diversify into business opportunities other than core operations. The advanced technological and management skills of Shougang placed it in a good position to initiate such mergers. Finally, the 'positioning' process was motivated by the opportunism of Shougang in taking advantage of its bargaining power with local governments to acquire a large number of firms to 'increase the size of its business empire'. This is looked upon as positioning because it is done 'in anticipation of a possible future move towards more concrete private property rights being permitted over former state owned enterprises' (Nolan 1996: 45–6).

All three merger processes have been at work since 1982 in Shougang's amalgamation. The key to all three processes is, however, state mediation. Nolan called these operations 'administrative mergers' (Nolan 1996: 12).[16] Typically, such mergers are realised by administrative order sometimes from just the local government (Beijing) and sometimes from both the central and the local government. There is no doubt that the attention that the Shougang experiment received from the top leadership helped smooth the way for state mediation in Shougang's merger operations.

The first administrative merger took place as early as 1 January 1982 when the Beijing government decided to 'put under Shougang's management' Beijing No. 1 Steel Rolling Plant previously managed by Beijing Metallurgy Bureau (Hao Zhen *et al.* 1992: vol. 1, 279). On 1 January 1983, through the administrative orders of the Beijing government, a further seventeen enterprises and institutes with a total of about 40,000 employees formerly under the Beijing Metallurgy Bureau became subsidiaries of Shougang. By 1988, the Shougang experiment was so successful that in June 33 loss-making large state-owned enterprises around the country were merged with Shougang, including thirteen military enterprises, located in such remote provinces as Gansu and Heilongjiang.[17] The 1988 merger is seen as a typical operation of profit-making firms taking over loss-making firms as part of the solution to reforming state-owned enterprises (Zhou Guanwu 1992: 14–15; Hao Zhen *et al.* 1992: vol. 1, 299, vol. 2, 5; Nolan 1996: 12–14, 1998: 36–8).[18] Through these mergers, Shougang not only expanded and consolidated its own backbone business, but quickly diversified, in its domestic operations, into machine building, shipbuilding and the electronics industry, among others. Shougang's employees grew from around 70,000 in 1983 to more than 200,000 in the early 1990s (Shirk 1993: 232). From 1980 to 1995, more than a hundred large and medium-sized factories were merged with Shougang (Nolan 1998: 36).

Shougang was certainly 'exceptional' in the first decade of China's economic reforms in the sense that it received wide publicity and was highly visible in the winding course of earlier economic reforms. Ironically, the apparent success of the much- trumpeted Shougang experiment and controversies surrounding it contributed to both Shougang's fame and its notoriety. Shougang is exceptional also because it managed to obtain and retain a high degree of enterprise autonomy by maintaining its profit contract with the government. As we will see in later discussions, Shougang actively cultivated its exceptional position in China's enterprise reforms in an attempt to transnationalise, and would fall a victim to its own successes, when in 1992 Deng Xiaoping offered explicit personal patronage during his visit to Shougang at the age of 88.

First international businesses

Import and export

Shougang conducted no international business at all before 1979. Like many other Chinese firms, it quickly took early initiatives to cultivate opportunities presented by reform and opening, in particular the decentralisation of the foreign trade system. As early as March 1979, Shougang submitted its first application for the rights to engage in foreign trade to both the Beijing Municipality Government and to the Ministry of Metallurgy.[19] On 7 August 1979, after Shougang was selected as one of eight large-scale state-owned enterprises for experimenting with enterprise reforms, it submitted a request for enterprise autonomy to the State Economic Commission, which included, among others, the rights to sell its own products on the market and to engage in export of its products (Interviews).

It took more than two years for Shougang's application to come through. On 25 December 1981, the State Import and Export Commission approved Shougang's application largely as part of the profit contract package. Shougang Import and Export Co. Ltd was subsequently set up in February 1982 as a subsidiary of the China National Metallurgical Import and Export Corporation (Kang *et al.* 1996: 127). For the first time, Shougang had an arm with which to engage the international market. This could be regarded as the first modest, yet significant step towards its internationalisation. In 1987, Shougang's export earnings would reach $6.7 million from $1.2 million in 1980 (Kang *et al.* 1996: 117).

Imports, particularly of advanced technology and equipment (compared with what Shougang had at the time), were also an important part of Shougang's early international operations, as it strove for technological renovation. As early as 1983, Shougang imported computer hardware worth $700,000 from the United States in order to automate production in its sintering plant. From 1984 onwards, a series of imports of second-hand equipment from Europe and from the United States were planned and carried out. Although Shougang had to work within severe financial constraints in its technological innovation, it was fortunate that in the 1980s there was, in Nolan's words, 'an international flea market' of steel-making equipment, and 'a large amount of second-hand equipment was waiting to be bought, typically at less than one-fifth of the original price' (Nolan 1998: 50). As the *China Daily* reported in October 1990, in the 1980s Shougang imported 512 items of advanced technology and equipment with a total value of $315 million. By the end of 1992, Shougang had incorporated sixteen major pieces of imported second-hand equipment into its production facilities (Nolan 1996: 22–4).

Joint ventures

Some of Shougang's early international operations could be said to be accidental. In the early 1980s, technological renovation was the key for

Shougang to enhance efficiency as well as to seek the expansion of its production capacity. After all, Shougang would have to realise 20 per cent annual growth of profit in order to fulfil its contract with the state as well as its envisaged investment plan and other welfare goals (Nolan 1996: 7). The dilemma here was acute. Renovation and modernisation of Shougang, which would make possible Shougang's continued expansion of its steel output, needed huge capital investment on the one hand. On the other, Shougang has to rely almost entirely on its own limited resources to finance its modernisation. Although Shougang enjoyed a high degree of autonomy in making investment decisions, it was constrained by the capital it could raise from its retained profits, particularly in the early years. In 1984, Shougang decided to buy the Seraing Works of Belgium and ship it back to China. The equipment and the workshop weighed over fifty thousand tons. To ship them back to China, the ocean shipping cost quoted by Chinese shipping companies was more than $6 million at $120 per ton. By Shougang's own calculation, if it bought second-hand ocean-going vessels to ship this equipment back by its own fleet, it could save up to $3 million. In February 1985, with an initial investment of $1.05 million, Shougang formed a joint venture company, Beijing Aisiji Shipping Co. Ltd, with the Hong Kong Hongda Shipping Company. The joint venture bought three ocean-going freight ships for $3.9 million. On 3 June 1985, the Shougang Ocean Shipping Co. Ltd was established. By the end of 1991, this joint venture had a fleet of seven ships with a total capacity of one million dwt (Shougang Corporation 1993: 282–3, Nolan 1998: 71–2).[20]

Shougang's early international operations also included attracting foreign investment and forming joint ventures in China. In May 1985, Shougang formed its first joint venture with a Swedish partner and established Shoudu Kang Tai Er Limited. In 1986, Shougang's No. 3 Steel Rolling Mill, a heavy polluter, located in the eastern suburbs of Beijing, was moved out of the city. Shougang and its Danish partner, supported by the Danish Foundation for Industries of Developing Countries, successfully redeveloped the site into the now much-acclaimed Dong Hu Lake Villas, a premium real estate development project in Beijing (Interviews).

Up till 1987, Shougang's international business was still very much restricted to what may be called 'inward-looking' operations. Exports were to increase the foreign currency earnings of the firm. Imports of second-hand equipment were one of the main thrusts of Shougang's technical renovation in the modernisation of its production facilities. The establishment of the ocean-shipping joint venture was first and foremost to serve the purpose of shipping back second-hand equipment purchased from Belgium. Even the two early joint ventures mentioned above were by no means aimed at expanding Shougang's operations overseas. In other words, the level of involvement of Shougang in international markets was fairly low. It is certainly clear that up till then, there was little evidence to suggest that Shougang had conceived a clearly worked-out strategy for expanding overseas. Shougang was still at a very early stage in the internationalisation process.[21]

The inward-looking orientation of Shougang's corporate strategy in those years is perhaps understandable, given all the constraints it had to overcome in operating as a profitable firm, its antiquated technology and its lack of expertise. One particular constraint that severely affected Shougang's early international operations needs emphasising here. In the early years of the Shougang experiment, particularly from 1982 to 1984, the profits retained by Shougang were quite small in absolute terms. As Zhou Guanwu reported in January 1991,

> In the first three years of our profit contract, Shougang had a very difficult time. Before the profit contract, the state had provided investment funds for Shougang in the region of 140 million yuan per annum on average. After the profit contract, the state stopped providing any investment fund to Shougang, with the exception of funds to finish off existing projects. In the first year of the profit contract, Shougang's retained profits amounted to only 40.08 million yuan, and in the second year, 96.25 million yuan. It was only in the third year that the retained profits reached 136 million yuan. But after deducting 81 million yuan which was used for welfare and bonuses, only 55 million yuan was left, which was much smaller than the investment fund the state used to provide Shougang with.
>
> (Zhou Guanwu 1992: 8)

Perhaps not surprisingly, as Steinfeld observed, 'in the early 1980s, the firm focused on low-cost investments that would increase efficiency and pay for themselves within a matter of weeks or months' and 'Shougang simply did not have the resources to engage in wholesale modernization of equipment'. Financial limitations, Steinfeld argued, conditioned the behavioural patterns of Shougang's investment (Steinfeld 1998: 200–1). They also constrained Shougang's entry into international business.

From technology-seeking to technology-exporting

Acquisition of Mesta

The year 1988 may be regarded as the first high water mark in Shougang's internationalisation, particularly because of two significant developments. In July, Shougang invested $3.4 million and purchased a 70 per cent equity share of Mesta Engineering Co. Ltd of Pittsburgh in the United States. By this single acquisition, Shougang made its first substantial outward investment and acquired its first overseas subsidiary. In September, Shougang restructured its section that dealt with international business. The Department of International Economic Cooperation and Trade (*guoji jingmao bu*) was established to replace Shougang Import and Export Co. Ltd that had been established in 1982. Consequently, a division of international economic cooperation and trade was established in all Shougang's subsidiary factories (*fen chang*) (Hao Zhen *et al.* 1992: vol. 1, 299; Kang *et al.* 1996: 128). Shougang's purchase of Mesta Engineering Co. Ltd gave Shougang a firm footing beyond the Chinese border. Shougang's transnational operations began to take shape. The restructuring of Shougang's corporate set-up for dealing with international business signalled a transition in Shougang's international operations from simple import–export to multidimensional international business, a tentative yet important step towards its transnationalisation.

The purchase of Mesta amounted to a Great Leap Outward by Shougang. It is interesting to note that the first significant outward investment made by Shougang was in the United States, a technologically much more advanced country than China, and that the entry mode of Shougang into that market was by direct acquisition of a reputable company. Further, the purchase was a typical technology-seeking investment. It would prove to be pivotal in enhancing Shougang's capacity to export later its technology and equipment.

The apparent purpose in acquiring Mesta, as reported in the *Beijing Review*, was for Shougang to combine Mesta's design capability and technology with Shougang's machine-manufacturing capability to make large continuous casting and steel rolling equipment (10–16 October 1988). In early 1988, Mesta became Shougang's takeover target. In April 1988, Shougang registered a wholly owned subsidiary in Pittsburgh in preparation for its acquisition of Mesta (Interviews). At the time of Shougang's acquisition, Mesta Engineering was a leading firm in metallurgical machinery design. Established in 1898,[22] Mesta Engineering had been involved in the design and manufacture of more than 50 per cent of all hot rolling machines in the world at the time. The investment gained Shougang access to more than 400,000 design blueprints and microfilms, 46 computer software packages, 41 still effective licensed patents, and two trade mark registrations. Soon after the acquisition, Shougang's engineers participated in Mesta Engineering's designing of a technologically advanced 2060 mm hot rolling mill for Shougang, which was to give Shougang the capacity to produce a high-quality steel product for the motor vehicle industry in China. As Zhan writes, 'Masta [*sic*] became Shougang's research-and-development basis overseas. This investment has significantly strengthened Shougang's abilities to design and manufacture heavy metallurgical equipment and increased the international competitiveness of China's iron and steel industry' (Zhan 1995: 89). In September 1989, Shougang established a wholly owned subsidiary – Beijing Mesta Engineering Co. Ltd – to tap into the domestic market (Shougang Corporation 1993: 286, Nolan 1996: 38, Kang *et al.* 1996: 118–28).

Technology exports in the 1990s

The combination of Mesta Engineering's technological know-how and international reputation with Shougang's machine manufacturing capability proved to be a winning formula and won Shougang a number of important contracts in the early 1990s in India, Indonesia, Macao, Malaysia, the Philippines and even the United States and Switzerland. Shougang quickly turned from importing technology to exporting technology.[23] Small wonder it is that in November 1990 Zhou Guanwu called for the promotion of Shougang's exports and foreign currency earnings to be integrated into the corporate strategy at the Congress of Shougang Workers Representatives (Hao Zhen *et al.* 1992: vol. 1, 306).

Major technology exports of Shougang in the early 1990s included the following. From 1990 through to 1991, together with Mesta Engineering, ten engineers from Shougang 'carried out the design, programming and engineering of two computerised supervisory and processing control systems for seven basic oxygen furnaces of USX, the leading steel maker in the US and for the Geneva Steel Works in Switzerland' (Nolan 1996: 37). In September 1991, Shougang exported and installed for the PT Master Steel Manufacturing Company of Indonesia a complete set of steel rods production equipment, which were designed and manufactured by Shougang. This complete set of equipment, capable of producing 100,000 tons of steel rods per annum, included 458 different machines with a total weight of 1,870 tons. This is claimed to be the first ever export of a complete set of heavy machinery equipment by China's metallurgical industry (Shu 1993).

In 1992, Shougang won a contract to design, manufacture and supply a 500 cubic metre blast furnace to the Indian steel maker Naco Industrial Company. Also in 1992, Shougang provided automation system technology to Chagra Steel of Indonesia, for $1.5 million, to regulate the automatic control system of the steel-rolling production line Chagra had imported from Germany in 1992 (Shu 1993). Perhaps more significantly, in September 1992, Shougang won the bid to design and manufacture a bolt plate leveller for the Portland Plant of Morgan Steel Mills Incorporation in the United States. While Mesta, with its internationally renowned technical capability, was responsible for the design, the leveller was manufactured in Shougang. It is often claimed that this was the first time that metallurgical equipment produced in China was exported to a developed country (Shougang Corporation 1993: 284–6, Zhan 1995: 89, Kang *et al.* 1996: 119, Nolan 1996: 4).

In the early 1990s, Shougang continued to engage in technology-seeking investment while exporting technology. In July 1990, Shougang and NEC Corporation set up a $200 million joint venture, Shougang NEC Electronics Co. Ltd (SGNEC), in Beijing to produce 50 million integrated circuits a year, with Shougang holding 60 per cent of the controlling share. This was Shougang's largest technology-seeking investment in its non-core business, and represented a major diversification into a high-tech industry. It established Shougang once and for all as a major player in manufacturing computer chips in China (Nolan 1998: 67, Shougang Corporation 1993: 283).[24] SGNEC remains the largest chip manufacturer in China with the most advanced technology. New investment was made by NEC and Shougang in the late 1990s for further expansion, as will be discussed later.

Growth of export

The enhanced technological capability of Shougang through its acquisition of Mesta Engineering and through its continuous technical renovation and innovation, and the diversification of Shougang's core business through mergers and acquisitions, strengthened Shougang's capacity to export. In the early 1980s, when Shougang was first allowed to export, its trading list had no more than fifteen unprocessed or semi-processed products, such as pig iron, steel billet, castings and cast iron pipes. By the end of 1991, it was exporting around 109 products from bicycles and farm machinery to a complete set of metallurgical equipment. By 1993, 260 different products were on its export lists, including knowledge-related products (Shougang Corporation 1993: 283, Nolan 1996: 41). Naturally, its exports in value terms grew very quickly. In 1991, its exports were valued at $210 million, more than three times that of the previous year. In 1992, Shougang's foreign exchange earnings had reached $350 million. This figure represented 17 per cent of Shougang's total volume of sales. The export of machinery and electronic equipment amounted to $94 million (Shu 1993: 17–18, Shougang Corporation 1993: 283–4). In 1993, Shougang's export earnings jumped to $620 million. Nolan noted that Shougang's exports rose rapidly from 0.10 per cent of the national total in 1990 to 0.68 per cent of that in 1993. Putting Shougang's achievement in interesting comparative perspectives, Nolan further observed:

> Shougang had become much the most important single exporting [manufacturing] firm in China's manufacturing sector. A decade previously, it had been of negligible importance. Shougang's exports in 1993 were larger than the entire export earnings of most low income developing countries, and were on a par with those of middle income countries such as Belarus, Panama, Bolivia, Lithuania and Paraguay.
>
> (Nolan 1996: 41–2)

By 1992, Shougang's transnational operations were taking shape and its transnationalisation was at a critical juncture. It is at this stage that Shougang was pulled into the whirlwind of China's reform politics. Deng Xiaoping's May 1992 visit to Shougang would effect another high water mark of Shougang's transnationalisation. Unfortunately, however, it would also prove to be the beginning of the end of the Shougang experiment.

Deng Xiaoping and Shougang, 1992

Deng's 'Shougang card'

China's post-1989 elite politics is not the major concern of this study. Suffice it to say that the political battle had been intensely played out in Beijing from 1989 to 1992 between the two 'centres': the 'economic construction centre' and the 'struggle against peaceful evolution centre'. The threat of this intense battle to the general orientation of China's economic reform was such that Deng Xiaoping, who had formally retired from his last official post as the Chairman of the CCP's Central

Military Commission in November 1989, had to reappear to defend and rescue the reforms he had personally launched thirteen years before. From 17 January to 20 February 1992, at the age of 88, Deng toured extensively in areas of Guangdong Province as well as Shanghai. This quasi-imperial tour by Deng[25] amounted to a preemptive strike against the anti-reform forces within the CCP before the Fourteenth Party Congress, which was to take place in autumn 1992. Deng's strategy of bypassing Beijing and cultivating local support for his reform policies proved highly effective. By March and April 1992, Deng had not only won the public opinion battle, but had laid down the general line of accelerated economic reform which was to be adopted in a few months' time at the Fourteenth National Congress of the CCP.[26]

By May 1992, Deng's efforts to resurrect the reform initiatives had achieved definitive victory. The Party leadership fell generally in line with the 'economic construction centre'.[27] The ideological wrangling as to whether reforms were 'capitalist-oriented' or 'socialist-oriented' was largely over. At the Fourteenth Party Congress a few months later, the socialist market economy was enshrined as the final goal of China's economic reform, and outward investment was officially sanctioned as an integral part of China's development strategy. The victory, however, had been achieved largely by outflanking the formal power hierarchy in Beijing. This reflected the craftiness of Deng, but also exposed both the strength and weakness of his political power. For Deng, therefore, a mini-visit to a model enterprise of reform in Beijing would serve a dual political purpose: to confirm his victory in the political battle and to institute a new breakthrough in reform initiatives.

On 22 May 1992, Deng made a highly publicised visit to Shougang, in sharp contrast to his tour of the south.[28] This was also only a few months before his last public appearance. Deng reportedly spoke highly of the Shougang experiment, as well as its achievements, especially its international operations, during his inspection tour. As one Shougang researcher recalled in an article published in the *Beijing Review*:

> Deng praised the success of Shougang's transnational operations saying it was encouraging and highly significant that the corporation has been able to expand exports and hold its market in both developing and developed countries. He stressed that enterprises should be granted *real decision-making power*.
>
> (Shu 1993: 20, italics my own)

New enterprise autonomy for Shougang

There is no doubt that Deng's visit threw Shougang immediately into the limelight of Chinese politics. However, Deng's visit would have had only limited significance had it not been followed closely by a series of decisions by the State Council in July 1992 to grant Shougang further unusual enterprise decision-making power, which some regarded as 'inappropriate privileges' (Steinfeld 1998: 213).

A State Council circular issued on 23 July 1992 granted Shougang three special 'privileges' as a package for expanding Shougang's enterprise autonomy in investment and transnational operations (Interviews). First, Shougang was given expanded power in investment decision-making. It was permitted to undertake investment projects with its own retained capital and with funds raised if it was within Shougang's own capability to carry out both construction and production for those projects. Shougang was also granted autonomy to decide on its own overseas investment of up to $10 million per project, and up to 200 million yuan in joint venture investment per project in China.

Second, Shougang was granted extensive power to handle foreign trade and foreign economic cooperation. The State Council approved specifically that China Shougang International Trade and Engineering Co. Ltd be established. The new entity had extended power to engage in importing and exporting, including trading second-hand equipment, technology and mineral ores. It was also permitted to conduct processing, assembling and compensation trade. More importantly, it was permitted to carry out certain transnational operations, such as developing mines abroad and the opening of overseas offices as well as entering the international market of engineering and labour services.

Third, and rather unusually, Shougang, an industrial enterprise, was allowed to enter into a full range of financial services and to raise funds for expansion, including engaging in domestic and overseas financing and leasing, trusts, proxies, guarantees, discounts and credit checks as well as securities and insurance. For that purpose, Shougang was permitted to establish its own bank to handle savings accounts and loans, and to accept remittances both in RMB and foreign exchange. The State Council even agreed to allow Shougang either to establish or to purchase a bank in Hong Kong (Shougang Corporation 1993: 287–8, Shu 1993: 21).

As a result of these new particularistic policies, Shougang had the 'highest level of autonomy of any Chinese industrial enterprise'. Zhou

Guanwu made clear the special status Shougang had achieved in 1992 when he said in an interview in the spring of 1994, 'We do not have to deal with bureaucracy, we have a direct line to the State Council. As far as loans, we have our own bank' (*South China Morning Post*, 22 February 1994).

1992 and the Shougang experiment

Following the State Council circular, Shougang first restructured its Department of International Economic Cooperation and Trade into China Shougang International Trade and Engineering Co. Ltd in August 1992. On 18 October 1992, Hua Xia Bank, Shougang's financial subsidiary, went into operation with an initial capitalisation of one billion yuan (Shu 1993: 21, Kang *et al.* 1996: 128–9). Shougang became the first industrial enterprise in China to own a commercial bank. The establishment of Hua Xia Bank afforded Shougang rare access to financial services and to a long credit line. In the second half of 1992, Shougang quickly launched its large-scale acquisition operations in Hong Kong.

Both in its rapid expansion in transnational operations, and in its spectacular collapse three years later, 1992 was a crucial year for Shougang. What did Deng's visit to Shougang do for Shougang's development strategy? Directly, Deng's visit resulted in a package of more particularistic policies for Shougang, a package that granted Shougang expanded and extensive decision-making power in investing at home and abroad as well as in international trade and economic cooperation. It also gave Shougang ready access to capital, a rare and exceptional privilege for an industrial enterprise, which would eventually prove to contain the seeds for the destruction of the Shougang experiment.

Indirectly, Deng's visit may have inspired a too ambitious, often not at all practical, plan for Shougang to go transnational. It may have also fired Zhou Guanwu's personal ambition in his twilight years. In the wake of Deng's visit, Shougang pronounced a 'new grand goal' for its development. It was to raise its annual output of iron and steel products to 10 million tons by 1994, and 20 million tons by the turn of the century. Shougang was also expected to 'speed up' its foreign currency earnings from its exports and overseas sales from $350 million in 1992 to $1 billion in 1995. By the turn of the century, Shougang's foreign exchange earnings were to reach 50 per cent of total sales (Shougang Corporation 1993: 288, Shu 1993: 21). Shougang even let it be known in 1993 that it aimed to be one of the ten largest steel producers in the world and to be listed in the *Fortune Global* 500 (Nolan: 1998: 25). Given the predominant role of Zhou Guangwu in deciding Shougang's corporate strategy (see Steinfeld 1998: 202–6), and 'personalised' state-ownership of Shougang, the aggressive and more often reckless and opportunistic investment behaviour of Shougang at home and abroad in the wake of Deng's visit to Shougang should not be too much of a surprise.[29]

If Deng's visit had largely freed Shougang from the usual bureaucratic intervention in its management and from the dictates and constraints of state commands, it may have also put Shougang beyond the normal supervisory purview of state agencies such as the Ministry of Metallurgical Industry. After Deng's visit, it appeared to be politically incorrect to stand in the way of the Shougang experiment. The story of Shougang from 1992 to 1995 is that of a dramatic advance in its transnationalisation followed by the spectacular collapse of the whole of the Shougang experiment.[30]

From Hong Kong to Peru

Within just a year of the State Council affording unprecedented autonomy to Shougang in July 1992, through aggressive overseas acquisitions, most importantly in Hong Kong and also in Peru, Shougang became a multinational in the true sense. Its outward investment soared and its overseas fixed assets quickly grew to hundreds of millions of dollars. The eighteen-month period from August 1992 to December 1993 saw a dramatic advance in Shougang's transnationalisation. During the boom in the Chinese economy in 1992–93, single-handedly engineered by Deng Xiaoping, Shougang turned quickly from 'inward-looking' to 'outward-looking' in its investment and expansion strategy.

Expansion into Hong Kong

In October 1992, Shougang stormed international markets with three large acquisitions in Hong Kong, the United States and Peru. In Hong Kong, it acquired a controlling stake in Tung Wing Steel Holdings in a strategic alliance with Hong Kong billionaire Li Ka-shing's Cheung Kong (Holdings) and with CEF Holdings. On 30 October, Shougang signed a contract in Los Angles to buy the No. 2 Converter Steel Making Plant of California Steel Industries.[31] On the same day, at an auction in Lima, Peru's failing state-owned iron mining company was sold to Shougang as the highest bidder. On 4 December, the exchange of documents for Shougang to purchase the Hierro Peru took place in Lima. While Shougang's purchase of the Californian steel plant amounted to buying second-hand equipment and thus has limited significance for our discussion here, the acquisitions by Shougang in Hong Kong and Peru signalled the beginning of its aggressive transnationalisation (Shougang Corporation 1993: 286–7; *Financial Times*, 14 January 1993).

Shougang's acquisition of Tung Wing Steel Holdings in Hong Kong turned Shougang overnight into a significant player in Hong Kong's steel market and beyond. Before the acquisition in October 1992, Tung Wing Steel Holdings had been one of the major suppliers of steel products in Hong Kong, listed on the Hong Kong Stock Exchange, with more than a 35 per cent share of the local steel market. Its main business was in trade, storage, transportation and engineering services of steel products. Shougang's acquisition was made together with Li Ka-shing's Cheung Kong. Of the total of the 77 per cent interest of Tung Wing acquired with $31.05 million, Shougang acquired 51 per cent with an investment of $20 million. The acquisition made Shougang Tung Wing's majority shareholder (*Financial Times*, 11 November 1992).

Shougang's acquisition of Tung Wing Steel merits particular attention here for several reasons. First, this is the first direct acquisition by Shougang in Hong Kong, which was to be followed by a trail of Shougang acquisitions. Further, direct acquisition of a listed company was to become Shougang's preferred entry mode into the Hong Kong market. Moreover, Shougang's first large-scale acquisition was carried out in strategic alliance with Li Ka-shing and his highly reputable local firm, Cheung Kong Holdings. This strategic alliance not only minimised the risks of Shougang diversifying into an unfamiliar market,[32] but immediately established Shougang as a credible force to be reckoned with in Hong Kong. This would prove invaluable when Shougang used its listed companies to raise capital on the local market. In 1993 and 1994, Shougang-controlled companies in Hong Kong raised about HK$7 billion in bonds and shares for the purchase of Shougang's mainland assets (*Financial Times*, 21 February 1995).

Second, the apparent purpose of this acquisition was clearly market-seeking. As mentioned earlier, Tung Wing Steel had more than one-third of Hong Kong's steel market at the time of Shougang's acquisition. The acquisition, therefore, would no doubt facilitate Shougang's exports to Hong Kong. For example, in 1994, 50 per cent of rolled steel in the Hong Kong market was supplied by Shougang's shareholding companies (*Business Weekly*, 12 February 1995). It would also give Shougang a firm foothold for expansion into Southeast Asian markets. At the same time, Tung Wing Steel could serve as an import channel for China's much-needed special steel products (Interviews).

The acquisition of Tung Wing, however, also served another equally important purpose. It is sometimes claimed that Shougang's acquisition of Tung Wing Steel was the first back-door listing of a Mainland Chinese firm on the Hong Kong Stock Exchange (Kang *et al.* 1996: 124). Regardless of whether this claim can be substantiated or not, it is clear that in addition to market-seeking, the acquisition also had the explicit purpose of tapping the capital market in Hong Kong for Shougang's domestic as well as overseas expansion. The so-called 'back-door listing' enabled Shougang to inject a pile of state assets into its Hong Kong subsidiaries. For example, in June 1994, Shougang Concord International Enterprises bought from its parent company, Shougang Corporation, a 51 per cent stake of the Qinhuangdao Shougang Steel Plate Mill for HK$478.2 million (*South China Morning Post*, 3 June 1994). With injected state assets, the total capitalisation of Shougang-controlled listed companies on the Hong Kong Stock Exchange quickly reached HK$11 billion by early 1995 (*Financial Times*, 21 February 1995).

Third, and clearly, Hong Kong was used as a springboard for Shougang's transnationalisation, a point repeatedly emphasised by Shougang's top executives. As Zhang Yusheng, managing director of Shougang HK Holdings, confirmed a few months after Shougang secured its footing in Hong Kong, 'We have set our foothold in Hong Kong, for expansion in Asia and the world' (*South China Morning Post*, 27 February 1993). In March 1993, Pan Huayuan, Vice-President of Shougang, claimed that the purchasing of overseas companies and shares was only part of Shougang's advance to become a first-rate transnational company and that Shougang was 'preparing to set up branches in New York, London, Moscow and some other big cities abroad' (Xinhua, 21 March 1993). In January 1994, Luo Bingsheng, President of Shougang, reiterated that Shougang-controlled companies listed in Hong Kong would be used as the base for Shougang's overseas expansion (*South China Morning Post*, 29 January 1994).

Fourth, the acquisition of Tung Wing Steel was followed by a string of intensive acquisitions by Shougang in 1992–93. In February 1993, Shougang started its takeover bid of East Century Holdings, a firm principally engaged in the trading of ferrous and non-ferrous metals and minerals, in particular manganese ore and manganese ferro-alloys widely used in the production of steel. Shougang initially bought a 25.12 per cent stake of the firm with an investment of HK$164 million. Through further manoeuvring in September, it successfully acquired a controlling stake of 50.6 per cent of East Century Holdings by the end of November. In July, it acquired the entire issued share capital of

Firstlevel Holdings Limited, whose sole assets were its 65 per cent interest in each of three joint ventures with Shougang in Beijing.[33]

Two other acquisitions signalled a significant diversification of Shougang's investment in Hong Kong. In May, a consortium led by Shougang Holdings (Hong Kong) bought a listed developer in Hong Kong with its purchase of 74 per cent of Kader Investment's shares and warrants with a deal of HK$582 million. The acquisition of Kader Investment soon formed the basis for the establishment of Shougang Concord Grand Group, a subsidiary of Shougang Concord International Enterprises specialising in property development in both Hong Kong and China. In July, Shougang bought 50.3 per cent of a loss-making electronics firm, Santa Manufacturing Limited, specialising in manufacturing telephone accessories, printed circuit boards and other electronics products. On the basis of this acquisition, Shougang Concord Technology would eventually emerge (Shougang Concord International Enterprises 1993: 6–9).

Clearly, from the second half of 1992 to the end of 1993, Shougang was making a fast-track bid to become a multinational through its Hong Kong acquisitions. It even contemplated purchasing a bank in Hong Kong as early as November 1992, and had in fact looked at the Overseas Trust Bank, which was put up for sale after a rescue operation by the Hong Kong government in the 1980s (*Financial Times*, 11 November 1992). Shougang's top executives in Hong Kong made public its investment strategy in Hong Kong as early as February 1993 after its acquisition of stakes in East Century Holdings. The managing director of Shougang (HK), Zhang Yusheng, did not mince words when he told the press that 'our form of investment will become diversified and more extensive and will probably include the purchase of a bank, when we are allowed to acquire banks here', and 'our investment will not be bounded by the steel business'. He also indicated that Shougang's investment in Hong Kong would be made through two channels. In his words, 'Shougang Corp's own investment in Hong Kong will be made through Shougang HK Holdings, as happened when we bought East Century. The other line will be through Tung Wing and will be jointly carried out with Cheung Kong and CEF' (*South China Morning Post*, 27 February 1993).

In January 1994, Zhou Beifang, newly appointed Chairman of Shougang's Hong Kong arm, reiterated that 'our aim is to become a multinational, world class enterprise by the year 2000' (*Financial Times*, 27 January 1994). In the 1993 annual report of Shougang Concord International Enterprises, Zhou stated, not without satisfaction, that

A series of successful acquisitions transformed the Company into a multifaceted conglomerate with significant presence in the businesses of trading in metal and construction materials, manufacture and sale of steel and electronic products and trading in ferrous and non-ferrous metals.

(Shougang Concord International Enterprises 1993: 6)

By the end of 1993, with all the above acquisitions and the establishment of a shipping company, a corporate structure emerged of Shougang's business interests in Hong Kong under the umbrella of Shougang Concord International Enterprises Co. Ltd.[34] As *China Daily Business Weekly* reported (29 May 1994), Shougang had by then amassed HK$ 4 billion ($512 million) of fixed assets in Hong Kong and its controlling assets exceeded HK$12 billion ($1.54 billion).[35] With controlling interests in five listed companies on the Hong Kong Stock Exchange, Shougang had become almost instantly a significant player on the Hong Kong market. According to a Reuters report in August 1995, based on its sales figure in 1994, Shougang Concord International 'was the 20th largest company listed on the Hong Kong Stock Exchange as of 31 August 1995'.[36]

Acquisition of Hierro Peru

Expansion into Hong Kong, however, constituted only part of Shougang's bid to become a multinational in 1992–93. Shougang also attracted world attention with its acquisition of Hierro Peru, the Peruvian state-owned mining company, at an auction in Lima on 30 October 1992. Shougang's winning bid was a total package of $312 million, with a cash payment of $120 million, a commitment of $150 million over the next three years and the repayment of $42 million debt. With this single investment, Shougang became the second largest foreign investor in Peru (*Financial Times*, 14 January 1993). Shougang formally took over Hierro Peru on 1 January 1993. It was reported that in its first year of operation, Shougang's Peruvian mine substantially increased its output; it made more than $5 million in profit (*China Daily*, 5 December 1994; Kang *et al.* 1996: 119).[37]

Shougang's purchase of Hierro Peru is a classic case of natural resource-seeking investment. As discussed in Chapter 4, natural resource-seeking investment accounts for a large portion of the total of China's outward investment. Investment in iron ore mines by Chinese firms had already been quite significant before Shougang's acquisition of the Peruvian company. As early as 1988, the China Metallurgical Import and Export Corporation invested $180 million in the Channar Mine in Australia, which went into operation in January 1990 (Zhang Jijing 1998: 415–24). Anshan Iron and Steel Complex (An'gang), China's largest steel producer, had also invested heavily in iron ore mines in Australia (*Financial Times*, 8 February 1995). As industrialisation in China quickened its pace in the 1990s, and as China became the world's largest steel producer in 1996 (*Financial Times*, 7 January 1997), China's demand for iron ore rose sharply.[38] From 1988 to 1993, China's imports of iron ore increased from 10.76 million tons to 33.02 million tons, when China's output of steel rose from 59.43 million tons to 88.31 million tons.[39] Almost every iron and steel complex needed a supply of imported ore for production. Chinese researchers estimated that by 2000 China would need to import 60 million tons of iron ore (Wang and Tang 1995: 40).[40] In the wake of what seemed to be the successful acquisition of Hierro Peru, one official from the Ministry of Metallurgical Industry told *China Daily* in January 1993 that 'China imported about 25 million tons of ore in 1992, mostly from Australia, Brazil and India' and that by 1995, China would need 'to import about 50 million tons of ore, nearly 24 per cent of world trade'. Beijing indicated that it would, therefore, take a more active role in developing mines overseas to satisfy its iron ore needs (*Reuters*, 17 January 1993).

Securing reliable sources of iron ore has long been an acute problem for Shougang. As Nolan noted, as early as the 1950s, Shougang 'had to "scour the country" searching for iron ore'. Only in 1960 was it allowed to own its iron ore mine in Qian'an in Hebei Province (Nolan 1998: 39). Iron ore from Qian'an, however, was of poor quality by international standards, and would not be sufficient for Shougang's ambitious expansion anyway. Acquiring a stable overseas supply through investment was obviously a preferred option. Before its acquisition of the Peruvian mine, Shougang had already investigated, from 1985 to 1992, many other sites around the world, including Australia, Bolivia, Brazil, India and even Vietnam for possible acquisition. Three months before its acquisition in Peru, in July and August 1992, Shougang was still looking at possible sites in the Russian Far East. Three visits were made by Shougang's team in the three months prior to October 1992 when Shougang made its bid (Wang and Tang 1995: 40–3).[41]

Given Shougang's ambitious plan to raise its annual output to 10 million tons in 1995 and to 20 million tons by the turn of the century, and given the short supply of iron ore in China, it was only natural that Shougang should have sought such a large-scale upstream acquisition as Hierro Peru to achieve vertical integration in its production. The acquisition was essential to compensate for Shougang's existing supply of poor-quality ore in its domestic mine in Qian'an. More importantly, it was to ensure a long-term stable supply of high-quality ore for its new plant under construction, Qilu Steel Mill in Shandong Province.

Controversies, which centred on two issues, over Shougang's purchase of Hierro Peru began to surface soon after its acquisition. One was that Shougang had paid too much, as it was revealed that Shougang's $312 million bid was much higher than that offered by the next bidder. The other was that the ore in the Peruvian mine had a high sulphur content (Wang and Tang 1995: 43). It was reported that Shougang 'was quite strongly criticised afterwards', and '[T]op levels of the leadership said they had acted foolishly' (*South China Morning Post*, 26 September 1993). In all likelihood, Shougang's bid was put together in haste, which elicited criticisms that Shougang rushed into the bid without adequate knowledge and careful assessment of the value of the Peruvian company. As late as June 1995, researchers from Shougang were still trying to defend publicly Shougang's purchase of Hierro Peru (see Wang and Tang 1995).

Looming liquidity crisis

By late 1993, hard on the heels of an aggressive acquisition trail, Shougang began to experience a liquidity crisis for the first time. In November 1993, a 400 million yuan package was put together by a consortium of Chinese banks as 'emergency loans' to Shougang to maintain its current production level. Shougang's liquidity problem may not be entirely of its own making. The government's credit tightening in 1993, as Zhou Guanwu explained on 14 November to a group of fund managers and investment analysts from Hong Kong on a special tour of Shougang, resulted in the inability of Shougang's customers to pay a total of 3.6 billion yuan owed to Shougang. However, Shougang's aggressive acquisitions were at least partially responsible. As one investment banker remarked at the time, '[t]hey [Shougang] have diversified left, right and bloody center. If it is a cash flow problem, it's because these boys have been playing fast and loose with their money. The slow payments by customers is only an excuse' (*Business Times*, 5 November 1993). As detailed by Steinfeld's study, already in 1994, as its ambitious expansion plan unfolded, Shougang began to accumulate quickly large amounts of short-term debt and soon started to default on these loans (Steinfeld 1998: 219). The investigation conducted by the Ministry of

Metallurgical Industry eventually concluded that '[F]rom the end of 1992 to the end of 1994, Shougang poured approximately RMB 13.5 billion into fixed assets, ongoing construction, and long-term investment'. Shougang thus 'expanded its short-term borrowings by approximately RMB 8.26 billion' to finance long-term investment (Steinfeld 1998: 209). With hindsight, the two incidents, the controversies over Shougang's purchase of Hierro Peru and the first liquidity crisis of Shougang, were the first indications of the beginning of the economic and political undoing of the Shougang experiment.

Whither Shougang as a multinational corporation post-1995?

The collapse of the Shougang experiment

In early 1995, just as Shougang started to operate like a multinational company, the Shougang experiment suddenly collapsed. In discussing the investment overstretch of Japanese companies in the 1980s, Bill Emmott concluded metaphorically, '[H]ubris followed by nemesis: it is a familiar and inevitable story' (Emmott 1992: 176). This may well be applied to Shougang's indulgent expansion of its transnational operations in 1992 and 1993. There is no doubt that, by 1995, Shougang was financially insolvent. However, what triggered the collapse of the Shougang experiment was not the explosion of its hidden financial crisis, but the sudden resignation of Zhou Guanwu, the long-serving Chairman and Party Secretary of Shougang, on 17 February 1995, and the arrest in Beijing the next day of Zhou Beifang, head of Shougang's Hong Kong operations and son of Zhou Guanwu.[42] Even if the financial crisis resulting from what Steinfeld called 'managerial bungling' (Steinfeld 1998: 219) is the deeper structural explanation of the spectacular collapse of Shougang, it is the 'scandal politics' that brought the Shougang model to an abrupt end.

The end of the Shougang experiment therefore has its political and economic explanations. Among the 'confluence of several disparate trends' that brought on the collapse are the personal ambition of Zhou Guanwu, and unfettered access to soft credit. Steinfeld is also scathingly critical of Shougang's investment in the Qilu project (Steinfeld 1998: 210–13). It is not clear from Steinfeld's study, though, how much Shougang's exceptional overseas expansion in the early 1990s, in particular its large-scale investments in Peru and in Hong Kong in 1992–93, contributed to its financial collapse in 1995. A post-mortem diagnosis of the economics of Shougang's collapse offered by Steinfeld is, never-theless, worth quoting in full:

> Once Shougang's insulation from malfunctioning external gover-nance mechanisms ended, the internal reform package that had worked fairly well in the past thoroughly collapsed. The flaws, which that reform package had always contained, now became crucial, thor-oughly undermining market-based incentives. Contracts that force firms to hit profit targets are fraught with problems, but contracts that force firms to hit profit targets in an environment of limitless subsidies are recipes for financial disaster. Once the budget constraint was softened, Shougang's profit contract enabled managers to engage in reckless investment, unfettered expansion of capacity and output, and firm-level asset destruction.
>
> (Steinfeld 1998: 168)

Following the sudden retirement of Zhou Guanwu, uncertainty hung over the future of Shougang. The Hua Xia Bank was soon taken from Shougang and put under the ownership of three industrial firms, with Shougang retaining only 20 per cent of equity in the bank. One billion yuan had to be injected into the bank for recapitalisation. Shougang's construction of the huge Qilu Steel Mill in Shandong Province was halted and Qilu is now virtually dead. Shougang's plans to diversify into ship-building and motor vehicle manufacturing, so often and so closely associated with Zhou Guanwu, were immediately shelved. As Nolan noted, the events in early 1995 'may mark the end of an extraordinary epoch in Shougang's history, and the start of a new direction' (Nolan 1996: 1).

The transnational operations of Shougang were immediately and seri-ously troubled by the scandal.[43] For example, shares in Shougang's five listed subsidiaries, which had been worth HK$11.4 billion prior to Zhou Beifang's arrest in February 1995, slumped by a fifth within a few days (Interviews). As the *South China Morning Post* aptly put it, Shougang's Hong Kong operations 'shone briefly but burned brightly'. If the scandal did not immediately undo Shougang's transnational operations, it abruptly halted and froze the transnationalisation of Shougang.

To all intents and purposes, the Shougang experiment collapsed in the wake of the scandal. Shougang disappeared among a sea of 'ordi-nary' and 'normal' large-scale industrial enterprises in China, as its con-tract with the government happened to expire in 1995. The Shougang model now carried an extreme negative connotation. In mid-1996, the

Beijing Review carried an article that openly criticised Shougang's pre-1995 experiment, and also told of the unwinding of the Shougang experiment. In its words, 'When Shougang had a contract system, it inappropriately pursued output and disregarded market demand, resulting in over-production, shortages of funds, and a production and management impasse.' Shougang also 'arbitrarily expanded its business scale'. All this 'resulted in numerous financial problems', which made Shougang 'unable to pay its debts, including taxes owed to the state'. Shougang's contract system was, therefore, brought to an end in 1995. 'Since 1995, Shougang has suspended the construction of 10 major projects and reduced investments in fixed assets totaling 10.7 billion yuan.' In 1996, Shougang was 'implementing reforms mandated by the state' and was in a transition 'from the contract system to the new tax system' (*Beijing Review*, 17–23 June 1996: 18–22).

Perhaps understandably, Shougang's output stagnated after 1995. According to the International Iron and Steel Institute (IISI), Shougang was the eighteenth largest steel producer in 1995 in the world with 8 million tons of crude steel output, the nineteenth largest with 7.9 million tons in 1996, the twenty-third largest in 1997 and twenty-first largest in 1998, both with 8 million tons (www.worldsteel.org/trends_indicators/companies.html). Even towards the end of the 1990s, Shougang's annual production output seemed to be still hovering around 8 million tons, far from the ambitious target envisaged by Zhou Guanwu in 1992, which was 10 million tons by 1995 and 20 million tons by the end of the century.

Shougang's transnational operations at the end of the 1990s

Whither Shougang in its transnational operations then in late 1990s? Available evidence suggests that Shougang still held on to its overseas operations and that Shougang's transnational operations have had at best mixed fortunes. In Peru, by the end of 1995, Shougang had failed to fulfil its commitment to invest $150 million in the Peruvian mine over the three years after its acquisition. The Peruvian government privatisation commission, believed that Shougang by then had invested less than $50 million. An agreement was eventually reached between Shougang and COPRI on restructuring Shougang's investment commitment, which required Shougang to fulfil its investment commitment of $150 million by 1999. If the commitment was not fulfilled, Shougang would be subject to heavy penalties (*Americas*, 22 and 28 August 1996; *South China Morning Post*, 8 May 1996).

Shougang's Hong Kong operations, which have been contracting,[44] suffered heavy losses in 1998. Shougang Concord International Enterprises, the listed flagship of Shougang in Hong Kong, reported a net loss of HK$414.34 million (*South China Morning Post*, 22 May 1999). As of March 1998, four Shougang companies, Shougang Concord International Enterprises, Shougang Concord Technology, Shougang Concord Grand and Shougang Concord Century, were still incorporated into the Hang Seng China-affiliated Corporations Index.

On the shipping side, there is a new venture. In April 1998, Shougang entered into an agreement with the Peninsular and Oriental Steam Navigation Company (P&O) to merge their respective bulk shipping operations and formed a new company, Associated Bulk Carriers Limited (ABC). ABC was to be owned 50 per cent by P&O, 25 per cent by Shougang Holdings (Hong Kong) and 25 per cent by Shougang Concord International Enterprises. As a result of the merger, ABC now has one of the world's largest independent fleets of giant dry bulk carriers with tonnage in excess of 4 million dwt (P&O Press Release, 24 April and 7 July 1998). Shougang's joint venture with NEC in Beijing, SGNEC, has also seen some positive movement. NEC, undeterred by the scandal politics troubling Shougang, invested another 12 billion yen in 1996 in its largest joint venture in China. The investment aimed at upgrading SGNEC's technology to enable the joint venture to produce circuits of less than one micron in China (*Beijing Review*, 18–24 March 1996: 30).

World Investment Report 1999 still lists Shougang as the nineteenth largest transnational from developing countries ranked by foreign assets based on the 1997 figures. According to the report, Shougang's foreign assets amounted to $1,600 million against its total assets of $6,640 million. Of its total sales of $4,390 million in 1996, $1,040 million was foreign sales. Shougang's transnationality index is 16.2 per cent, ranked 41 among the top fifty transnationals from developing countries (UNCTAD 2000: 86).[45]

Summary

The politics surrounding the controversial rise and spectacular fall of the Shougang experiment makes this institutional story extraordinary and exceptional. It is exceptional in the sense that it is the reform politics that in the first instance made it possible for Shougang to embark on transnational operations in the 1980s and to engage in aggressive transnationalisation after 1992. It is also the politics of reform, as much as the economics of Shougang's reckless and opportunistic investment behaviour, that has not only unwound the Shougang experiment, but also negated Shougang's transnationalisation, both in principle and in practice. Particularistic policies, in more than one sense, have been responsible for both making and breaking the Shougang experiment.

Politics aside, however, the Shougang case remains an interesting one to look at in an examination of the transnationalisation of Chinese manufacturing firms. The transnationalisation of Shougang seems to have followed the classic path identified in the existing literature. The sequential process and the evolutionary progress of Shougang's international business moved through several identifiable stages. The start of Shougang's own export operations in 1982 can be regarded as the first stage. The second stage saw the level of Shougang's international involvement increase substantially as it engaged in importing technology and setting up joint ventures in China in the mid-1980s. In the third stage, Shougang embarked on odd foreign acquisitions (typically Mesta Engineering) and began to export technology. The fourth stage was marked by Shougang's full expansion of its transnational operations, from large-scale market-seeking investment in Hong Kong to resource-seeking investment in Peru. It is also worth noting that organisational changes in the corporate structure were initiated at each stage to cope with the increasing level of internationalisation of Shougang.

The Shougang experience has also a few other things to commend it. Shougang's acquisition of Mesta Engineering in 1988 was a typical success in technology-seeking investment. Its entry mode into the Hong Kong market through direct acquisition in a strategic alliance with the most reputable local firms, such as Cheung Kong, minimised its risk and transaction costs. In the light of the acute shortage of iron ore deposits in China, seeking vertical integration by acquisition of foreign mines, as Shougang's move into Peru did, may prove pivotal for the expansion and transnationalisation of China's iron and steel firms. Perhaps, the most intriguing puzzle concerning the Shougang experiment in terms of its transnationalisation is not so much about its sudden collapse, but how and why a state-owned manufacturing enterprise in a transitional command economy could have gone so far in such a short span of time in transnationalising.

8
Conclusion

Quietly but surely global businesses originating in China are in the making. Over the 1990s, a growing number of such businesses have taken the entire globe as their markets and operating theatre and are becoming ever more aggressive and assertive in the global economy. 'The spread of China Inc.' has increasingly captured the world's attention and imagination (*Newsweek*, 3 September 2001). As this book goes to print, Shanghai Automobile Industry Corporation (SAIC) made the headline story in the *South China Morning Post* on 14 October 2002 by its acquisition of 10 per cent of GM Daewoo Auto and Technology worth $57.9 million. SAIC has thus become the first Chinese mainland automaker to expand overseas (*South China Morning Post*, 14 October 2002). Following Premier Zhu's call for implementing a strategy for Chinese enterprises to 'go out' and invest beyond Chinese borders, Minister Shi Guangsheng claimed at the 2002 Forum on International Investment in September that the globalisation of the world economy, China's entry into the WTO and economic reform in China combined 'have created right conditions and ripe opportunities' for Chinese firms to engage in 'going out' strategy. After more than ten years experimenting in outward investment and transnationalisation, Chinese enterprises are also 'ready' to implement such a strategy (*Xinhua*, 8 and 9 September).

It is true that China cannot boast yet any famous global brand.[1] Neither can it claim yet any home-grown world-class multinational company. This compares unfavourably with such developing countries as Mexico and Brazil, not to speak of Korea. Yet considering the short and fast journey that the transnationalisation of Chinese companies has just made, and in view of the nature of China's transitional economy and its political system, it is still enviable that China has become a primary Third World investor on a par with Korea in terms of its outward investment stocks. A number of China's multinational corporations have found their places in the *Fortune* Global 500 and UNCTAD's list of the 50 largest TNCs from developing countries.

The stories surrounding China's emerging global businesses are surely captivating as a tale of the past. The changing political economy for the policy regime and regulatory framework for China's outward investment and the reform politics that is closely bound up with the trials and tribulations of the transnationalisation of the three firms examined constitute an intriguing dimension of China's reform experience. Economic transformation in the form of rapid economic restructuring, uncompromising liberalisation of markets and sustained economic growth induced by the globalisation of world economy, it is often argued, underlie the aggressive expansion of outward investment from new investors from the developing countries over the 1980s and 1990s. To the extent that this argument is valid, the rise of China's global businesses is symbiotic with the radical transformation of the Chinese economy.

The importance of telling this story of the past as we have done in this study, however, lies in how much it informs us of the future trajectory of China's growing global businesses. This is particularly true when the pace of the transnationalisation of Chinese companies has appreciably accelerated and the scale has expanded in the last few years of more fundamental economic transformation in China. In view of Premier Zhu's explicit call to implement a strategy for Chinese firms to go overseas and invest, and as China responds more proactively to economic globalisation, particularly in the instance of its embrace of WTO membership, the general trajectory of China's growing outward investment and its expanding global businesses will not be difficult to envisage, though the exact speed and scope of such a trajectory is anyone's guess.

One of the main purposes of this book is to provide an analytical account of the emergence and growth of China's global businesses against the particular background of the political economy of China's opening and economic reform. The analytical account provided has addressed three closely related dimensions of this subject in some detail. The three dimensions are the evolving general and particularistic policies of China that foster and nurture the transationalisation of Chinese enterprises; the scale and the scope of transnational operations and outward investment by Chinese firms; and finally, the dynamics of interactions between policies and firm-level initiatives in the evolution and expansion of global businesses originating in China. In considering these, we seek to overcome an embedded bias in the existing literature on the transformation of the Chinese economy as well as China's integration into the global economy. More broadly, we look at the rise of China's global businesses as China's adjustment, initially reluctant but increasingly enterprising, to the exigencies of the world economy, and as China's creative response to globalisation. In so doing, we seek to address questions concerning the internationalisation and globalisation of the Chinese state.

The inexplicable puzzle, as we set out at the beginning, is why and how such a distinctive and sustained outward orientation of the transitional Chinese economy and such a creative response to economic globalisation by China have received so little attention. It is particularly surprising when other aspects of China's foreign economic relations – China's bid for WTO membership, the impact of its accession and FDI in China in particular – have received, and continue to attract, unremitting attention in the study of China's economic transformation. China's outward FDI is therefore a 'novel dimension' of China's integration into the global economy (Cai 1999) only in so far as it has been just recently and belatedly brought to our attention.

To all intents and purposes, the transnationalisation of firms located in the PRC has only a short history. Its beginning can best be traced back to 1978–79 at the launch of China's economic reform and opening, although a small number of government-directed firms did carry out some business operations beyond Chinese borders before then. The PRC's exclusion from the international economic system probably best explains why and how Chinese firms did not and could not engage in meaningful transnational operations prior to that period. There are two facets of this exclusion. While the PRC pursued a self-reliance strategy in its economic development, barring the participation of international capital in its economy and maintaining minimum trade as the only tenuous linkage with the world economy, sanctions against the PRC imposed mostly by the United States were in place throughout the 1950s and the 1960s. Even in 1978, the PRC was still excluded from all key functioning international economic organisations. The emergence of China's multinationals, like its integration into the world economy, is therefore contingent upon the relaxation of systemic constraints as well as the liberalisation of domestic policies.

By 1978, most sanctions against the PRC had been lifted. The establishment of the diplomatic relations between China and the United States in December 1978 paved the way for China's participation in the World Bank and the IMF in 1980 (Jacobson and Oksenberg 1990). Also in 1978, the general orientation of the Chinese economy radically changed. Among the earliest reform policies aimed at opening China for trade and investment was tentative liberalisation that allowed Chinese firms to set up subsidiaries overseas. A series of innovative policies were swiftly introduced and implemented in 1978–79 to organise purpose-built companies designated to conduct transnational operations and to encourage existing trading firms to go overseas. Although government policies towards outward investment are ambivalent at first and ambiguous at best, a clear thrust is discernible.

It is here that the genesis of China's multinational corporations is to be found. Many state-owned enterprises actively cultivated and creatively responded to the gradual liberalisation of government policies towards foreign trade and outward investment by moving quickly to set up trade subsidiaries and joint ventures overseas. The origin of the multinationals headquartered in China owes, therefore, most to dynamic interactions between government policies and the firms' responses. It is less attributable to enhanced technological capability or market failure (Dunning 1983). Nor can it be attributed to large export of capital, which, Stopford argues, usually occurs long before the emergence of multinational corporations (Stopford 1974).

Three important historical and systemic features of the Chinese economy in 1978 – China's post-1949 experience in the international economic system, the nature of its socialist planned economy and the public ownership of Chinese enterprises – constitute the unique background against which the emergence and growth of China's global businesses must be evaluated and appreciated. As the state plays a prominent role in the economic developmental process in China, government policies were most instrumental in inducing the beginning of outward investment from China post-1978. This refers first and foremost to the CCP's decision to open up China for trade and foreign investment in 1978, followed by a period of limited liberalisation. What is of great interest is how quickly and enthusiastically a number of firms responded in starting their international businesses notwithstanding lack of funds, limits of expertise and shortfall of information and of knowledge of the international market, and in spite of the systemic constraints of China's transitional economy.

Constraints and impediments embedded in and generated by China's domestic political and economic system are formidable for the emergence of Chinese multinationals. For one thing, it is through a long and agonising process that multinational corporations as an economic institution have been first intellectually accepted and later incorporated into

China's economic development strategy. For another, for more than thirty years, the development strategy was underlined by the ideology of self-reliance. The central planning system meant control from Beijing in managing the economy, from allocation of resources to distribution of goods. The absence of even elementary market mechanisms did not encourage any entrepreneurship. These are among the conditions out of which China's global businesses had to emerge and the significant modification of which they have eventually contributed to. The political economy of pre-1978 China provides explanations for China's total absence from the first wave of outward FDI from Third World countries which saw a surge in the late 1960s and the 1970s. Equally importantly, it explains why the transnationalisation of Chinese firms only started towards the end of the 1970s.

It is also important to note that, since the 1970s, the context for world development has seen some fundamental changes largely induced by globalisation. This does not refer only to an accelerated pace of technological change, phenomenal increase of cross-border flows of capital and services and shrinking economic space, but also to a more humanised concept of 'development', which now encompasses not just economic but, more importantly, social, political, environmental, sustainable and many other dimensions. This new context for global development has resulted in and is accompanied by a new understanding of the role of both inward and outward FDI, particularly on the part of developing countries. If in the 1970s, FDI and multinationals were largely seen as a problem from the perspective of developing countries, FDI as a package of tangible and intangible assets that embody the transfer of knowledge, technology and skills is now mostly perceived as the solution to intractable developmental problems by governments of the developing world (UNCTAD 2000: 149–55). The changing context of global development and changing attitude of developing countries toward FDI combined encourage developing countries to engage in outward FDI at the same time as they open up more opportunities for such investment.

The rapid growth of China's outward investment happened at such a conjunction when cross-border capital flows increasingly became the new instrument of intensified international economic integration and globalisation and when there was a surge of outward investment from developing economies (see for example, UNCTAD 1999, 2000, 2001). The emergence and growth of multinationals from developing countries, it is argued, 'constitute one of the more recent fundamental changes in the geographical pattern of international production' and 'have led to increased geographical diversity and competing sources of foreign direct investment' (Tolentino 1993: 360). It is exactly for this reason that 'a fundamental shift in both the character and motivation of much outward FDI from certain developing countries' has taken place.[2]

It is more than coincidence, though, that China joined the elite league of the so-called 'primary Third World investors' in less than twenty years.[3] As Dunning *et al.* (1998) show, in 1980 China accounted for as little as 0.82 per cent of the total developing country outward FDI stocks. In 1993, it accounted for as much as 10.89 per cent. By comparison, Argentina's share decreased in the same period from 20.41 per cent in 1980 to 0.89 per cent in 1993,[4] whereas India's share decreased from 2.68 per cent to 0.55 per cent.[5] At the same time, the total of outward FDI stocks from developing countries increased from $4.8 billion in 1980 to $108.4 billion in 1993. The absolute increase of China's outward FDI stocks is therefore statistically more striking, from $40 million to $11.8 billion in the same period (Dunning *et al.* 1998: 258–60). According to the *World Investment Report*, by 1998, China's outward FDI stocks reached $22.7 billion, behind Hong Kong, Singapore and Taiwan, but ahead of Korea and Malaysia.[6] It increased to $27.2 billion in 2000. As a percentage of GDP, it reached 2.2 per cent in 1997 and 2.5 per cent in 1999 from 0.7 per cent in 1990 (UNCTAD 2000: 521, UNCTAD 2002: *Country Fact Sheet: China*).[7] It is China's outward FDI, to paraphrase Stopford, that has sowed the seeds of Chinese multinational corporations (Stopford 1974: 305). It is a quantum leap that China has taken from going through intellectual agonies over its acceptance of the positive role of multinationals in economic development in the 1970s to being a home country to a dozen of largest multinationals from developing countries in the 1990s.

Yet what is still difficult to comprehend is the speed with which so many Chinese SOEs have gone transnational in such a short time. Hundreds, if not thousands, of Chinese companies have developed themselves into what could be regarded as modern multinational corporations in structural terms and in operational mode. Some of them, like Sinochem and CITIC examined in this study, have grown into a big business even by world standards. More important to our discussion here, these companies, like other multinational corporations, are actively moving across borders factors of production, such as capital, technology, skills and even labour force. Just look at the active operations of numerous Chinese engineering and construction multinationals on the world scene. Just watch the recent moves by China's oil giants on the global merger and acquisition markets. For this simple reason, Chinese multinational corporations, as active players in the world economy, are now playing a special role for China to engage the global economy.

How to explain then the quantum leap that China has made since 1978 in its outward FDI and in the transnationalisation of Chinese firms? The transformation of the Chinese economy and its sustained economic growth are necessary but not sufficient explanations. They certainly cannot explain either the speed or the scope of China's outward FDI. Ambiguous and often confused ownership of public assets by the SOEs and 'informal privatization through internationalization' of those assets may explain property transfer offshore by some Chinese firms and mushrooming of China's 'window' companies in Hong Kong and overseas (Ding 2000). However, it cannot account for the sustained transnationalisation of Chinese firms and their strategic investment overseas. Industrial reconfiguration in China and upgrading of industrial structure and ownership advantages of firms do not seem to be an explanation either, for the simple reason that the main thrust of China's outward investment has not been so far conducted by manufacturing firms. There are also reasons to be sceptical about the generalisations advanced by the investment development path (IDP) as explanations. China's net outward investment (NOI) position, for example, fluctuated violently in the 1990s (see Table 8.1), and by no means conforms to the recently revised IDP pattern (Dunning and Narula 1996: 2–3). China's investment behaviour is widely different from that predicted by the IDP for Stage 2 countries (Dunning *et al.*, 1998).

Table 8.1   GNP per capita and NOI of China and the four Asian tigers, 1997 (in $ million except for GNP per capita)

	GNP per capita	Inward stocks	Outward stocks	NOI*
China	760	217,341	20,416	−196,925
Hong Kong	23,520	26,869	137,512	+110,643
Korea	8,490	14,832	18,044	+3,212
Singapore	29,610	78,062	43,400	−34,662
Taiwan	13,198**	19,848	34,178	+14,330

* Net outward investment.
** This is for 1997. All other GNP per capita figures are for 1999.
Sources: Taiwan Statistical Data Book, 1999: 328, UNCTAD (1999: 376, 382), and www.worldbank.org/data.

The answers, we suggest, lie in the unfolding of the reform politics, the particular role of the state and government policies, which, it has been argued, constitute more important explanatory variables for China's quantum leap. What is often called a 'government-controlled investment scenario' is applicable to China's inward FDI as much as to its outward FDI. It explains not only the rapid take-off of outward FDI from China, but also the unusual direction of its main thrusts. The important role of the government in promoting both inward and outward investment of developing countries is nothing new. The difference here is that because of the special circumstances that are peculiar to the political economy of China's reform years, the state and government policies have assumed a disproportionately significant role in fostering, encouraging or restraining outward FDI, hence the transnationalisation of Chinese firms.

In exploring these explanatory variables, we have noted a number of policy innovations introduced and implemented by the Chinese government in 1978–79 and examined how important they are in initiating the early thrusts of transnational operations of Chinese SOEs. We have also discussed in detail the gradual construction by the Chinese government of a general regulatory framework for outward investment and transnationalisation of Chinese firms, largely in response to initiatives at the firm level in pioneering and conducting international businesses in the 1980s. Our discussions have questioned the effectiveness and credibility of the general regulatory framework. Nevertheless, the general policy regime does set out basic objectives for government-approved outward investment and draws the boundaries for administrative intervention. The evolution of these policy regimes is, however, slow, eclectic and haphazard. Even now, they are not well-defined.

In addition to the general policy regime, particularistic policies are another focal point of our discussions. These are occasional policies initiated by the top Chinese leadership and applicable only to specific firms, hence particularistic. They are usually preferential. Pending overall liberalisation of the economy, they have been used, with considerable skill, by the Chinese leadership to facilitate the transnationalisation of selected firms. The application of particularistic policies also seems compatible with the incremental and experimental approach characteristic of China's overall economic reform. In any case, up till 1995, particularistic contracting was widely practised in China's economic reform (Shirk 1993, Yang 1996). Without particularistic policies, neither CITIC's success nor Sinochem's experiment and expansion would be imaginable.

A more intriguing question for us is, therefore, how individual Chinese SOEs respond to and cultivate challenges and opportunities offered by economic globalisation in general and by Chinese economic reforms and opening in particular to transnationalise and to build themselves into a global business. In the institutional investigations conducted in Part III, we have carefully traced the pathways through which three firms, namely, CITIC, Sinochem and Shougang, transnationalise and effect their global reach. The three 'contemporary business histories' clearly show that the pathways they have taken are conspicuously different. The three firms enjoy different degree of success in their transnationalisation experience. Yet there is also obvious commonality in their experience. All three are at the forefront of the Chinese government experiment with economic reforms in their sectors throughout the period of our discussions. Not surprisingly, all three enjoy different sets of particularistic policies that are indispensable for encouraging and sustaining their global expansion. Equally importantly, all three have taken innovative firm-level initiatives to respond to the changing policy milieu and the unfolding economic reforms and engaged in a creative experiment in transnationalisation. Their cases bear out our assertions of the extraordinary importance of the state and of government policies in fostering the emergence of Chinese global businesses.

Their institutional investigations also highlight the limits of the role of the state and government policies. As the trying circumstances of Sinochem and Shougang demonstrate, reform politics and particularistic policies can make as well as break seemingly successful experiments of the transnationalisation of Chinese firms. The specific government policies on outward investment, as well as increasingly fundamental transformation of the Chinese economy in general, create conducive and necessary conditions for the rise of China's global businesses. They do not induce sufficient conditions. Rapid transnationalisation of all three firms under different and exacting circumstances is only ensured by entrepreneurship at the firm level, embodied in particular in their respective CEOs: Rong Yiren, Zheng Dunxun and Zhou Guangwu.

From the broader perspectives of history and political economy, integration of China with the global economy at the start of the twenty-first century is unprecedented. It is clear that China's outward FDI has played its due part in China's sometimes agonising search for its integration into the international economic system. The importance of the rise and the growth of China's multinational corporations in the last two decades of the twentieth century, however, goes far beyond integrating China into the global economy. It is a story of China's embracing a particular capitalist-invented institution in its pursuit of economic development, and a story of Chinese firms going out of their way to engage the global economy. In this light, the emergence of global businesses headquartered in China should be viewed as nothing short of a creative response to economic globalisation by Chinese firms as well as the Chinese state.

The emergence and growth of China's global businesses then begs a more profound question. If China seems to have so far successfully accommodated the exigencies of the global economy in order to incorporate the transnationalisation of firms into its development strategy, what does this inform us of the internationalisation and globalisation of the Chinese state?

Susan Strange once warned that '[N]o longer can any state today afford to opt out of the global market economy ... But the consequences of opting in, of acknowledging the constraints of opting in, so to speak, are fundamental and for the foreseeable future, irreversible' (Strange 1995: 160–1). China has obviously opted in. Internationalisation has noticeably increased the sensibility and vulnerability of the Chinese economy to global changes. Opting in, as in the instance of China's embracing this particular economic institution, has already introduced new opportunities and constraints in China's economic transition that influence the behaviour of firms and condition government policy preferences. The big question is whether and how the Chinese state in its present guise can continue to accommodate successfully those constraints and adjust itself to the exigencies of globalisation. Strange continues,

> Competing for world market shares, whether oil or semiconductors or air travel, means accepting the established structures and customs of those markets. Competing for foreign capital means accepting the terms and conditions set by the major financial centres and the major international banks, insurance firms, law firms and accountants. It means becoming vulnerable to the ups and downs and the consequent risks of an intrinsically volatile and not particularly rational market. It means accepting the imperative of negotiating with foreign firms which have more control than national governments over access to major world markets, and have ownership of and control over advanced technologies; and whose co-operation can also gain access to the foreign human and financial capital necessary for economic growth and a secure balance of payments.
>
> (Strange 1995: 260–1)

It is beyond doubt that China's emerging global businesses, acting as agents for internationalising the Chinese economy, are creating a special set of social and economic relations between China and the global economy as never seen before. By facilitating China's opting in, these agents are also turning the Chinese state inside out. Evaluated from this perspective, the rise and expansion of China's global businesses take China one step further towards globalisation, and constitute an indispensable dimension of China becoming a globalised state. The impact of such a transformation of China on the global economy needs to be carefully considered.

Notes

Introduction

1 See, for example, 'Taking on the World', *Business China*, vol. 26, 20 November 2000; 'Bank of China Thinks Global', *Far Eastern Economic Review*, 7 December 2000; 'China Business Goes Global', *Far Eastern Economic Review*, 28 March 2002; and 'Chinese Insurer Targets Global Markets', *Wall Street Journal*, 18 January 2000.

2 One of the most recent is Kevin Cai's 'Outward Foreign Direct Investment: A Novel Dimension of China's Integration into the Regional and Global Economy', in *China Quarterly* (Cai 1999). Otherwise, there are two technical papers published by the Organisation for Economic Cooperation and Development (OECD), one by Yun-Wing Sung (1991) on *Chinese Outward Investment in Hong Kong: Trends, Prospects and Policy Implications*, and the other by David Wall (1996) on *Outflows of Capital from China*. Other essays have made their way into *Transnational Corporations*, including James Zhan's 'Transnationalisation and Outward Investment: The Case of Chinese Firms' (1995). There are also some book chapters, most notably by Tseng Choo-Sin (1994, 1996), and Haiyan Zhang and Daniel van den Bulcke (1994, 1996). We may add to the list three working papers published by the Strathclyde International Business Unit. Occasional discussions on the international business conducted by individual Chinese firms also appear in such studies as Nolan (1996, 1998) and Steinfeld (1998). The primary focus of these studies is not, however, the transnationalisation of the firm concerned.

3 Throughout this study, we use 'firms', 'enterprises' and 'companies' in the Chinese context interchangeably and advisably to avoid definitional problems associated with the transitional nature of China's industrial organisation. See Nolan (1998: 6).

4 The respective figures are: for Hong Kong, $154.856 billion; Singapore, $47.63 billion; Taiwan, $38.003 billion. See UNCTAD (1999: 497–8). The figure for China's outward FDI here obviously does not include China's investment stocks in Hong Kong.

5 For example, in recognition of this fact, UNCTAD began to list the top 50 multinational corporations from developing countries in the *World Investment Report 1995*. Also in 1995, *Fortune* Global 500 included eight multinational corporations from Korea alone. Daewoo, which is listed as the largest multinational corporation from developing countries in both the 1997 and 1998 *World Investment Report*, is comparable in its foreign assets and transnationality index to many of the top 100 multinational corporations from developed countries.

6 Geoffrey Jones adopts a similar practice in defining multinational traders most recently. In his words, 'A multinational trading company engages in trader intermediation between countries, and owns assets in more than one country' (Jones 1998: 2).

7 Hong Kong's membership in the ADB and APEC, and its guaranteed membership in the WTO when eventually admitted, further reinforce its special status as a separate economic entity in the region.
8 It is interesting to note how Dunning defines what is 'foreign' in analysing the internationalisation process of firms. In his words, 'by foreign, we mean outside the physical confines of a particular country. Using this definition, colonies and overseas possessions are treated as foreign territories' (Dunning 1993: 133).

1   Economic Reform and the Internationalisation of the State

1 Italics in original text. Contributors to the same book also try to grapple with multiple definitions of internationalisation. In Richard Falk's formulation, for example, internationalisation has three dimensions: the projection of power, political, economic, cultural and whatever, beyond national boundaries; the degree of openness or closedness which reflects receptivity of a society to ideas and practices coming from beyond its borders; and the increasing porousness of states, even strong states. Shuichi Kato refers to internationalisation simply as 'a country's closer relations with foreign partners, or integration into the international community, whose members share some common values' (Falk 1992).
2 Others offer similar definitions. For example, Welch and Luostarinen define internationalisation as 'the process of increasing involvement in international operations' (1993: 157).
3 I have explored elsewhere the political and economic explanations of this anomaly of China in international society post-1949 (see Zhang 1998: chapters 2 and 3). China's limited trade and investment activities in this period are discussed in Chapters 2 and 4 respectively.
4 Take G7 members as an example. Before 1970, only France had full diplomatic relations with China after its recognition of the PRC in 1964. Britain recognised the PRC in January 1950. However, full diplomatic relations between Britain and China were not possible until 1972. The other five G7 members only recognised the PRC in the course of the 1970s: Canada and Italy in 1970, Germany and Japan in 1972 and the United States in 1978.
5 The six NICs identified by Milner and Keohane (1996: 11) as the 'first NICs' are Brazil, Mexico, Hong Kong, South Korea, Singapore and Taiwan.

2   The Internationalisation of the Chinese Economy: Empirical Evidence

1 For a simpler discussion of China and globalization, see Pang Zhongying (1999), 'Globalisation and China: China's Response to the Asian Economic Crisis'; and Moore, Thomas G. (1999), 'China and Globalisation', both in *Asian Perspective*, vol. 23, no. 1.

2   These figures are in current US dollars. Except otherwise indicated, $ in this study means US dollar.

3   China moved up to be the tenth largest in 1998. In 1999, China was ranked by WTO as the ninth largest (WTO 2000: 19).

4   In 1978, China's exports accounted for a meager 0.75 per cent of the world export total. Within a decade, in 1988, this had increased to 1.43 per cent and by 1996 to 2.93 per cent.

5   In 1997, the ratio was 41.6 per cent (*Beijing Review*, 30 March–5 April 1998: 10).

6   In 1993, their share increased to 27.5 per cent at $25.24 billion; and in 1994 to 28.7 per cent at $34.71 billion. These figures are from State Statistics Bureau (1995: 537–9, 553). The calculation is my own.

7   The importance of foreign-funded firms in China's foreign trade is also captured nicely by the World Bank. According to its report, already in 1995 'one third of China's exports and half of its imports involved joint ventures between Chinese and foreign partners' (World Bank 1997b: 90).

8   According to Lardy, in 2000, foreign-funded enterprises exported $119.4 billion, 48 per cent of China's total exports of $249.2 billion (Lardy 2002: 7). According to MOFTEC, in 1999, foreign-funded enterprises exported $88.63 billion, 45.5 per cent of China's total exports of $194.93 billion (www.moftec.gov.cn/moftec_cn/tjsi/wztj).

9   At the same time, only 10 per cent of commercial bank lending flowed into China.

10 It is also important to note that in the 1990s, FDI became the largest single source of capital inflow into China. It is in 1992 that, for the first time, FDI inflows surpassed the total of capital inflows from other sources put together, including loans from commercial banks, export credits, international bond issues, intergovernmental loans and loans from international organisations (Lardy 1994: 63) .

11 China's trade minister Shi Guangsheng is particularly proud of this achievement when he claimed that in six consecutive years, from 1993 to 1998, China was the world's second largest FDI recipient country, second only to the United States (Shi 1999).

12 According to Barnett's calculation, from 1970 to 1977, China's total borrowing was $4.86 billion, with $3.74 billion (77 per cent) in short-term loans 'generally for periods ranging from six to eighteen months' (see Barnett 1981: 225–6).

13 In an earlier report, the World Bank noted, however, that on a per capita basis, total lending to China amounts to only $2.50, *the lowest proportion of lending per capita in the entire East Asia region.*

14 Lardy noted that the only other transition economy which has ready access to international capital markets is the Czech Republic (Lardy 1995: 1065).

15 It was a Yen bond issued by the Bank of China (BOC) in Tokyo. At the same time, CITIC was also negotiating for the issue of another 20 billion Yen bond on the Tokyo market.

16 The *China Daily* reported on the same day that China was considering allowing Chinese enterprises to issue bonds on international capital markets.

17 B-shares are shares quoted in RMB in both the Shanghai and the Shenzhen stock exchanges, but settled in American dollars in Shanghai and in Hong Kong dollars in Shenzhen. They are not, however, convertible to A-shares which are traded in RMB mostly by domestic investors. This restricts their liquidity.

18 The nine companies are Qingdao Breweries, the Shanghai Petrochemical Complex, the Yizheng Joint Corporation of Chemical Fibre, the Kunming Machine Tool Plant, the Maanshan Iron and Steel Company, the Dongfang Electric Company, the Tianjin Bohai Chemical Industry Company, the Beijing Renmin Machinery General Plant, and the Guangzhou Shipyard International Co. Ltd. Six of them were successfully floated in 1993, and the other three, in 1994.

19 By the end of September 1995, seventeen Chinese companies had been floated on the Hong Kong Stock Exchange, raising a total of HK$19.09 billion (Davis 1996: 63, Lin and Jian 1995: 33–4).

20 Liu's figure of Chinese companies floated on the New York Stock Exchange seems to be inaccurate. According to Lees and Liaw, quoting the *Wall Street Journal* (22 February 1995), by the end of 1994, six Chinese companies were listed on the New York Stock Exchange: Brilliance China Automotive Holdings, China Tire Holdings, EK Chor China Motorcycle, Shanghai Petrochemical, Shandong Huaneng Electrical Power and Huaneng Power (Lees and Liaw 1996: 72–3).

21 N-shares refers to shares of the Chinese companies listed on the New York Stock Exchange in the form of American depository receipts (ADR).

22 For further details, see Liu Yan (1997) and Liu *et al.* (1998).

23 Chinese companies are also listed on stock exchanges other than Hong Kong and New York. Lees and Liaw (1996: 73) noted, for example, that in 1995 one Chinese company, the Guangdong Corporation, was listed on the Australian Stock Exchange.

24 It should also be pointed out that official aid from the Chinese government as a form of international capital flow is not to be included in this discussion.

25 For example, from 1991 to 1995, MOFTEC's figures of its approved FDI were only around $1.4 billion (MOFTEC 1997: 434), whereas the total listed in the same period, as in Table 2.6, is $13.13 billion.

26 For further discussions of China's capital flight, see Gunter (1996) and Wall (1996).

27 In another estimate, Xinhua News Agency reported that by the end of 1994, China's investment in Hong Kong was $19.2 billion.

28 There is also evidence to suggest that after the handover, there was more capital flight from the Mainland into Hong Kong. In 2000, the total FDI into Hong Kong reached an uncanny $64.3 billion, while at the same time, $62.9 billion were moved out of Hong Kong as outward FDI, mostly going to the Mainland (*Far Eastern Economic Review*, 21 June 2001).

29 The discussion here excludes financial services such as banking and insurance.

30 The first recorded contract for China's service trade is in 1976.

31 For China's aid programme before 1978, see Bartke (1989) and Shi Lin *et al.* (1989: 23–73).

3 Towards the Transnationalisation of Chinese Firms: Policies and Debates

1 For more detailed discussions of China's changing perceptions of important international institutions, see Zhang Yongjin (1998: 99–125). For China's limited exchange with the world economy see Barnett (1981).

2 The book was translated by the World Economy Research Group of the Institute of Economics of Nankai University. The Research Group was expanded into the Research Institute of World Economy of Nankai University in the mid-1980s, now one of the most prestigious research institutes of world economy in China.

3 Jilin University Press published *Meiguo de Kuaguo Gongsi* [American Multinationals], also in 1975 (Kang *et al.* 1996: 7).

4 In the preface to the publication of the Chinese version, the publisher, wary of political correctness, declared that multinational corporations 'are an important tool for imperialist countries to engage in foreign exploitation and aggression and in their rivalry for the sphere of influence', and 'are conducting economic plundering and political interference and sabotage in developing countries' (UN Department of Social and Economic Affairs 1975, Chinese edn).

5 Such an interpretation, tinted with ideological bias, was not surprising given the political constraints at the time. What is interesting is the fact that the early to late 1970s is also a time when what Fieldhouse called the popular alarmists, ideologues (Marxists and dependency theorists) and nationalists offered their severe critiques of multinationals in world development (Fieldhouse 1986: 17–21). Though there is no direct evidence to show that this literature influenced Chinese thinking on multinationals, there is good reason to believe that China's participation in the UN and its support of the New International Economic Order (NIEO) throughout the 1970s must have exposed Chinese officials and scholars to that literature.

6 Professor Ye Gang of Fudan University was to become one of the leading Chinese analysts of the development of China's multinational corporations.

7 A major publication which meant to provide practical guidance for Chinese firms in their outward investment in 1993 called for a 'revaluation and new understanding of merits and demerits' of multinational corporations in the world economy (see Li Yuesheng *et al.* 1993: 8–17).

8 The conference examined the dynamic relations between transnational corporations and China's open-door policy. Among the sponsors of this conference were UNESCO, Merrill Lynch, the Hong Kong and Shanghai Banking Corporation, and the AMAX Foundation. John Dunning, among a group of prominent foreign scholars, participated in and contributed to the conference (Teng and Wang 1988).

9 One Chinese scholar even claimed in the opening sentence of his paper, 'that the multinational enterprise (MNE) has become a positive and livening element in the modern world economy is no longer of any doubt' (Wang 1988: 191).

10 In 1987, in the Chinese edition of the *Encyclopaedia of the World Economy*, multinational corporations were still defined as 'an important tool for the

capitalist countries to export their capital and engage in foreign economic expansion' (Kang *et al.* 1996: 9).

11 For example, one study listed thirty publications from 1975 to 1993. Of this total, twenty were published in 1990–93 (Kang *et al.* 1996: 13–15). The list is obviously far from complete because it did not include, for example, one important publication of 1993, namely Li Yuesheng *et al.* (eds), *A Practical Handbook of Overseas Investment*.

12 For many years, Ma Hong has been the director of the Development Research Centre of the State Council, a major think-tank of the Chinese government.

13 It should be noted, though, that in the initial period of China's opening up and economic reform in the 1980s, the government's policy attention focused primarily on the policy environment for attracting FDI into China, not on the outward investment and transnational operations of Chinese firms.

14 The Chinese version of these documents is available in Chinese in Li Yuesheng *et al.* (1993): 123–9.

15 The approval came in particular from Li Xiannian and Deng Xiaoping, both Vice-Premiers at the time.

16 Sinochem, for example, established its first overseas office in Japan in April 1980. For further discussions, see Chapter 6.

17 MINMETAL led the way and in 1979 opened offices in West Germany, Japan, Britain and the United States (Wu Kuang 1994: 201). It was followed quickly in 1980 by the incorporation of MINMETAL's first overseas company – Kimet Corporation in the United States (Liu Zhongliang 1994: 10).

18 In an earlier document issued by the MOFERT in 1984, political needs had been stipulated as one consideration in obtaining approval for overseas investment projects. The stipulation was 'that it serves political needs and is economically viable'. The reason seems clear. In the 1984 document, Hong Kong and Macao were included as the investment destinations, while the 1985 document carefully dropped Hong Kong and Macao and made it applicable only to China's investment 'in foreign countries' (Li Yuesheng *et al.* 1993: 123–4).

19 According to Wells, 'Taiwan: regulations state that outward investments must meet one of the following requirements: promote the sales of domestic products; make available raw materials required by domestic industries; expand the market for the products of the investor whose domestic plant has excess capacity; be conducive to the export of technical know-how that may increase foreign exchange earnings; or promote international economic co-operation' (Wells 1983: 144).

20 The fourth major motivation is efficiency-seeking.

21 As is clear in the 1988 MOFERT document on trade-related investment, the control procedure is much looser, the requirements for approval are easier to meet, and the approval authorities are more decentralised.

22 As David Wall observed (1996: 34), in the late 1980s all five largest overseas investment projects by Chinese firms were in resource sectors.

23 The major document concerned is MOFTEC's *Regulations Governing Control and Approval Procedures for Opening Non-trade Enterprises Overseas* of March 1992 (see Liu Xiangdong *et al.* 1993: 1276–9).

24 The first regulations concerning the control of foreign exchange for China's overseas investment were not promulgated until March 1989. For the text of the document, see Li Yuesheng *et al.* (1993: 129–30).

25 MOFERT and the ministries concerned also reserved to themselves the responsibility for screening and approving all investment projects, big or small, in countries that had no diplomatic relations with China. The screening and approval of such projects are to be in consultation with the Foreign Ministry.

26 In an important study of the transnationalisation of Chinese firms, Zhan summarises these policy incentives well when he states: 'The methods by which the Government promotes these types of outward FDI include tax incentives, subsidies and privileged access to the domestic market for goods produced abroad by Chinese foreign affiliates' (Zhan 1995: 70).

27 Strong policy support to Chinese engineering and construction firms on international engineering and labour service markets was also offered by the State Council from the very start. The policy regime evolved to support such operations eventually included, among others, preferential loans in foreign currency to these firms offered by the Bank of China. Or alternatively, guarantees can be provided by the Bank of China for loans obtained from foreign banks by these firms. Tax exemption for the overseas earnings made by these firms is conceded for the first five years. A national fund for foreign economic cooperation has been established comprising both US dollars and RMB, under the rubric of which preferential loans were offered to firms undertaking such operations (Liu Xiangdong *et al.* 1993: 1228). Although not initially important, a series of general policies encouraging Chinese investment in Hong Kong emerged in the 1990s. Many such government-induced investments are out of political considerations.

28 CITIC issued a 10 billion yen bond in January 1982 in Tokyo, the first ever bond issue by a PRC entity after 1949. The funds raised were used to construct Yizheng Chemical Fibre, the largest polyester producer in China today.

29 For further details, see Chapter 7.

30 Liu Guoguang (ed.) (1984) is probably the first book that systematically discussed China's choices of economic development strategy.

31 Robert Hsu argues that development economics was 'functional economics for Chinese economists' in the 1980s (Hsu 1991: 106).

32 Wang Jian's original article was first published in the *People's Daily*, 5 January 1988.

33 For further discussions of the theory of the great international cycle, see Fewsmith (1994: 214–17) and Hsu (1991: 138–41).

34 For a brief but revealing discussion of politics behind the adoption of the coastal area development strategy, see Fewsmith (1994: 215–16).

35 In October 1991, a conference on 'Transnational Operations of Chinese Firms in the 1990s' was held in Shanghai jointly by the International Technological and Economic Research Institute of the State Council's Development Research Centre and the Transnational Corporation Committee of the Shanghai Association of World Economy. One hundred and three people participated in the conference. A seminar, 'Strategies to Develop Transnational Operations of Chinese Firms', was held in Qingdao in Shandong Province in November 1992.

36 Some were published within six months of the conference.

37 Two people from SCRES, including Vice-Minister Gao Shangquan, published their papers presented at the symposium in *Guanli Shijie* (Management World).

38 Li also emphasised that the pluralisation of China's export markets had a political dimension, that is, that China is in a strong position to withstand political and economic pressure from the West. In Li's words, 'The Central Committee attached great importance to this, and MOFERT made preparations and plans for the same purpose'.

39 Almost all discussion in China on the transnational operations of Chinese firms mentions this concern, but stops at discussing the impact of exported capital on the domestic economy.

40 As will be discussed in some detail in Chapter 6, China's petrochemical industry has to undergo painful reorganisation to rid itself of the traditional divisions.

41 It is interesting to note that these goals are precisely what the Korean government spelt out for Korean overseas investment (see Kumar and Mcleod, 1981: 68).

42 Only projects involving Chinese investment of over $30 million now need the State Council's approval.

43 The phrase is borrowed from Nicholas Lardy. For a detailed analysis of China's financial reforms in the 1990s, see Lardy (1998).

44 In presenting this package, Jiang Zemin, the Chinese President, stated: 'Establishing a socialist market economic structure requires giving full play to the market's basic role in the allocation of resources under state macro-economic control. Both state macroeconomic control and the role of market mechanisms are essential requirements of the socialist market economic structure' (*Beijing Review*, 31 January–6 February 1994, enclosure).

45 The State Development Bank was set up in June 1994, the Agricultural Development Bank in November 1994 and the Import and Export Bank also in 1994. For a brief discussion of these three policy banks, see Lardy (1998: 76–80). See also Mehran *et al.* (1996: 14).

46 China has committed to eliminate these quotas and licences by 2005.

47 By 1996, the presence of foreign financial institutions in China was such that the People's Bank of China felt it necessary to publish *A Directory of Foreign Financial Institutions Resident in China*. It is 360 pages long and gives contact addresses of those institutions (over 340) and their branches (over 600) in China (PBOC 1996). For further discussions of the presence of foreign banks in China, see Lardy (2002: 114–19).

48 The other three thrusts are preparing China for its accession to the WTO; further expanding China's imports and exports; and cultivating better utilisation of foreign direct investment in China.

4   China's Multinational Corporations: Then and Now

1 Geoffrey Jones poignantly reminded us of this bias even in 1998 in a groundbreaking study of what he calls 'multinational traders'. In his words, 'The paucity of literature on trading companies reflects a more general bias in the

literature on international business towards the manufacturing sector, even though by the 1990s upwards of 50 per cent of world foreign direct investment (FDI) was in services' (Jones 1998: 7).

2 Another example is that in June 1967, the China Ocean Shipping Company (COSCO) formed a joint venture with the Tanzanian government, Chinese–Tanzanian Joint Shipping Co., known as SINOTASIP (www.cosco.com.cn/about/overseas.asp).

3 Chu Kong Shipping, established in 1962, is another example.

4 Prior to 1982, it was the Ministry of Foreign Economic Cooperation that supervised such activities. In 1982, it merged with the Ministry of Foreign Trade to establish the Ministry of Foreign Economic Relations and Trade (MOFERT).

5 In 1988, the China State Construction and Engineering Company Ltd, the largest construction engineering firm in China, was ranked 27 and the China Civil Engineering and Construction Corporation 132 on the list according to their annual turnover.

6 China Merchants was established in 1872, BOC HK Branch in 1917 and China Travel in 1928.

7 Lin and Jian (1995) also provide explanations about the restricted operations of those firms from the perspectives of China's international environment and domestic politics.

8 For example, Jiyou Bank, a small retail bank established in 1947 in Hong Kong, also passed into the hands of the Chinese government (Lin and Jian 1995: 7).

9 It is further estimated that the net worth of the BOC Group was $1,556 million at the end of 1980. On the other hand, the net worth of non-financial Chinese companies was estimated conservatively at $400 million (see Sung 1996: 16).

10 Zhang and Van Den Bulcke call them 'Foreign Business Oriented Companies' (FBOCs) (Zhang and Van Den Bulcke 1994: 144).

11 According to *Engineering News Record*, in both 1994 and 1995 23 Chinese companies were among the largest 225 engineering and constructions firms in the world (MOFTEC 1997: 129).

12 Sinotrans is a corporation directly under the MOFTEC, specialising in shipping and other transportation business. Like others, it has diversified into a wide range of business activities. One example, as will be mentioned later, is its investment in forestry in New Zealand in 1990.

13 According to one study conducted in the early 1990s, Shenzhen did not establish its first overseas enterprise until September 1983. By the end of 1988, it had set up 110 overseas enterprises in Hong Kong and Macao and twelve enterprises in other countries (Ye and He 1993: 170).

14 This assessment is based on MOFERT statistics. An official evaluation by MOFERT is worth quoting here in full. According to MOFERT, 'By the end of 1988, China has approved 526 non-trade related investment projects overseas. The total amount of the investment involved in these projects are $1.898 billion, with Chinese investment of $0.715 billion, 37.6% of the total. These projects are scattered in 79 countries and regions all over the world ... They are mainly, however, concentrated in the United States, Thailand, Australia, Japan, Canada, West Germany, Singapore, Mauritius, as well as

Hong Kong and Macao . . . Of 526 approved ventures, 376 are already opened for operation. 90% of them have very good and good economic returns' (MOFERT 1990: 55). Please note that there are some small discrepancies between figures in Table 4.1 and the figures quoted here.

15 James Zhan cautioned, for example, that 'The two main sources of data on China's outward FDI are the IMF and MOFTEC . . . The data-collection and estimation methods of these two institutions give rise to large discrepancies in the outward FDI values reported' (Zhan 1995: 72). Such inconsistency, of course, is not unique to the estimation of China's outward FDI. Dunning *et al.*, for example, noted a huge discrepancy in the statistics compiled by the US Department of Commerce and UNCTAD of the total outward FDI stocks from developing countries in 1980 (Dunning *et al.* 1998: 257).

16 Interestingly, MOFTEC did not begin to register systematically China's trade-related investment until 1993. MOFTEC statistics show that from 1993 to 1995, 202 trade-related overseas subsidiaries were approved with an investment total of $58.01 million (MOFTEC 1997: 454). But as previously noted, according to the *Beijing Review*, from 1979 to 1993, China's trade-related investment overseas was $3.47 billion. That is an annual average of $248 million! This figure does seem to have included China's trade-related investment in Hong Kong (see *Beijing Review*, 21–27 March 1994: 18).

17 An earlier 'rescue' operation was the acquisition of Congli Investment by the Bank of China and the China Resources Ltd (see Lin and Jian 1995: 30).

18 For further discussion of CITIC's rescue operation of Ka Wah Bank, see Chapter 5.

19 Geoffrey Jones (1998) recently argued very strongly for the importance of 'relational networks' in the evolution and expansion of multinational traders.

20 It is hyperinflation only in the Chinese context.

21 According to the IMF, Chinese financial entities issued only $150.4 million worth of bonds in 1989 in comparison to $1,415.2 million in 1987 and $911.6 million in 1988. No bond issue by Chinese financial entities was recorded in 1990 (see Goldstein *et al.* 1992: 75).

22 Lardy (1992: 105–47) provides an analytical account of China's trade system reforms both before and after June 1989.

23 The statistics here from the *China Statistical Yearbook* do not include the portfolio investment China made overseas. Portfolio investment listed under the category of 'purchase of foreign bonds and securities' in the statistical yearbook of 1990–95 was $200 million in 1990, $300 million in 1991, $500 million in 1992, $600 million in 1993, $400 million in 1994 and $100 million in 1995. Note, too, that they do not include reinvestment or investment raised by Chinese firms on the international capital market. It is related only to the direct export of capital from China. It is also safe to assume that the statistics, either from China's State Statistical Bureau or UNCTAD, only include a small portion, if any, of China's outward investment in Hong Kong and Macao.

24 This list does not include China's investment in Hong Kong and Macao.

25 The export total in 1998 was $183.76 billion, compared with $182.70 billion in 1997.

26 Pang further argued that the Asian financial crisis issued a clear warning to China that it needs more than capital inflows, technology transfer and

management expertise to succeed in its economic transformation. In his words, 'an appropriate economic structure, such as a healthy banking system, efficient corporate governance, a prevalent rule of law, a clean government, and a workable democracy are at the heart of China's success. As the largest emerging market in the world, China faces a serious test in balancing the benefits and costs of globalization' (Pang 1999).

27 It should be noted that the Chinese statistics still register a significant outward investment in 2000 at $2.36 billion (*China Statistics Yearbook* 2001: 80).

28 It is reported that some research in China comes up with much higher estimates at $36 billion in 1997 and $38.6 billion in 1998 (*Taipei Times on line*, 1 October 2000).

29 According to CNN, the price tag for Husky Energy, Canada's fifth largest integrated oil company, is $4 billion for PetroChina. Husky Energy is controlled by Li Ka-shing and Hutchinson Whampoa.

30 To further complicate any attempt to find definitive answers, there is a need to carefully differentiate China's *outward* investment from its *overseas* investment, though so far we have largely used these phrases interchangeably. Both concern China's investment beyond Chinese borders. Strictly speaking, however, the former involves direct capital export, whereas the latter does not necessarily do so. Capital raised on international capital markets outside China by Chinese firms does not involve direct capital export from China but is still counted as overseas investment.

31 Even MOFTEC candidly admitted in a recent White Paper that 'there are no detailed statistics about trade related investment before 1992' (MOFTEC 1997: 454).

32 The intriguing question here is what portion of Hong Kong's outward FDI flow, which was estimated by Wall at an annual average of $15.8 billion in 1992–94 and $42.5 billion in 1995, is red chips' reverse investment in China and in 'third' economies. One estimate claims that in the first nine months of 1993, four Mainland-controlled companies in Hong Kong, namely, the Bank of China Group, the China Resource Group, the China Travel Service Group and the China Overseas Group, invested $1.5 billion, 14 per cent of China's utilised FDI in the same period.

33 The respective figures compiled by the IMF for the late 1990s are $2,114 million for 1996, $2,563 million for 1997, $2,634 million for 1998, $1,775 million for 1999 and $916 million for 2000 (IMF 2001: 356–7).

34 *Far Eastern Economic Review* claimed in 1988 that already by the end of 1987, Chinese investment in Hong Kong reached $10 billion, higher than the estimated American investment at $6 billion (No. 23: 64–6).

35 In the same report, the Hang Seng Bank estimated that the United States and Japan invested $8.5 billion and $11.5 billion respectively in the same period. China therefore became the 'top HK investor'.

36 This includes mostly finance and trade services.

37 The primary exception is again Shougang's acquisition in Peru.

38 The reason for the low-level technology-seeking investment from China may lie in the fact that the main agent for technology transfer for upgrading China's industrial structure is the FDI inflow into China.

39 Based on MOFTEC figures (1984–93), Zhang and Van Den Bulcke claim that the average Chinese investment per project is less than $1.2 million (1996:

402–3). This claim should be taken with a large pinch of salt, because, as noted, MOFTEC in fact only records a small portion of China's overseas investment.

40 They are ranked by transnationality index respectively as follows: Sinochem at 17, the China State Construction and Engineering Corporation at 31, China MINMETAL at 32, the China Harbour Engineering Company at 42 and the China Shougang Group at 44.

41 In making this change, the managing editor of *Fortune*, John Huey, observed, 'we made this change for one simple reason: The world of business is rapidly transforming itself – and blurring once-valid distinctions between industrial and service companies – as a new information economy takes hold' (*Fortune*, 7 August 1995: 6).

42 There are two interesting comparisons here. First, compared with Australia's three multinationals in *Fortune Global 500*, namely BHP (ranked 303), Coles Myer (ranked 347) and News Corporation (ranked 488), the Chinese three have a much higher ranking and have far larger combined revenues and assets. The figures for the combined total of the Australian three are $30.87 billion for revenues and $45.28 billion for assets. Second, while China has three multinationals in *Fortune Global* 500, Hong Kong has only one and Taiwan two. For further discussions, see Zhang Yongjin (1997: 429–42).

43 The four companies involved are, respectively, the China Machinery and Equipment Import and Export Corporation, the China Textile International Economic Cooperation Corporation, the China Water Conservancy and Electric Power International Economic and Technical Cooperation Corporation and the China Civil Engineering and Construction Corporation.

44 Jianlibao, a non-state-owned soft drinks company, for example, has invested in New Zealand. Many non-state-owned firms such as township and village enterprises (TVEs) from SEZs investing in Hong Kong and Macao, to quote another example, can also be theoretically counted as multinationals. Chinese statistics (quoted in Zhang and Van Den Bulcke 1996: 409) show that overseas subsidiaries of TVEs rose from 15 in 1991 to 130 in 1992. But generally they are small in scale and are rather restricted in their transnational operations in China's peripheral states and economies.

45 The PLA also runs a number of trading firms to conduct, in particular, arms trade. The most prominent of them are the China Xinxing Corporation under the General Logistics Department, Polytechnologies (also known as Baoli), founded by the General Staff personnel, and New Era (Xinshidai), jointly managed by the PLA and the Commission for Science, Technology, and Industry for National Defence (COSTIND) (Bickford 1994: 464–5). These firms also conduct large-scale transnational operations.

46 There is also the People's Insurance Company of China (PICC). Established in 1950, PICC's early overseas operations were mainly concerned with the reinsurance business in India, Indonesia, Burma and Ceylon (now Sri Lanka). The transnationalisation of PICC started in 1979. By 1990, it had eight subsidiaries established in Hong Kong and Macao, China Insurance (UK) in London and representative offices in New York, Hamburg and Tokyo. The premiums of its overseas operations increased from $25 million in 1979 to $120 million in 1990 (Jin 1992: 15).

47 In 1992, the Sanjiu Enterprise Group controlled 34 military-affiliated companies and had a reported profit of $162 million (Bickford 1994: 466).

48 It should also be noted that many subsidiaries of Chinese parent firms, whether they are located overseas or inside China, have become multinationals in their own right. There are plenty of examples of these even if we look just at those subsidiaries in Hong Kong, say, for example, the COSCO (HK) Group and Shougang Concord International. Of CITIC's subsidiaries, CITIC Pacific and CITIC Australia are true multinationals. Even CITIC Development Co. Ltd has investment in real estate in the USA and in a fishing joint venture in Morocco, and trade-related investment in Tokyo, Paris and New Zealand.

5 CITIC: A Pioneer of Chinese Multinationals

1 The actual figure in CITIC's annual report is, however, 3.6 billion yuan.

2 In its annual report of 1998, CITIC candidly admits that 'the amount of CITIC's overseas investment and the results of the Company's business declined significantly compared with previous years due to the Asian financial crises and the volatility in the international market. As a result, the Company's overall profit decreased compared with last year'. It did not, however, given any quantitative details (CITIC 1998: 6).

3 They are MAC-Fishery in Morocco, CITIC MINGYU Company Ltd, and Dong Hua Fund, both in Tokyo, BBU Mezzanine Fund and CITIC Ambanc Scottsdale Airport Limited Partnership, both in the USA, China Partners S.A. in Paris and Three Rings Ltd in Christchurch in New Zealand (see http://www.chinabusiness.net/citicdev/projects.html)

4 According to CITIC's veterans, it took around three years to get just half of the promised capital actually transferred to the kitty of CITIC (Interviews).

5 Unless otherwise specified, the following account of Rong and the establishment of CITIC is largely drawn from Wen (1990), Huang (1994) and Ma (1997).

6 In a recently published biography of Rong Yiren, it is claimed that Deng originally intended to see Rong alone. It was at the request of the Department of the United Front of the CCP Central Committee that Deng met the five as a group (Ji Honggeng 1999: 199). All five were members of the Chinese People's Political Consultative Conference (CPPCC) at the time.

7 Italics my own. The full text (in Chinese) of Deng's talk with the group is published in *Selected Works of Deng Xiaoping*, Vol. II, pp. 156–7.

8 The Rong family was, perhaps not surprisingly, nicknamed 'the King of Cotton Yarn' (*miansha dawang*), and 'the King of Flour' (*mianfen dawang*). Mao Zedong was quoted to have remarked that 'of all China's indigenous capitalists, the Rong family's business interests were the largest. It owned China's only "conglomerate" by the world standard'.

9 Ten years later, in 1959, Rong made public his fears and worries in a speech at the National People's Congress, published in the *People's Daily* (Ji Honggeng 1999: 88–9).

10 Among them were Zi Yaohua, Xu Guomao, Yang Xishang and Wang Jianshi, who were all financiers in pre-1949 Shanghai. Wang and Zi were to become directors of the first board of CITIC.

11   The other two persons appointed together with Rong were Lei Renmin and Wu Zhichao. Lei was later appointed deputy managing director of CITIC in October 1979.

12   Three of them, George C. Tso, Li Ka-shing and Fok Yingtung, were still on the board of directors in 1998.

13   As discussed earlier, when entrusting Rong to set up and then to manage CITIC, the CCP leadership recognised that Rong's reputation and personal contacts, as well as his networking with the overseas Chinese business community, were invaluable assets. In 1986, Deng would acknowledge this publicly in Beijing, when he personally received more than 200 members of the Rong clan from all over the world.

14   The *Financial Times* (7 March 1994) reported that 'Imperial Chemical Industries of the UK and Amoco of the US have each taken strategic stakes of 2.5 percent in the Yizheng Chemical Fibre Company, China's biggest polyester producer, which is being floated on the Hong Kong Stock Exchange. The stakes are worth $6 million apiece. Yizheng is claimed to be the world's fifth biggest polyester producer.'

15   My interviewees gave a figure of 'millions' of yuan. I was not able to get the exact figure from other sources either.

16   One of my interviewees, who had worked in the Overseas Investment Department until its dismantlement, said that in those two years he had travelled to almost all the large copper mines in the world.

17   As the guarantee for the loan, half of CITIC's share of the pulp mill was mortgaged to the Royal Bank of Canada; a long-term sales contract was signed with its parent company in China (Interviews). See also Zhang Jijing (1998: 407–13).

18   Detailed discussions of project financing of these two investments can be found in Zhang Jijing (1998), particularly 397–414.

19   CITIC's acquisitions in Hong Kong also stand testimony to this.

20   *Euromoney* described CITIC's acquisition of the Ka Wah Bank as 'Red Calvary came to the rescue' (*Euromoney*, February 1986: 15).

21   In 1985–86, CITIC Hong Kong also made a number of investments in trading, garment-making and real estate (Ye Gang 1993a: 307).

22   One point of contention was whether CITIC should behave more like a commercial firm or a government organisation.

23   Zhao's instructions were 'Let us do as proposed. No more quibbles among ourselves' (Ji Honggeng 1987).

24   Deng Xiaoping seems to have intervened, too, in the early years of CITIC. An article in the *Beijing Review* in 1994 made the interesting claim that 'Whenever he met difficulties, Rong wrote letters to Deng, who always fully supported him by answering his letters with detailed instructions, and asking concerned departments to give Rong the green light' (Huang 1994: 23).

25   The actual capital injection, according to Larry Yung, is between HK$230 million and HK$250 million (see *Reuters*, 26 March 1997; Ma Kefeng 1997: 286).

26   Before he accepted the appointment, Yung insisted that he be granted autonomy (1) to recruit his managers, and (2) to make most local investment decisions. According to Kraar, this is 'a degree of autonomy unheard of in other PRC government corporations (Kraar 1997: 38; see also Ma Kefeng 1997: 285).

27 Larry Yung recalled that there were different opinions in CITIC Beijing as to how CITIC Hong Kong should position itself in Hong Kong. He is quoted as saying that 'In the beginning, the business of CITIC Hong Kong did not develop rapidly. This is largely because the headquarters [in Beijing] are divided as to which direction CITIC Hong Kong should go' (Ma Kefeng 1997: 285; see also Ye Gang 1993a: 307).

28 In an interview with the *Financial Times* in 1993, Wei Mingyi, the newly appointed Chairman of CITIC 'dated the organization's drive abroad to the credit squeeze of 1988, when China clamped down on most business activity. It was then that CITIC made its push into Hong Kong, leading to stakes in Hong Kong Telecom (12 per cent), Cathay Pacific (12.5 per cent) and Dragon Air (46.2 per cent)' (1 May 1993). This account is not accurate, as will be seen in the following discussion. CITIC's first big push into Hong Kong started in 1987, well before the 1988 credit squeeze.

29 Cable & Wireless and Hutchinson Whampoa eventually quit AsiaSat in December 1998, and their shares were bought by CITIC and ASTRA of Luxembourg. The combined shareholdings of CITIC and ASTRA are 68.95 per cent of AsiaSat (CITIC 1998: 11).

30 Beijing was reluctant initially because of the amount of capital involved. Larry Yung eventually obtained Beijing's consent, but had to raise the funds to finance the deal without relying on Chinese banks. It has been said that it took one and half day's debate within the State Council before Li Peng and others approved the acquisition. There was, however, no Chinese bank in the syndication group that lent the money to Larry Yung (Ma Kefeng 1997: 289–91; *Euromoney*, June 1991: 31).

31 In the initial take-over, Li Ka-shing took 19 per cent of Hang Chong, Robert Kwok's Kerry Trading 7 per cent, and Larry Yung 6 per cent (*Financial Times*, 4 September 1991).

32 In the same interview, Rong also admitted that, so far, CITIC had mainly invested in the industrial sector and would like to make some progress in the finance and service sectors.

33 Details of the full package were publicised in the *People's Daily* on 27 July 1992. As will be discussed in Chapter 7, it is important to note that the State Council also granted much broader autonomy to Shougang in its transnational operations, at approximately the same time.

34 Fuller discussions of CITIC Australia's acquisitions and its eventual exit from Australia's meat-processing industry are found at the end of this chapter.

35 It has also looked at possible sites in Russia.

36 The *South China Morning Post*, for example, claimed as early as 1996 that CITIC Pacific was one of a small number of Hong Kong firms that 'blazed a trail as high quality investment vehicles for China projects' (1 November 1996).

37 CITIC Pacific also has subsidiary companies registered in China. In manufacturing, for example, there are Jiangyin Xingcheng Special Steel Works Co. Ltd and Wuxi Huada Motors Co. Ltd, and in trade and distribution, Shanghai DCH Jiangnanfeng Co. Ltd and Shanghai DCH Jinshan Co. Ltd (see CITIC Pacific 1998: 100–1).

38 In January 1996, for example, CITIC Pacific placed HK$3.24 billion worth of new shares, of which HK$800 million were earmarked for its Shanghai pro-

jects of toll bridges and roads, and HK$400 million, to fund the second phase of the Ligang power station in Jiangsu Province (*Financial Times*, 5 January 1996).

39 As reported in the *Beijing Review*, CITIC's initial plan was to issue $150 million. But it had to increase the amount to $250 million because of the huge demand in America. Even so, the *Wall Street Journal* reported that 'the total bond issued was sold out on the very first day' (*Beijing Review*, 30 August–5 September 1993: 25).

40 In 1986, when CITIC first took over the Celgar Pulp Mill, the cost of timber was about 30 per cent of the total production. In 1995–96, it rose to 60 per cent. Severe restrictions on lumbering due to environmental concerns and deforestation are blamed for the rise (Interviews).

41 As early as 1993, the *Far Eastern Economic Review* noted that Celgar was beset by 'labour problems' and 'the recession in the United States' (23 January 1993: 51).

42 CITIC Australia's earlier investment in Australia also incurred considerable losses. According to the *Far Eastern Economic Review*, CITIC Australia's investment in Southern Aluminium in Tasmania, a producer of aluminium alloy wheels, was mainly responsible for CITIC Australia's loss of A$10.4 million in 1992. It had to divest itself of its stake there in September 1992 (23 February 1995: 60).

43 This has also affected its domestic investment priority. As one senior CITIC official put it, 'What China needs, CITIC will do, even though we are aware that this sometimes might not be profitable' (*Far Eastern Economic Review*, 21 January 1993: 50).

44 In January 1988, 541 General Plant, a military enterprise, was transferred to CITIC and renamed CITIC Machinery Manufacturing Co. Ltd. In December 1993, Luoyang Mining Machinery Plant was merged with CITIC and is now CITIC Heavy Machinery Ltd. Both however have been 'big headaches', to quote one of my interviewees, for CITIC (Interviews).

45 In October 1996, CITIC's group executive director, Chang Zhenming, admitted in an interview with Reuters that 'manufacturing [of CITIC's businesses] is having a hard time' (*Reuters*, 28 October 1996).

46 CITIC's executive directors are however still appointed by the State Council.

47 Curiously, its Chinese name remains the same, Zhongxin Taifu.

48 For CITIC Pacific's purchase of China L & P and controversies surrounding the deal, see 'CITIC deal reflects balance of HK power' (*Financial Times*, 29 January 1997).

49 An interesting comparison here is that Singapore Airlines was ranked 23rd in its foreign assets, and the Malaysian Airline Berhad was ranked 12th in its transnationality index.

50 On the controversial issue of CITIC Pacific's disposal of 17.6 per cent of Dragonair to the China National Aviation Corporation (CNAC) in 1996, for example, Yung insisted that 'CITIC Pacific made the decision. No pressure from Beijing' (*Financial Post*, 16 November 1996).

51 The remaining 2 per cent came from 'real estate and other investments'.

52 In comparison, CITIC Australia's turnover in 1986 was only A$1.1 million.

53 CITIC Australia was also reported to have acquired substantial stakes in the grain and wool business by obtaining majority stakes in Ambiack Pty Ltd

in north-western Australia in 1995 (*Australian Financial Review*, 21 December 1995).

54 CITIC Australia sought outright the controlling interest of Portman Mining in its bid and was rejected by the shareholders. As CITIC's top executives later admitted, such a strategy was not the optimal one (Interviews).

55 In addition, CITIC Australia also holds a 50 per cent share in C&S Joint Venture, which is involved in active exploration activities in Queesland (www.citic.com.au/about/index.html).

56 The joint venture also led to the establishment of CITIC Australia (Singapore) Pte Ltd

57 Symbol Australia Geo-Services Pty Ltd is a joint venture between CITIC Australia and the Ministry of Geology and Mineral Resources of the PRC. It had two joint ventures in 1995, involved in the manufacturing and trading of bentonite products in China, as well as the exploration and development of mining and mineral projects in China and Australia.

6 Sinochem: Global Reach

1 Before 1995, *Fortune* had separate lists for industrial and services companies.

2 Though we do not attempt to address directly the theoretical questions raised by Jones in this case study, we believe that such a case study of a Chinese multinational trader is likely to help answer three theoretical questions identified by Jones concerning multinational trading companies, namely: Why are such firms used in trade intermediation? Why do they exhibit a constant tendency to diversify, and what are their competencies? And how are they able to reinvent themselves? (Jones 1998: 16).

3 The other two are the Bank of China and COFCO, as mentioned earlier.

4 The ranking is based on the total turnover only of imports and exports in 1994.

5 Sinochem's domestic trade figures in 1990–95 are not included in this chart. They vary between $800 million and $1.3 billion in those years.

6 The other chunk is the turnover of Sinochem's domestic operations, $995 million in 1995 and $1.46 billion in 1996.

7 Three indexes suggested by UNCTAD to measure a firm's transnationality are the percentages of foreign sales in the total turnover, of foreign assets in total assets and of foreign employees in total employees. The three percentages combined are used as the index of transnationality of a firm. In 1996, the respective figures for Sinochem are foreign assets $3.2016 billion, total assets $6.1668 billion; foreign sales $7.9656 billion, total sales $17.955 billion; and foreign employees 828, total employees 6,466 (UNCTAD 1999: 48).

8 For example, Sinochem International Engineering and Trade Co. Ltd, established in 1993, dispatched over 600 persons to Japan, Singapore, Korea and Spain in labour services from 1994 to 1996. The total turnover in 1996 reached $13 million (see Sinochem 1997: 17).

9   Zhan's study pointed out that, in 1994, Sinochem's foreign assets were just $1.915 billion (Zhan 1995: 84).

10 Detailed discussion of Sinochem's most recent efforts at conglomeration follows later in this chapter.

11 For details of Sinochem's subsidiaries and their geographical distribution in 2000, see Figure 6.7.

12 The only exception is the small-scale border trade already approved by the central government.

13 For a detailed discussion of China's pre-reform trade system, see Lardy (1992: 16–36) and World Bank (1988: 18–24).

14 For a detailed discussion of the beginning of China's export of crude oil, see Shen *et al.* (1992: vol. II, 110–13).

15 The representative office of the China Import and Export Corporation was established in July 1953 in East Berlin.

16 Lardy (1992), Naughton (1995) and Shirk (1993) provide essential reading for the understanding of China's economic reforms and the reform of trade regimes.

17 By the end of 1988, the total number of representative offices and trade subsidiaries that Chinese firms had established abroad reached 560, with 449 trading companies and 111 representative offices in 53 countries.

18 For more detailed arguments, see Jones (1998).

19 The exceptions were those defined by the government as 'mass commodities of vital strategic importance to the national economy and people's livelihood'.

20 China's exports of 'mineral fuels and related materials' amounted to $6.062 billion in 1984, 24.8 per cent of China's total exports, and $7.334 billion in 1985, 28.3 per cent of China's total exports. These exports dropped sharply to $3.582 billion (13.3 per cent of the total) in 1986 (*China Statistical Yearbook* 1985–87).

21 The only exception was 1995 when it reached $9.583 billion with imports alone standing at $6.441 billion and imports of chemical fertiliser at $3.44 billion. The figures here are from Sinochem (1995: 82) and Sinochem (1996, 1997). The 1999 figures are $7.702 billion with $1.563 billion in exports and 6.139 billion in imports (www.sinochem.com).

22 This translation is from Susan Shirk. For further discussion by Shirk on the reform of China's foreign economic policies, see Shirk (1994: 34–54).

23 For more discussion on China's enterprise reforms, see Gao (1996: 69–98) and Naughton (1995: 99–109).

24 The italics are my own.

25 From my interviews with Sinochem executives, two factors seem to be decisive for the success and failure of these two enterprises. First, Sinochem did not have any expertise in managing the production facilities of an oil refinery. The problem is less severe with regard to Sinochem's management of the Florida-based fertiliser plant. Second, and I think more importantly, while the fertiliser produced by Sinochem's subsidiary USAC had a ready and almost insatiable market in China, oil products from the refinery had to compete on the world market.

26 The other two are Sinochem Oil (London) Ltd and Sinochem Oil (Hong Kong) Ltd (Sinochem 1997: 29).

27 In my interviews with Sinochem, however, it was emphatically pointed out that their futures trading is engaged to hedge, not to speculate.

28 We need to heed a note of caution here. The definition of so-called 'international operations' in Sinochem's annual report is rather ambiguous. By 1999, a new way of accounting seems to have settled in. Instead of dividing the total turnover into imports, exports, domestic sales and international operations, it is now divided into imports, exports, domestic sales, entrepôt trade and others (www.sinochem.com).

29 US Agri-Chemicals Company also had a very successful year in 1995. It earned $30 million US on a turnover of $1.074 billion. In the same year, USAC invested in a MAP (fertilizer) plant with an annual capacity of 300,000 tons in order to maximise profitability.

30 As early as 1991, Sinochem's Corporate Strategy Study Group had already emphasised that Sinochem's investments should concentrate on domestic manufacturing sectors to realise vertical integration (see Sinochem Corporate Strategy Study Group 1991: 282).

31 On 21 December 1999, however, Sinochem International was floated on the Shanghai Stock Exchange, with the issue of 120 million A-shares. Sinochem calls it 'a breakthrough in capital operation' (www.sinochem.com/b-jingying.html).

32 The most important part of the restructuring was that FOTIC handed over its business concerning foreign government loans to the China Export and Import Bank.

33 For further details of Shougang's merger operations, see Nolan (1996: 10–12).

34 This is a new oil and gas exploration company established in January 1997 to commercialise the activities of oil bureaus and research institutes under the Ministry of Geology and Mineral Resources. It was established after years of battling with opposition from existing oil companies. It is to engage in both onshore and offshore exploration for oil and gas (*Financial Times*, 27 January 1997).

35 An example often boasted about by Sinochem of its own investment in such a project is its investment in Dalian West Pacific Petrochemical Co. Ltd Sinochem's investment in the Pacific Oil Refinery, as discussed earlier, was largely a failure.

36 Lin further argued that as China's financial system and banking system are undergoing their own reform and transformation, the requisite conditions for trading conglomerates to play an essential role in finance, as has happened in Japan and Korea, are yet to emerge. By the same token, government support for Sinochem's pilot project in enhancing its role in finance has its limitations. He also acknowledged that formidable systemic constraints severely limit the effectiveness of the government policy in support of Sinochem's pilot project for conglomeration. Further, the limited policy support is not clearly spelt out. Clearly, Sinochem by itself would not be able to break free from these systemic constraints.

37 In 2000, Sinochem's exports only accounted for 9.58 per cent of its total turnover. Export of crude oil was valued at only $380 million, 22 per cent of its total exports, but only 2.1 per cent of its total turnover (Sinochem 2001).

7   Shougang: Going Transnational

1   As mentioned in the previous chapter, CNPC has recently embarked on large-scale investment overseas. But it is in the extractive rather than the manufacturing industry.

2   For a broad and detailed discussion of Shougang in China's economic reforms, see Nolan (1996, 1998) and also Steinfeld (1998).

3   Unless otherwise indicated, the following historical profile of Shougang has been drawn from Nolan (1996, 1998), Kang *et al.* (1996: chapter 9), Steinfeld (1998: chapter 6), Shirk (1993) and Fewsmith (1994).

4   This date is given by Shougang researchers. Based on Gardner Clark's research, Nolan, however, writes that 'the furnace did not go into operation until 1936'. Shougang researchers also provide different explanations (from Nolan's) as to why the Shijingshan Iron Factory did not go into production between 1922 and 1938. In their words, this was due to 'lack of funds, the Chinese civil war and the Japanese occupation of Beijing after July 1937'. Nolan believes that 'this was due to the decline of iron prices after World War I' (Nolan 1998: 21, Kang *et al.* 1996: 115).

5   Nolan uses the expression adopted from the Chinese, 'the museum of metallurgical history', to describe Shougang's production facilities in 1978. He further noted that 'Two generators manufactured by Siemens in the 1920s were still in use. Siemens offered to replace them with new ones free of charge because they wanted to use the old ones to advertise the company's sixty years' quality production' and that 'Some boilers and steam turbines, which had been imported in 1918, when the company was first established, were still in use' (Nolan 1998: 48).

6   While Steinfeld pointed out specifically that Magang (Maanshan Iron and Steel Corporation) was offered the same contract but did not take it up, Nolan noted 'a few' state-owned enterprises in other industries, too, were offered a similar contract.

7   Steinfeld (1998) and Nolan (1996: 10–17) both noted instances of such friction. Nolan further noted that the state continued to coordinate and control Shougang's input and output and its expansion as well as management appointment. In Nolan's words, Shougang only enjoyed 'autonomy within constraints' (Nolan 1998: 33–43).

8   The rest, that is, the other 40 per cent of profit retained, is supposed to be used to pay for bonuses (20 per cent) and for welfare (20 per cent), such as housing, for Shougang's employees. This is the so-called 6:2:2 formula.

9   Nolan pointed out, however, that the actual annual rate increase of Shougang's total handovers to the government, including profits and various taxes, amounted in fact to 13 per cent (Nolan 1998: 27).

10   Such a claim was mostly spread by the media, especially after the collapse of the Shougang experiment, Nolan believes (1998: 25). Both Nolan and Steinfeld tried strenuously to counter this view.

11   Wan Li's relationship with Zhou Guanwu can be traced back not only to the 1950s when Wan was the deputy mayor of Beijing, but further back to the 1930s and 1940s when Zhou was a county military commander in the Jiluyu (Hebei–Shandong–Henan) area controlled by the CCP, where Wan Li was one of the senior leaders.

12 For example, during one of Wan Li's visits to Shougang in 1980, he asked explicitly 'Do we have a credible approach to enterprise reform?' (Interviews).

13 Shougang's proposal, which was submitted to the Party Leading Group of the Ministry of Metallurgy, was also copied to Deng, Hu and Zhao. In the proposed plan, Shougang was to increase its industrial output fourfold in value terms by 1995. To realise this, Shougang proposed to raise capital itself to build a new iron and steel complex. At the same time, it also asked to continue its profit contract as originally approved until 1995 (Hao Zhen *et al.* 1992: vol. 1, 288–9). Hu endorsed this plan with his comments: 'I think this is a very good thing. I would like to see it actively carried out as soon as possible.'

14 Italics my own. Shougang's own chronology recorded serious controversies in 1983 and 1984 surrounding Shougang's retention of profits, at least one of which was directly generated from the Ministry of Finance. In both cases, Shougang had to reach the top leadership to explain its case and to dispel the allegations (Hao Zhen *et al.* 1992: vol. 1, 285, 289).

15 Since the 1990s, this top-down process has also aimed at maximising the size of China's large conglomerates so as to enhance their competitive edge on the world market.

16 A more recent example of such an administrative merger in China's iron and steel industry is the merger between Shanghai Baogang (Baoshan Iron and Steel, the newest iron and steel complex with the most advanced technology built in the 1980s) with Shanghai Metallurgical Holdings (see *Financial Times*, 25 November 1997).

17 They were labelled as 'burdens that cannot be cast away, holes that cannot be filled, rusty locks that cannot be unlocked'. In the first half of 1988, their operational loss was 44.88 million yuan and in the second half more than 60 million yuan.

18 Altogether 33 large enterprises were merged with Shougang, among which were the Kaifeng Combine Harvester Plant, the Jinzhou Electronic Computer Plant and the Zhenjiang Ship Building Company (Nolan 1996: 13).

19 Indeed, one of the problems that Shougang faced in its earlier reform efforts was that it had to deal with both the local government of Beijing and the Ministry of Metallurgy of the central government.

20 According to Nolan, that capacity increased to 2.4 million tons by the end of 1994.

21 According to conventional theories, the internationalisation process is a dynamic process as well as an incremental process: that is, from low involvement to high involvement in foreign markets. This relates to different stages through which a company may pass as it develops in foreign markets, normally beginning with indirect/*ad hoc* exporting leading to active exporting and/or licensing, joint equity investment in foreign manufacturing and full-scale multinational marketing and production. As involvement in foreign markets and risks are high in the case of FDI, firms generally will only engage in this process after acquiring knowledge of the foreign market through the first and second stages (Buckley and Tseng 1997: 3).

22 Nolan's paper has mistakenly put it as 1888.

23   In addition to the examples of export of technology by Shougang mentioned below, Nolan also noted that 'A number of patent technologies [of Shougang], such as bell tops for blast furnaces, top burning hot air induction stoves and pulverised coal injection furnaces, have been transferred to some developed countries, including the United States, Japan, Britain and Luxembourg' (Nolan 1996: 41).

24   SGNEC started full operations in 1994. In 1995, its output of integrated circuits accounted for 10 per cent of the national total, while its sales, which amounted to 900 million chips, represented 20 per cent of China's total sales volume of the year (*Beijing Review*, 18–24 March 1996: 30).

25   In Chinese, Deng's tour was described as *nan xun*. While *nan* means South, *xun* is largely reserved for describing an emperor's inspection tour in Chinese history, and more recently Mao's tour of provinces in the 1950s and the 1960s.

26   Zhao Suisheng (1993) provides an excellent detailed analysis of political manoeuvring by Deng. The broad summary in this paragraph is largely extracted from his study.

27   As Zhao noted, as early as 12 March 1992, *Renmin Ribao* published a communiqué of an Enlarged Politburo Plenary Session convened in Beijing on 9–10 March, which called for 'the necessity' to uphold 'one center' of economic development, and for accelerating 'the pace of reform and opening up to the outside world' (Zhao 1993: 752).

28   Not only were very few journalists allowed to follow Deng's southern tour in January and February 1992, but Deng's visits to local enterprises, and more importantly his speeches, were not reported in the national press until after March 1992.

29   Nolan argued that 'Zhou Guanwu was an exceptional powerful leader, capable of deep strategic thinking and possessed of a high level of motivational and organisational skills'. He did not comment, though, on the impact of such a personality on Shougang's aggressive investment overseas (Nolan 1998: 32).

30   Shougang also started some reckless domestic investment projects. One of the most ambitious, but also disastrous, is Qilu Steel. Since Shougang's domestic investment projects are not the focal point for this investigation, they are not going to be discussed in any detail. For further details of Qilu Steel, see Nolan (1998).

31   The *Financial Times* reported that Shougang bought the plant 'for an undisclosed sum' (11 November 1992). As reported by both Xinhua and Reuters, the purpose of Shougang's purchase of the Californian steel plant was to dismantle the whole plant and ship it back to China to build one of Shougang's own mills in Shandong. Shougang was to send 300 workers to dismantle the plant, which would take two years to finish. Shougang's purchase also included design and technology (*Reuters*, 3 November 1992 and 7 November 1992).

32   The *Financial Times* described Li Ka-shing's role vividly in retrospect: 'in 1992, Mr. Li had acted as midwife to Shougang's entry into Hong Kong when he helped the mainland steel maker secure control of Tung Wing Steel' (*Financial Times*, 21 February 1995).

33   The three joint ventures are, respectively, Beijing Shougang-Posheng Strip Steel Co. Ltd, Beijing Shougang-Liwoh Bar Steel Co. Ltd and Beijing Shougang-Gitane Alloy Materials Co. Ltd.

34   The acquisition activities of Shougang in Hong Kong are described in detail in the Shougang Concord International Enterprises annual report of 1993 as follows: 'In order to develop and diversify its existing business and to expand its product mix, the Company has made a series of acquisitions. In July 1993, the Company also acquired a controlling interest in Santa Manufacturing Limited. The acquisitions of Firstlevel and Santa were financed by way of a rights issue amounting to approximately HK$1928 million. In November 1993, the Company acquired a controlling interest in Eastern Century Holdings Limited. The Company also established a transportation and shipping division in November 1993. After the completion of the above acquisitions and establishment, the activities of the Company are now diversified into the following business sectors: namely trading in metal and construction materials; manufacture and sale of steel products; manufacture and sale of electronic products; – trading in ferrous and non-ferrous metals; transportation and shipping' (Shougang Concord International Enterprises 1993: 6–7).

35   The estimate of Shougang's fixed assets in Hong Kong here seems to be an exaggeration. Most other estimates put Shougang's fixed assets towards the end of 1994 at HK$2 billion, just half of what was claimed in the *China Daily Business Weekly*. The estimate of Shougang's controlling assets here, however, agrees largely with other estimates, which are around HK$10–12 billion.

36   The ranking is based on the sales figure for 1994. The list does not include banks and finance houses in Hong Kong.

37   The other figure is $7 million (see Wang and Tang 1995: 41).

38   China's import of iron ore from Australia, for example, increased from A$216 million in 1990–91 to an estimated A$470 million in 1993 (*Financial Times*, 8 February 1995).

39   Domestic production of iron ore in the same period also increased, but at a slower pace, from 167.7 million tons to 224.85 million tons (Wang and Tang 1995: 40).

40   One study in Australia forecasts that 'China will need to import 90 million tons of iron ore by 2005'.

41   In all likelihood, these visits were made in haste. One of the criticisms was indeed that Shougang rushed into the bid without adequate knowledge and careful assessment of the value of the Peruvian company.

42   Zhou Beifang was eventually convicted on charges of corruption and sentenced to death, which was later commuted to life imprisonment.

43   When the scandal besetting Shougang broke in February 1995, the new Chairman of Shougang, Bi Qun, who was also Vice-Minister of the Ministry of Metallurgical Industry, hastened to go out of his way to defend Shougang's transnational operations. In an unusual report carried in the *China Daily* on 21 February 1995, Bi tried to assure the world through Xinhua that, first, all subsidiaries of Shougang listed on the Hong Kong Stock Exchange had been approved by the relevant government departments. The implications of this affirmation are that the so-called 'back-door' listings and the subsequent

injection of assets from the parent firm were in full compliance with the pre-vailing laws and regulations of both the PRC and Hong Kong at the time. Second, Shougang would continue to strive to become a transnational company. Naturally, Shougang would further expand its Hong Kong busi-ness and fulfil all contracts signed. It would try to increase its export earn-ings to $1 billion in 1995. And it would further strengthen its management of the Shougang–Peru Mining Corporation.

44 For example, in 1996, the total turnover of Shougang Concord International Enterprises was HK$5.7 billion, which represented a 22 per cent decrease from 1995. The operating profit before exceptional items was HK$128.4 million as compared to HK$341.8 million (see Shougang Concord Interna-tional Enterprises, 1996).

45 It must be noted that the growth of Shougang's total assets, foreign assets, total sales and foreign sales stagnated in 1997. In comparison, the 1998 figures are, respectively, $1,582.6 million (foreign assets), $6,630 million (total assets), $4,385.3 million (total sales), and $1,032.7 million (foreign sales). The report of 1999 did not give the number of Shougang's foreign employees. But in 1996, only 1,623 Shougang employees out of its total of 221,961 were employed overseas (UNCTAD 1999: 48–9).

8   Conclusion

1 Kenichi Ohmae predicts more recently, however, that 'over the next decade, Chinese companies will develop their own global brands for their best goods – appliances, electronics, processed foods, possibly automobiles, and perhaps new technological innovations in energy or materials' (*Toronto Star*, 7 July 2002).

2 Elsewhere, Dunning and Narula observed 'some shifts in the rationale for FDI'. In particular, 'some strategic asset acquiring FDI implies that firms may engage in outward FDI from a position of weakness' (Dunning and Narula 1996: 14–15).

3 Other 'primary Third World investors' identified by Dunning and others include the four Asian tiger economies, Hong Kong, Korea, Taiwan and Singapore, as well as some newly industrialising countries (NICs) in Latin America such as Brazil and Argentina. Dunning *et al.* (1998) further identi-fied the four Asian tigers and China as 'primary second wave Third World investors' in the 1990s. In 1998, for example, the total of outward FDI stocks from these five economies is $284.064 billion, accounting for 72.7 per cent of the developing countries' total!

4 This particular estimate is based on Dunning *et al.* (1998). Other estimates differ. See UNCTAD 2000.

5 In terms of value, India's outward FDI stocks in fact increased from $130 million to $601 million, while those of Argentina contracted from $990 million to $960 million in the same period (Dunning *et al.* 1998: 261).

6 The respective figures of the outward FDI stocks for those economies are: Hong Kong $154.86 billion, Singapore $47.63 billion, Taiwan $38 billion, Korea $21.51 billion and Malaysia $14.65 billion. See *World Investment Report*

UNCTAD (2000: 497–8). The figure for China's outward FDI here obviously does not include all of China's investment stocks in Hong Kong.

7   China's share in the developing countries' total, though, dropped to around 5.65 per cent (*World Investment Report 1999*: 495–7). This is not because outward FDI from China has declined. On the contrary, as is clear from the above statistics, it almost doubled between 1993 and 1998. It means that some other developing countries increased their FDI outflow even faster than China. It may also be attributable to statistical discrepancies. For example, whereas Dunning and others put the total of outward FDI of developing countries in 1980 at $4.8 billion, according to recent UNCTAD figures it was $15.40 billion (UNCTAD 1999: 379).

Bibliography

Internet sites and online services

www.adb.org
www.asia.cnn.com
www.chinabusiness.net
www.chinabusiness.net/citicdev/overseas.html
www.citic.com
www.citic.com.au
www.citicpacific.com
www.cosco.com.cn
www.dch.com.hk
www.dp.cei.gov.cn
www.enr.com/dbase
www.fortune.com
www.icbcasia.com
www.moftec.gov.com.cn
www.news.sohu.com
www.shougang.com
www.sinochem.com
www.unctad.org
www.worldbank.org
www.worldsteel.org
Reuters Business Briefing
Xinhua News Agency

Newspapers and periodicals

Asia Week
Asian Wall Street Journal
Beijing Review
Business Week
China Daily
Far Eastern Economic Review
Financial Times
Gaige (Reform)

Guanli Shijie (Management World)
Guoji Jingji Hezuo (International Economic Cooperation)
Guoji Jingrong Yanjiu (Studies of International Finance)
Guoji Maoyi (Intertrade)
Guojihua Jingying Zhanlue Yanjiu (Studies of Strategies for Internationalisation)
Jingji Ribao (Economic Daily)
Jingji Yanjie (Studies of Economics)
Newsweek
Shijie Jingji Wenti (Essays on the World Economy)
South China Morning Post
Renmin Ribao (RMRB) (People's Daily)
Wall Street Journal
Yatai Jingji (Asia-Pacific Economies)
Zhongguo Waizi (Foreign Investment in China)

Books and articles

Afriyie, Kofi (1998) 'Foreign Direct Investment in China's Emerging Market Economy', in John H. Dunning (ed.), *Globalization, Trade and Foreign Direct Investment* (Amsterdam: Elsevier) pp. 217–36.

Anastassopoulos, Jean-Pierre *et al.* (1987) *State-Owned Multinationals* (translated by Velarie Katzaros) (Chichester: John Wiley & Sons).

Andersen, Otto (1993) 'On the Internationalisation Process of Firms: A Critical Analysis', *Journal of International Business Studies*, 2, 209–31.

Asian Development Bank (ADB) (2002), *Annual Report 2002* (www.adb.org/Documents/Reports/Annual Report/2001/default.asp).

Bank of China (1995) *Annual Report*.

Barnet, Richard J. and Ronald E. Muller (1974) *Global Reach: The Power of the Multinational Corporations* (New York: Simon & Schuster).

Barnett, A. Doak (1981) *China's Economy in Global Perspective* (Washington, DC: Brookings Institution).

Bartke, Wolfgang (1989) *The Economic Aid of the PR China to Developing and Socialist Countries*, 2nd rev. edn (München/New York: K.G. Saur).

Bell, Michael W. *et al.* (1993) *China at the Threshold of a Market Economy* (Washington, DC: International Monetary Fund).

Bergsten, Fred (1999) 'Preface', in Daniel Rosen, *Behind the Open Door: Foreign Enterprises in the Chinese Marketplace* (Washington, DC: Institute for International Economics) pp. xi–xiii.

Bergsten, Fred C., Thomas Horst and Theodore H. Moran (1978) *American Multinationals and American Interests* (Washington, DC: Brookings Institution).

Bickford, Thomas J. (1994) 'The Chinese Military and Its Business Operations: The PLA as Entrepreneur', *Asian Survey*, 34(5), 460–74.

Bodinger, Pamela (1991) 'Help China Prosper: Interview with Rong Yiren', *China Business Review*, November–December, 42–3.

Brahm, Laurence (1996a) *Red Capital: Hong Kong '97: China Money Takes Centre Stage* (Hong Kong: NAGA Publishers).

Brahm, Laurence (1996b) *China as No. 1: The New Superpower Takes the Centre Stage* (Singapore: Butterworth-Heinemann Asia).

Brahm, Laurence (ed.) (2001) *China's Century: The Awakening of the Next Economic Superpower* (Singapore: John Wiley & Sons).

Buckley, Peter J. and Mark Casson (eds) (1992) *Multinational Enterprises in the World Economy: Essays in Honour of John Dunning* (Aldershot: Edward Elgar).

Buckley, Peter J. and Pervez N. Ghauri (eds) (1993) *The Internationalization of the Firm: A Reader* (London: Academic).

Buckley, Peter J. and C. S. Tseng (1997) 'Foreign Direct Investment by PRC Enterprises – The Success and Failure of First-time Investors Abroad: A Comparison with Their Counterparts in the UK', paper prepared for the Conference and APJM secial isue on 'The Asian MNC', mimeo.

Bulatov, Alexander S. (1998) 'Russian Direct Investment Abroad: Main Motivations in the Post-Soviet Period', *Transnational Corporations*, 7(1), 69–82.

Cai, G. Kevin (1999) 'Outward Foreign Direct Investment: A Novel Dimension of China's Integration into the Regional and Global Economy', *China Quarterly*, 160 (December), 857–80.

Cao Jianming (1992) 'On Developing Overseas Chinese Enterprises: Training the Enterprises to Think and Operate Globally and to Become More Competitive', *Intertrade* (August), 17–19.

Casson, Mark (1998) 'The Economic Analysis of Multinational Trading Companies', in Geoffrey Jones (ed.), *The Multinational Traders* (London/New York: Routledge) pp. 22–47.

Chai, Joseph (1997) *China: Transition to a Market Economy* (Oxford: Clarendon Press/New York: Oxford University Press).

Chai, Joseph, Y. Y. Kueh and Clement A. Tisdell (eds) (1997) *China and the Asian Pacific Economy*, Economice Conference Monograph No. 3 (Brisbane: Department of Economics, University of Queenland).

Chan, Anthony (1996) *Li Ka-shing: Hong Kong's Elusive Billionaire* (Hong Kong: Oxford University Press).

Chan, Hing Lin (1995) 'Chinese Investment in Hong Kong: Issues and Problems', *Asian Survey*, 35(10), 941–54.

Chen Dongqi and Qin Hai (1997) 'Zhongguo Ziben Shichang de Jianjinshi Guojihua Fenxi' [Gradualism in the Internationalisation of China's Capital Markets], *Jingji Yanjiu* (Studies of Economics), 7, 12–24.

Chen Ronghui (1997) *Qiye Kuaguo Jingying Lun* [A Study of Transnational Operations of Firms] (Shanghai: China Textile University Press).

Chen Yongcai (1992) Zhongguo Qiye Kuaguo Jingying de Shijian yu Zhengce [Transnational Operations of Chinese Firms: Practice and Policies], *Guanli Shijie* (Management World), 1, 49–52.

Chen Yinjang (1988) 'Transnational Corparations as World Development: An Evolutionary View', in Teng Weizao and N. T. Wang (eds), *Transnational Corporations as China's, Open Door Policy* (Lexington, Mass.: Lexington Books), 33–46.

Chen, Edward K. Y. (1986) 'Multinationals from Hong Kong', in Sanjaya Lall (ed.), *The New Multinationals: The Spread of Third World Enterprises* (Chichester/New York: John Wiley & Sons) pp. 88–136.

Chow, Gregory (2000) 'China's Economic Reform and Policies at the Beginning of the Twenty-first Century', *China Economic Review*, 11, 427–31.

Christoffersen, Gaye (1998) *China's Intentions for Russian and Central Asian Oil and Gas*, NBA Analysis 9:2 (Seattle, Wash.: National Bureau of Asian Research).

CITIC (China International Trust and Investment Corporation) (1995) *Corporate Profile* (no publishing details).

CITIC (China International Trust and Investment Corporation) (1995–2001) *Annual Report* (Beijing: CITIC).

CITIC Australia (1995a) *CITIC Australia: A Profile* (Melbourne: CITIC Australia).

CITIC Australia (1995b) 'Jianshe Xiandaihua de Haiwai Daxing Qiye Jituan' [Building up a Modernized Group Company Overseas], in Wen Jinping (ed), *Wo yu Zhongxin, 1979–1994* [CITIC and I 1979–1994] (Beijing: CITIC Press) pp. 236–47.

CITIC Pacific (1993–9) *Annual Report* (Hong Kong: CITIC Pacific).

Cox, Robert (1987) *Production, Power and World Order: Social Forces in the Making of History*, (New York: Columbia University Press).

Davis, Ken (1996) *Hong Kong after 1997* (London: The Economist Intelligence Unit).

de Bettignies, Henri-Claude (ed.) (1996) *Business Transformation in China* (London: International Thompson Business Press).

De Trenck, Charles *et al.* (1998) *Red Chips* (Hong Kong: Asia 2000).

Deng Hongguo (ed.) (1996) *Zhongguo Jingrong Shichang Fazhan yu Guojihua* [Development and Internationalisation of China's Financial Markets] (Beijing: China Finance Press).

Deng Xiaoping (1987) *Selected Works of Deng Xiaoping, vol. II* (Beijing: Foreign Languages Press).

Di Weiping (1997), 'Zhongguo Jingrong Duiwai Kaifang Shiqi Nian' [Seventeen Years of the Opening of China's Financial Sector], *Guoji Jingrong Yanjiu* (Studies of International Finance), 1, 11–15.

Dicken, Peter (1992) *Global Shift: The Internationalization of Economic Activity*, 2nd edn (New York: Guilford Press).

Ding, X. L. (2000) 'Informal Privatization Through Internationalization: The Rise of Nomenklatura Capitalism in China's Offshore Businesses', *British Journal of Political Science*, 30, 121–46.

Dobson, Wendy and Siow Yue Chia (eds) (1997) *Multinationals and East Asian Integration* (Ottawo: International Development Research Centre).

Duan Yuncheng (1995) *Zhongguo Qiye Kuaguo Jingying yu Zhanlue* [Transnational Operations of the Chinese Enterprieses and Their Strategies] (Beijing: China Development Press).

Dunning, John and Rajneesh Narula (1996) 'The Investment Development Path Revisited: Some Emerging Issues', in John H. Dunning and Rajneesh Narula (eds), *Foreign Direct Investment and Governments: Catalysts for Economic Restructuring* (London: Routledge) pp. 1–41.

Dunning, John H. (1981) 'Explaining Outward Direct Investment of Developing Countries: In Support of the Eclectic Theory of International Production', in Krishna Kumar and Maxwell McLeod (eds), *Multinationals from Developing Countries* (Lexington, Mass.: Lexington Books).

Dunning, John H. (1983) 'Changes in the Level and Structure of International Production: The Last One Hundred Years', in Mark Casson (ed.), *The Growth of International Business* (London: George Allen & Unwin) pp. 84–139.

Dunning, John H. (1986) 'The Investment Development Cycle Revisited', in *Weltwirtschaftliches Archiv*, 122(4), 667–76.

Dunning, John H. (1992) 'The Competitive Advantage of Countries and the Activities of Transnational Corporations', *Transnational Corporation*, 1(1), 135–68.

Dunning, John H. (1993) *Multinational Enterprises and the Global Economy* (New York: Addison-Wesley).

Dunning, John H. *et al.* (1998) 'Third World Multinationals Revisited: New Developments and Theoretical Implications', in John H. Dunning (ed.), *Globalization, Trade and Foreign Direct Investment* (Amsterdam: Elsevier) pp. 255–86.

EIU (1997) *Country Report, China* (London: The Economist Intelligence Unit, 2nd Quarter).

EIU (1999) *Country Report, China* (London: The Economist Intelligence Unit, 1st Quarter).

Emmott, Bill (1992) *Japan's Global Reach: The Influences, Strategies and Weaknesses of Japan's Multinational Companies* (London: Century).

ESCAP/UNCTC Joint Unit on Translational Corporations (1985) *Transnational Corporations from Developing Asian Economies* (Bangkok: United Nations).

ESCAP/UNCTC Joint Unit on Translational Corporations (1988) *Transnational Corporations from Developing Asian Economies: Host Country Perspectives* (Bangkok: United Nations).

Falk, Richard (1992) 'American Hegemony and the Japanese Challenge', in Glen D. Hook and Michael A. Weiner (eds), *The Internationalization of Japan* (London/New York: Routledge): 32–60.

Fan Qimao and Peter Nolan (eds) (1994) *China's Economic Reforms: The Costs and Benefits of Incrementalism* (New York: St Martin's Press).

Fang Hanting (1997) 'Zhongguo Waizi Jingrong Jigou Fenxi' [Foreign Financial Institutions in China], *Guanli Shijie* (Management World), 1, 67–77.

Fewsmith, Joseph (1994) *Dilemmas of Reform in China: Political Conflict and Economic Debate* (Armonk, NY: M. E. Sharpe).

Fieldhouse, D. K. (1986) 'The Multinational: A Critique of a Concept', in Alice Teichova *et al.* (eds), *Multinational Enterprise in Historical Perspective* (Cambridge: Cambridge University Press) pp. 9–29.

Folkerts-Landau, David *et al.* (1995) *International Capital markets: Developments, Prospects and Policy Issues* (Washington, DC: International Monetary Fund).

Frieden, Jeffry A. and Ronald Rogowski (1996) 'The Impact of the International Economy on National Policies: An Analytical Overview', in Robert O. Keohane and Helen Y. Milner (eds), *Internationalization and Domestic Politics* (Cambridge/New York: Cambridge University Press) pp. 25–47.

Fu Yong (1994a) 'Sinochem's Global Organisational Strategy', *Intertrade*, (April), 4–7.

Fu Yong (1994b) 'Zhonghua Quanqiu Zuzhi Zhanlue' [Sinochem's Global Strategy], *Guohihua Jingying Yanjiu* [Studies of Strategies for Internationalisation], 22, 1–5.

Fujita, Masataka *et al.* (1997) 'European Union Direct Investment in Developing Asia and Developing Asian Direct Investment in the European Union', *Transnational Corporations*, 6(1), 83–100.

Fukasaku, Kiichiro, Yu Ma and Qiumei Yang (1999) *China's Unfinished Open-Economy Reforms: Liberalisation of Services*, Technical Paper 147 (Paris: OECD Development Centre).

Fung, K. C. (1996) 'Mainland Chinese Investment in Hong Kong: How much, Why and So What?, *Journal of Asian Business*, 12(2), 21–39.

Fung, K. C. (1997) *Trade and Investment: Mainland China, Hong Kong and Taiwan* (Hong Kong: City University of Hong Kong Press).

Gao Shangquan (1992) 'Guanyu Kuaguo Jingying de Sikao' [Reflections on Transnational Operations of Chinese Firms], *Guanli Shijie* (Management World), 1, 38–40.

Gao Shangquan (1996) *China's Economic Reform* (London: Macmillan).

Gao Tianjie (1994) 'Zou Zonghe Shangshe Zhi Lu, Chuangjian Zhongguo Tece de Kuaguo Gongsi' [Establish Multinational Corporations with Chinese Characteristics by Following the Example of Sogo Shosha], *Guojihua Jingying Zhanlue Yanjiu* (Studies of Strategies for Internationalisation), 26, 7–10.

Garnaut, Ross and Liu Guoguang (eds) (1992) *Economic Reform and Internationalisation: China and the Pacific Region* (St Leonards, NSW: Allen & Unwin in association with the Pacific Trade and Development Conference Secretariat, the Australian National University).

Gilley, Bruce (1995) 'Great Leap Southward', *Far Eastern Economic Review* (23 November), 60–2.

Girardin, Eric (1997) *Banking Sector Reform and Credit Control in China* (Paris: Organisation for Economic Cooperation and Development).

Goldstein, M. *et al.* (1992) *International Capital Markets: Developments, Prospects and Policy Issues* (Washington, DC: International Monetary Fund).

Goodman, David S. G. and Gerald Segal (eds) (1994) *China Deconstructs: Politics, Trade and Regionalism* (London/New York: Routledge).

Guex, Sebastien (1998) 'The Development of Swiss Trading Companies in the Twentieth Century', in Geoffrey Jones (ed.), *The Multinational Traders* (London/New York: Routledge) pp. 150–72.

Gunter, F. R. (1996) 'Capital Flight from the People's Republic of China: 1984–1994', *China Economic Review*, 7(1), 77–96.

Haggard, Stephan (1995) *Developing Nations and Politics of Global Integration*, (Washington, DC: Brookings Institution).

Haggard, Stephan and Sylvia Maxfield (1996) 'The Political Economy of Financial Internationalization in the Developing World', *International Organization*, 50(1), 35–68.

Hamilton, Geoffrey (ed.) (1986) *Red Multinationals or Red Herrings? The Activities of Enterprises from Socialist Countries in the West* (London: Pinter).

Hamilton-Hart, Natasha (1999) 'Internationalisation: What Scholars Make of It?' Working Paper 1999/5 (Canberra: Department of International Relations, Australian National University).

Hao Zhen *et al.* (eds) (1992) *Shougang Gaige*, 3 vols [The Reform of Shougang Corporation, 3 vols], (Beijing: Beijing Press).

Harris, Stuart (2001) 'China and the Pursuit of State Interests in a Globalizing World', *Pacifica Review*, 13(1), 15–29.

Hennart, Jean-François (1982) *A Theory of Multinational Enterprise* (Ann Arbor: University of Michigon Press).

Hennart, Jean-François and Georgine M. Kryda (1998) 'Why Do Traders Invest in Manufacturing?', in Geoffrey Jones (ed.), *The Multinational Traders* (London/New York: Routledge) pp. 213–27.

Hertner, Peter and Geoffrey Jones (eds) (1986) *Multinationals: Theory and History* (Aldershot: Gower).

Hong Yuncheng (1995) 'Guoji Ziben Shichang Shang de Kailu Xianfeng' [A Pioneer on the International Capital Market], in Wen Jiping (ed.), *Wo yu Zhongxin, 1979–1994* [CITIC and I, 1979–1994] (Beijing: CITIC Press) pp. 1–10.

Hoogvelt, Ankie, (ed.) (1987) *Multinational Enterprise: An Encyclopedic Dictionary of Concepts and Terms* (London: Macmillan).

Hook, Glen D. and Michael A. Weiner (1992) 'Introduction', in Glen D. Hook and Michael A. Weiner (eds), *The Internationalization of Japan* (London/New York: Routledge).

Hsu, Robert C. (1991) *Economic Theories in China, 1979–1988* (Cambridge/New York: Cambridge University Press).

Hu Shuli *et al.* (2002) 'Wang Jun Jiepan Zhongxin' [Unpacking CITIC: An Interview with Wang Jun] (www.citic.com/wangjuncaifang.htm).

Huang Mei (1994) 'Mr. CITIC and PRC Vice-President', *Beijing Review*, (29 August–4 September), 22–3.

Huang, Yiping and Ronald Duncan (1997) *State Enterprise Reforms in China: A Critical Review of Policy* (Canberra: National Centre for Development Studies, Australian National University).

Institute of Developing Economies (1996) *IDE Spot Survey: Hong Kong 1997 – Society in Transition* (Tokyo: Institute of Developing Economies).

International Monetary Fund (1991) *International Capital Markets: Development and Prospect* (Washington, DC: International Monetary Fund).

International Monetary Fund (1999, 2000, 2001, 2002) *International Financial Statistics Yearbook* (Washington, DC: International Monetary Fund).

Islam, Iyanatu and William Shepherd (eds) (1997) *Current Issues in International Business* (Cheltenham: Edward Elgar).

Jao, Y. C. and C. K. Leung (eds) (1986) *China's Special Economic Zones: Policies, Problems and Prospects* (Hong Kong/New York: Oxford University Press).

Jacobson, Harold and Michael Oksenberg (1990) *China's Participation in the IMF, World Bank and GATT: Towards a Global Economic Order* (Ann Arbor: University of Michigan Press).

Jefferson, Gary H. (1997) 'China's Economic Future: A Discussion Paper', *Journal of Asian Economics*, 8(4), 581–95.

Ji Chongwei (1992) 'Kuaguo Jingying yu Woguo Dazhongxing Qiye Fazhan' [Transnational Operation and the Development of China's Large and Medium-Sized Firms], *Guanli Shijie* (Management World), 5, 85–9.

Ji Honggeng (1987) 'Qiaokeli Daxia de Maibo' [The Pulse of the Chocolate-coloured Mansion], *Remin Ribao* (People's Daily) (5 September).

Ji Honggeng (1995) 'Zai Zhan Hongtu Puxinpian' [Strive for New Achievements and Brighter Prospect], in Wen Jiping (ed.), *Wo yu Zhongxin 1979–1994* [CITIC and I 1979–1994] (Beijing: CITIC Press) pp. 257–63.

Ji Honggeng (1999) *Rong Yiren* [A Biography of Rong Yiren] (Beijing: Central Document Press).

Ji Shi (1994) 'Zonghe Shangshe Shidian Gongzuo Zuotanhui Jiyao' [Executive Summary of a Symposium on the Sogo Sosha Experiment], *Guojihua Jingying Zhanlue Yanjiu* (Studies of Strategies for Internationalisation), 24, 37–40.

Jiang Zemin (1992) 'Accelerating Reform and Opening Up', *Beijing Review*, 26 October–1 November, 9–32.

Jin He (1992) 'China's Foreign Insurance: PICC Forges Ahead with Vigor', *Intertrade* (May), 14–15.

Johanson, Jan and Jan-Erik Vahlne (1977) 'The Internationalization Process of the Firm – A Model of Knowledge Development and Increasing Foreign Market Commitments', *Journal of International Business Studies*, 8(1), 23–32.

Jones, Geoffrey (1986) 'Origins, Management and Performance', in Geoffrey Jones (ed.), *British Multinationals: Origins, Management and Performance* (Aldershot: Gower) pp. 1–23.

Jones, Geoffrey (1998) 'Multinational Trading Companies in History and Theory', in Geoffrey Jones (ed.), *The Multinational Traders* (London/New York: Routledge) pp. 2–15.

Kang Rongping *et al.* (1996) *Zhongguo Qiye de Kuaguo Jingying: Anli Yanjiu, Lilun Tansuo* [Transnational Operations of Chinese Enterprises: Case Studies and Theoretical Exploration] (Beijing: Economic Science Press).

Kato, Shuichi (1992) 'The Internationalization of Japan', in Glen D. Hook and Michael A. Weiner (eds), *The Internationalization of Japan* (London/New York: Routledge) pp. 310–16.

Katz, Jorge and Bernardo Kosacoff (1983) 'Multinationals from Argetina', in Sanjaya Lall (ed.), *The New Multinationals: The Spread of Third World Enterprises* (Chichester/New York: John Wiley & Sons) pp. 137–219.

Keohane, Robert and Helen Milner (eds) (1996) *Internationalization and Domestic Politics* (Cambridge: Cambridge University Press).

Keohane, Robert and Joseph Nye (eds) (1972) *Transnational Relations and World Politics* (Cambridge, Mass.: Harvard University Press).

Khan, Kushi Mohammed (ed.) (1986) *Multinationals of the South: New Actors in the International Economy* (London: Pinter).

Kraar, Louis (1987) 'Rong Yiren: China's Mister Right', *Fortune* (5 January), 109.

Kraar, Louis (1997) 'The Man to Know in Hong Kong', *Fortune* (13 January), 34–40.

Kumar, Krishna and Maxwell McLeod (eds) (1981) *Multinationals from Developing Countries* (Lexington, Mass.: Lexington Books).

Lall, Rajiv B. (1986) *Multinationals from the Third World: Indian Firms Investing Abroad* (Delhi/New York: Oxford University Press).

Lall, Sanjaya (1980) *The Multinational Corporation* (London: Macmillan).

Lall, Sanjaya (1996) 'The Investment Development Path: Some Conclusions', in John Dunning and Rajneesh Narula (eds), *Foreign Direct Investment and Governments: Catalysts for Economic Restructuring* (London: Routledge) pp. 421–41.

Lall, Sanjaya (ed.) (1983) *The New Multinationals: The Spread of Third World Enterprises* (Chichester: West Sussex/New York: John Wiley & Sons).

Lardy, Nicholas (1992) *Foreign Trade and Economic Reform in China, 1978–1990* (Cambridge/New York: Cambridge University Press).

Lardy, Nicholas (1994) *China in the World Economy* (Washington, DC: Institute of International Economics).

Lardy, Nicholas (1995) 'The Role of Foreign Trade and Investment in China's Economic Transformation', *China Quarterly*, 144, 1065–82.

Lardy, Nicholas (1998) *China's Unfinished Economic Rovolution* (Washington, DC: Brookings Institution).

Lardy, Nicholas (2002) *Integrating China into the Global Economy* (Washington, DC: Brookings Institution).

Lecraw, Donald (1992) 'Third World MNEs Once Again: the Case of Indonesia', in Peter J. Buckley and Mark Casson (eds), *Multinational Enterprises in the World Economy: Essays in Honour of John Dunning* (Aldershot: Edward Elgar).

Lecraw, Donald J. (1993) 'Outward Direct Investment by Indonesian Firms: Motivation and Effects', *Journal of International Business Studies*, 3, 589–600.

Lees, Francis A. and K. Thomas Liaw (1996) *Foreign Participation in China's Banking and Securities Markets* (Westport, Conn.: Quorum Books).

Li Cheng (1986) 'China's Foreign and Eurobond Issues', *China Business Review* (January–February).

Li Jianguo (1997) 'Zhongguo de Guoji Zhaijuan Rongzi' [China's International Bond Issues], *Zhongguo Waizi* (Foreign Investment in China), 8, 13–15.

Li Kui-Wai (ed.) (1997) *Financing China Trade and Investment* (Westport, Conn.: Praeger).

Li Lanqing (1992) 'Zhongguo Qiye Kuaguo Jingying Wenti' [Problems in the Transnational Operations of Chinese Firms], *Guanli Shijie* (Management World), 1, 33–37.

Li Rongxia (1996) 'Ongoing Overhaul at Shougang', *Beijing Review* (18–25 December).

Li Yining and Cao Fengqi (1996) *Zhongguo Qiye de Kuaguo Jingying* [Transnational Operations of Chinese Firms] (Beijing: China Planning Press).

Li Yuesheng *et al.* (eds) (1993) *Jinwai Touzi Shiwu Shouce* [A Practical Handbook of Overseas Investment] (Shanghai: Shanghai Far East Press).

Li Zhongping (1997) *Zhongguo Jingrong Guojihua Wenti Yanjiu* [A Study of Financial Internationalisation of China] (Beijing: China Finance and Economics Press).

Lin Congbiao and Jian Zeyuan (1995) 'Zhongzi Gongsi yu Xianggang Jingji' [China-Funded Companies and the Hong Kong Economy], paper delivered at the international conference on 'China's Economic Reforms and Opening', 24 October, mimeo.

Lin Danming (1996) 'Hong Kong's China Invested Companies and Their Reverse Investment in China', in John Child and Yuan Lu (eds), *Management Issues in China: Volume II, International Enterprises* (London: Routledge).

Lin Ye (1995) 'Shiyou Shengchan he Liutong Tizhi Bijiao Yanjiu' [A Comparative Study of Petroleum Production and Distribution Systems], *Guojihua Jingying Zhanlue Yanjiu* (Studies of Strategies of Internationalisation), 4, 1–5.

Lin Ye (1996) *Zhongguo Zonghe Shangshe Lun* [A Study of China's Emerging Sogo Shosha] (Beijing: China Youth Press).

Lin Ye (1997a) 'Zhongguo Zujian Zonghe Shangshe de Ruogan Lilun he Shijian Wenti Tantao' [Establishing Sogo Sosha in China: Theory and Practice], *Guoji Jingji Hezuo* [International Economic Cooperation], 3, 33–8; 4, 39–40.

Lin Ye (1997b) 'Zhongguo Zonghe Shangshe Shidian: Kunnan yu Xuanze' [China's Experiment of Organising Sogo Shosha: Problems and Choices], *Guoji Jingji Hezuo* (International Economic Cooperation), 1, 21–2.

Lin Ye (1997c) 'Zonghe Shangshe yu Waimao' [Sogo Shosha and Foreign Trade], *Guoji Maoyi* (Intertrade), 2, 15–16.

Ling, L. M. H. (1996) 'Hegemony and the Internationalizing State: A Post-

Colonial Analysis of China's Integration into Asian Corporatism', *Review of International Political Economy*, 3(1), 1–26.

Liu Guoguang (ed.) (1984) *Zhongguo Jingji Fazhan Zhanlue Wenti Yanjiu* [Studies of China's Economic Development Strategies] (Shanghai: Shanghai People's Press).

Liu Hongru *et al.* (1998) *Zhongguo Qiye Haiwai Shangshi Huigu yu Zhanwang* [Floating Chinese Enterprises on Foreign Stock Exchanges: Restrospect and Prospect] (Beijing: China Finance and Economics Press).

Liu Jun (ed.) (1994) *Zhongguo Jingji Jingrong Guojihua Wenti* [Studies of China's Economic and Financial Internationalisation] (Beijing: China Finance Press).

Liu Xiaming, Wang Chengang, and Wei Yingqi (2001) 'Causal Links between Foreign Direct Investment and Trade in China', *China Economic Review*, 12, 190–202.

Liu Xiangdong (ed.) (1994) *Dangdai Zhongguo Wai Jingmao Fazhan Zhanlue* [Contemporary China's Strategy for Developing Foreign Trade and Economic Cooperation] (Beijing: World Knowledge Press).

Liu Xiangdong *et al.* (eds) (1993) *Zhongguo Duiwai Jingji Maoyi Zhengce Zhinan* [A Guide to Chinese Policies on Foreign Economic Cooperation and Trade] (Beijing: Economic Management Press).

Liu Yan (1992) *Lun Zhongguo Qiye Guojihua* [On the internationalisations of Chinese Firms], *Guanli Shijie* (Management World), 1, 160–4.

Liu Yan (1997) 'Zhongguo Qiye Haiwai Shangshi Wenti Yanjiu' [A Study of How Chinese Companies Were Floated on the Stock Exchanges Overseas], *Gaige* (Reform), 6, 29–44.

Liu Zhongliang (1994) 'An Effort to Open Up International Markets', *Intertrade* (April), 10–11.

Lloyd, P. J. and Zhang Xiao-guang (eds) (2000) *China in the Global Economy* (Cheltenham: Edward Elgar).

Lu Caihong and Kou Yahui (1997) 'Dui Hongchougu Zican Jingying, Jianguan he Fazhan Fangxiang de Tantao' [Red Chips: Asset Management, Supervision and Future Development], *Gaige* (Reform), 6, 45–52.

Lu Chuanmin and Kang Yongping (1993) 'Shougang: China's Steel Magnate', *Intertrade* (June/July), 32–5.

Lu Jinyong *et al.* (1996) *Haiwai Qiye de Jingying yu Guanli* [Operation and Management of Overseas Enterprises] (Beijing: China Youth Press).

Ma Hong (1994) 'Guanyu Kuaguo Gongsi de Jige Wenti' [Several Comments on Multinational Corporation], in Zhu Ronglin (ed.), *Kuanguo Jingying: Zhongguo Jingji Fazhan Xinde Zengzhang Dian* [Transnational Operations: The New Growth Point of the Chinese Economy] (Shanghai: Shanghai Far East Press).

Ma Hong and Sun Shangqing (1993) *Zhongguo Jingji Xingshi yu Zhanwang, 1992–1993* [China's Economic Situation and Prospect: 1992–1993] (Beijing: China Development Press).

Ma Kai (1994) 'Jiji Wentuo de Fazhan Woguo Zonghe Shangshe' [Develop China's Sogo Shosha Actively and Steadily], *Guojihua Jingying Zhanlue Yanjiu* (Studies of Strategies for Internationalisation), 26 (December), 1–6.

Ma Kefeng (1997) *Rong Shi Jiazu: Hongse Zibenjia* [The Rong Clan: Red Capitalists] (Guangzhou: Guangzhou Press).

MacMillan, Carl H. (1987) *Multinationals from the Second World: Growth of Foreign*

Investment by Soviet and East European Enterprises (London: Macmillan – now Palgrave Macmillan).

Mathieson, Donald J. and Gary J. Schinasi (2000) *International Capital Markets: Developments, Prospects and Key Policy Issues* (Washington, DC: International Monetary Fund).

McCarty, E. and Stanley J. Hille (eds) (1993) *Research on Multinational Business Management and Internationalization of Chinese Enterprises* (Nanjing: Nanjing University Press).

Mehran, Hassanali *et al.* (1996) *Monetary and Exchange System Reforms in China: An Experiment in Gradualism* (Washington, DC: International Monetary Fund).

Milner, Helen V. and Robert O. Keohane (1996) 'Internationalization and Domestic Politics: An Introduction', in Robert O. Keohane and Helen V. Milner (eds), *Internationalization and Domestic Politics* (Cambridge/New York: Cambridge University Press) pp. 3–24.

Modelski, George (ed.) (1972) *Multinational Corporation and World Order* (Beverley Hills, Calif.: Sage Publications).

MOFERT and MOFTEC (1990–2000) *Zhongguo Duiwai Jingji Maoyi Nianjian* [Almanac of China's Foreign Economic Cooperation and Trade] (Beijing: China Foreign Economic Cooperation and Trade Press).

MOFTEC (1997) *Zhongguo Duiwai Jingji Maoyi Baipishu, 1997* [White Paper on China's Foreign Trade and Economic Cooperation, 1997] (Beijing: China Foreign Trade and Economic Cooperation Press).

MOFTEC Research Group (1993) Zonghe Shangshe – Qiye Guojihua, Jituanhua de Shenzhangdian [Sogo Shosha: The Growth Point of Transnationalisation and Corporatisation], *Guojihua Jingying Yanjiu* [Studies of Strategies for Transnationalisation], 19, 4–8.

Moore, Thomas G. (1999) 'China and Globalization', *Asian Perspective*, 23(4), 65–95.

Morrison, E. (1986) 'Borrowing on World Bond Markets', *China Business Review* (January–February), 18–20.

Nakai, Yoshifumi (ed.) (1998) *China's Roadmap as Seen in the 15th Party Congress* (Tokyo: Institute of Developing Economies).

Nambudiri, C. N. S. (1983) *Third World Multinationals: Technology Choice and Employment Generation in Nigeria*, Multinational Enterprises Programme Working Paper Series No. 19 (Geneva: International Labour Office).

Naughton, Barry (1995) *Growing Out of the Plan: Chinese Economic Reform, 1978–1993* (Cambridge/New York: Cambridge University Press).

Naughton, Barry (2000) 'China's Trade Regime at the End of the 1990s: Achievements, Limitations, and Impact on the United States', in Ted Galen Carpenter and James A. Dorn (eds), *China's Future: Constructive Partner or Emerging Threat?* (Washington, DC: Cato Institute) pp. 235–60.

Nolan, Peter (1996) *From State Factory to Modern Corporation? China's Shougang Iron and Steel Corporation under Economic Reform* (Cambridge: Department of Applied Economics, University of Cambridge).

Nolan, Peter (1998) *Indigenous Large Firms in China's Economic Reform: The Case of Shougang Iron and Steel Corporation* (London: Contemporary China Institute, School of Oriental and African Studies, University of London).

Nolan, Peter (2001) *China and the Global Economy: National Champions, Industrial Policy and the Big Business* (Basingstoke: Palgrave Macmillan).

Oborne, Michael (1986) *China's Special Economic Zones* (Paris: Development Centre, Organisation for Economic Cooperation and Development).

Okposin, Samuel Bassey (1999) *The Extent of Singapore's Investment Abroad* (Aldershot: Ashgate).

Organisation for Economic Cooperation and Development (OECD) (1992) *Financing and External Debt of Developing Countries, 1991 Survey* (Paris: Organisation for Economic Cooperation and Development).

Overholt, William (1993) *The Rise of China: How Economic Reform is Creating a New Superpower* (New York: W.W. Norton).

Pang Zhongying (1999) 'Globalization and China: China's Response to the Asian Economic Crisis', *Asian Perspective*, 23(4), 111–31.

Pearce, Robert D. (1993) *The Growth and Evolution of Multinational Enterprises: Patterns of Geographical and Industrial Diversification* (Aldershot: Edward Elgar).

Pei Guifen and Jin Dong (1995) *Kuaguo Gongsi yu Kuakuo Yinghang Jingying Zhanlue* [Corporate Strategies of Transnationals and Multinational Banks] (Beijing: People's Press).

People's Bank of China (1996) *Zhuhua Waizi Jingrong Jigou Minlu* [A Directory of Foreign Financial Institutions Resident in China] (Beijing: China Finance Press).

Perkins, Dwight (1986) *China: Asia's Next Economic Giant?* (Seattle: University of Washington Press).

Perlmutter, H. V. (1969) 'The Tortuous Evolution of the Multinational Corporation', *Columbia Journal of World Business* (January–February), 9–18.

Qiu Xichun (1992) 'The Organization of Foreign Trade Enterprise Groups: A Prerequisite to the Development of the National Economy', *Intertrade* (April), 13–15.

Rafferty, Kevin (1991) 'China's Enigmatic Conglomerate', *Euromoney* (June), 24–7.

Richter, Frank-Jurgen (ed.) (2000), *The Dragon Millennium: Chinese Business in the Coming World Economy* (Westport, Conn.: Quorum Books).

Rosen, Daniel H. (1999) *Behind the Open Door: Foreign Enterprises in the Chinese Marketplace* (Washington, DC: Institute for International Economics).

Ross, Madelyn (1995) 'China's International Economic Behaviour', in Thomas W. Robinson and David Shambaugh (eds), *Chinese Foreign Policy: Theory and Practice* (Oxford: Clarendon Press) pp. 435–52.

Rowley, Chris and Mark Lewis (eds) (1996) *Greater China: Political Economy, Inward Investment and Business Culture* (London: Frank Cass).

Schutte, Helmut (ed.) (1994) *The Global Competitiveness of Asian Firms* (New York: St Martin's Press).

Segal, Gerald (1999) 'Does China Matter?', *Foreign Affairs*, 5, 78: 24–36.

Shang Dewen (1997) 'Zhongguo de Haiwai Touzi yu Xianggang de dui Neidi Touzi' [China's Outward Investment and Hong Kong's Investment in the Mainland], *Yatai Jingji* (The Asia-Pacific Economies), 4, 53–7.

Shang Dewen (ed.) (1994) *Zhongwai Zhumin Qiye Guoji Touzi Anli Fenxi* [An Analysis of International Investment Projects by Chinese and Foreign Firms] (Beijing: Economic Daily Press).

Shen Jueren *et al.* (eds) (1992) *Dangdai Zhongguo Duiwai Maoyi*, 2 vols, [Contemporary China's Foreign Trade] (Beijing: Contemporary China Press).

Shi Guangsheng (1999) 'Great Achievements in Foreign Trade and Economic Cooperation in the Last Fifty Years since the Founding of the People's Republic of China', www.moftec.gov.com.cn.

Shi Lin *et al.* (1989) *Dangdai Zhongguo Duiwai Jingji Hezuo* [Contemporary China's Foreign Economic Cooperation] (Beijing: Contemporary China Press).

Shirk, Susan (1993) *The Political Logic of Economic Reform in China* (Berkeley, Calif.: University of California Press).

Shirk, Susan (1994) *How China Opened its Doors: The Political Success of the PRC's Foreign Trade and Investment Reforms* (Washington, DC: Brookings Institution).

Shirk, Susan (1996) 'Internationalization and China's Economic Reforms', in Robert O. Keohane and Helen V. Milner (eds), *Internationalization and Domestic Politics* (Cambridge/New York: Cambridge University Press) pp. 186–206.

Shougang Concord International Enterprises (1993, 1994, 1995, 1996, 1997) *Annual Report*.

Shougang Corporation (1993) 'Cong Shougang Kan Woguo Daxing Gongye Qiye de Kuaguo Jingying' [Transnationalisation of China's Large Industrial Enterprises: The Shougang Experience], in Wang Chuntao and Wu Zhongshu (eds), *Zhongguo Qiye Kuaguo Jingying Lilun yu Shijian* [Transnational Operations of Chinese Firms: Theory and Practice] (Beijing: Foreign Languages Press) pp. 281–90.

Shougang Concord International Enterprises (1994) *Annual Report 1993* (Hong Kong: Shougang Concord International Enterprises).

Shu Zhijun (1993) 'Shougang on the Road to Transnational Operation', *Beijing Review* (4–10 October), 17–22.

Sinochem (1995a) *Zhonghua Sishiwu Nian, 1950–1995* [Forty-five Years of Sinochem, 1950–1995] (Beijing: Sinochem).

Sinochem (China National Chemicals Import and Export Corporation) (1993–2000) *Annual Report* (Beijing: Sinochem).

Sinochem Corporate Strategy Study Group (1991) 'Guojihua Jingying Sannian Shijian yu Zhanwang' [Sinochem's Transnational Operation in the Last Three Years and Its Prospect], in Zhao Kunbi and Li Zheng (eds), *Kuaguo Jingying Zhilu* [The Pathway to Transnational Operation] (Beijing: China Social Sciences Press) pp. 273–83.

Song Ning *et al.* (1992) 'Zhongguo Qiye Kuaguo Jingying Zhengce Yantaohui Jiyao' [Executive Summary of the Symposium on Policies Concerning Transnational Operation of Chinese Firms], *Guanli Shijie* (Management World), 1, 53–5.

State Statistics Bureau (1995–2001) *Zhongguo Tongji Nianjian* [China Statistical Yearbook] (Beijing: China Statistics Press).

State Statistics Bureau (1995–2001b) *Zhongguo Tongji Zhaiyao* [A Statistical Survey of China] (Beijing: China Statistics Press).

Steinfeld, Edward S. (1998) *Forging Reform in China: The Fate of State-Owned Industry* (Cambridge: Cambridge University Press).

Stopford, John (1974) 'The Origins of British-Based Multinational Manufacturing Enterprises', *Business History Review*, 43(3), 303–35.

Stopford, John (1999) 'Multinational Corporations', *Foreign Policy* (Winter 1998–99), 12–24.

Strange, Susan (1995) 'Political Economy and International Relations', in Ken Booth and Steve Smith (eds), *International Relations Theory Today* (Cambridge: Polity Press) pp. 154–74.

Sun Weiyan (1991) 'China's Transnational Corporations: Who Are They and What Is Their Purpose?, *Intertrade* (January), 4–6.

Sun Weiyan (1992) 'Zhongguo Qiye Kuaguo Jingying de Fazhan Zhanlue' [Strategies for Transnationalisation of Chinese Firms], *Guanli Shijie* (Management World), 1, 41–8.

Sung, Yun-wing (1991) *The China–Hong Kong Connection: The Key to China's Open-door Policy* (Cambridge: Cambridge University Press).

Sung, Yun-wing (1992) *Non-Institutional Economic Integration via Cultural Affinity: The Case of Mainland China, Taiwan and Hong Kong* (Hong Kong: Hong Kong Institute of Asia-Pacific Studies, the Chinese University of Hong Kong).

Sung, Yun-wing (1996) *Chinese Outward Investment in Hong Kong: Trends, Prospects and Policy Implications*, Technical Paper 113 (Paris: OECD Development Centre).

Taipei Trade Centre in Hong Kong (1996) 'Zhongzi Qiye Ruzhu Xianggang Jiancheng Zhuliu' [China-funded Enterprises are Becoming Dominant Forces in the Hong Kong Economy], *Maoyi Zhoukan* (Trade Weekly, Taipei), 1714, 10–16.

Tam, Pui-Sun (1995) 'The Bank of China Group in Hong Kong: Its Changing Role and Future Direction', Master of Economics thesis, School of Economics and Finance, University of Hong Kong.

Teichova, Alice *et al.* (eds) (1986) *Multinational Enterprise in Historical Perspective* (Cambridge: Cambridge University Press).

Teng Weizao, 'Qianyan' [Foreword] in Zhang Yangui (1997) Zhongguo Qiye de Kuaguo Jinying [Transnationalisation of Chinese Firms] (Guiyang, Guizhou People's Press) :1–6.

Teng Weizao and N. T. Wang (eds) (1988) *Transnational Corporations and China's Open Door Policy* (Lexington, Mass.: Lexington Books).

Tolentino, Paz Estrella E. (1993) *Technological Innovation and Third World Multinationals* (London/New York: Routledge).

Transnational Corporations and Management Division (TCMD) (1993) *Transnational Corporations from Developing Countries: Impact on Their Home Countries* (Geneva/New York: United Nations).

Tseng, Choo-Sin (1994) 'The Process of Internationalisation of PRC Multinationals', in Helmut Schutte (ed.), *The Global Competitiveness of Asian Firms* (New York: St Martin's Press) pp. 121–8.

Tseng, Choo-Sin (1996) 'Foreign Direct Investment from the People's Republic of China', in Henri-Claude de Bettignies (ed.), *Business Transformation in China* (London: International Thomson Business Press) 85–114.

Tu, Jenn-Hwa and Chi Schive (1995) 'Determinants of Foreign Direct Investment in Taiwan Province of China: A New Approach and Findings', *Transnational Corporations*, 4(2), 93–104.

UNCTAD, Division on Transnational Corporation and World Development (ed.) (1996) *Companies Without Borders: Transnational Corporations in the 1990s* (London: Routledge).

UNCTAD (1996) *World Investment Report, 1995: Transnational Corporations and Competitiveness* (Geneva: United Nations).

UNCTAD (1997) *World Investment Report 1996* (New York/Geneva: United Nations).

UNCTAD (1997) *World Investment Report, 1996: Investment, Trade and International Policy Arrangements* (Geneva: United Nations).

UNCTAD (1998) *World Investment Report 1997: Transnational Corporations, Market Structure and Competition Policy* (New York/Geneva: United Nations).

UNCTAD (1999) *World Investment Report 1998: Trends and Determinants Overview* (New York/Geneva: United Nations).

UNCTAD (2000) *World Investment Report, 1999: Foreign Direct Investment and the Challenge of Development* (Geneva: United Nations).

UNCTAD (2001) *World Investment Report, 2000: Cross-border Mergers and Acquisitions and Development* (Geneva: United Nations).

UNCTAD (2002) *World Investment Report 2001: Country Fact Sheet: China*, www.unctad.org/wir/pdfs/wir01fs_cn.en.pdf.

United Nations Centre on Transnational Corporations (UNCTC) (1977) *Survey of Research on Transnational Corporations* (New York: United Nations).

United Nations Department of Social and Economic Affairs (1973) *Multinational Corporations in World Development* (Chinese edn 1975, Beijing: Commercial Press).

United Nations Transnational Corporations and Management Division (UNTCMD) (1993) *Transnational Corporations from Developing Countries: Impact on Their Home Countries* (New York: United Nations).

Vernon, Raymond (1992) 'Transnational Corporations: Where Are They Coming From? Where Are They Headed?' *Transnational Corporations*, 1(2), 7–35.

Vogel, Ezra F. (1991) *The Four Little Dragons: The Spread of Industrialization in East Asia* (Cambridge, Mass.: Harvard University Press).

Wall, David (1996) *Outflows of Capital from China*, Technical Paper 123 (Paris: OECD Development Centre).

Wang Chuntao and Wu Zhongshu (eds) (1993) *Zhongguo Qiye Kuaguo Jingying Lilun yu Shijian* [Transnational Operations of Chinese Firms: Theory and Practice] (Beijing: Foreign Languages Press).

Wang Congjun (1992) 'Reaching to the Outside World – Transnational Operation by a Chinese Corporation: CNFTTC Takes a Bold Initiative', *Intertrade* (May), 50–1.

Wang Hailan and Tang Xinyuan (1995) 'Shougang Shougou Mitie de Beijing ji Jingying Pingjia' [Shougang's Acquisition of Herrio Peru and Its Management: Assessments], *Guoji Jingji Hezuo* (International Economic Cooperation), 6, 40–3.

Wang Jinmei and Wang Bin (1994) 'Zhongguo Qiye Kuaguo Jingying Zhanyue' [Internationalisation Strategies of Chinese Firms], *Guojihua Jingying Zhanlue Yanjiu* (Studies of Strategies for Internationalisation), 24 (August), 8–15.

Wang, N. T. (1988) 'China's Learning Curve in Its Relations with Transnational Corporations', in Teng Wenzhao and N. T. Wang (eds), *Transnational Corporations and China's Open Door Policy* (Lexington, Mass.: Lexington Books) pp. 251–66.

Wang Xuebin (1997) 'Xinchun Zhuci' [New Year's Greetings], *Guoji Jingrong Yanjiu* (Studies of International Finance), 1, 4–5.

Watson, M. *et al.* (1986) *International Capital Markets: Development and Prospects* (Washington, DC: International Monetary Fund).

Wen, G. J. and D. Xu (eds) (1997) *The Reformability of China's State Sector* (Singapore: World Scientific Publishing).

Wei Mingyi (1995) 'Forewood', in Wen Jinping (ed.), *Wo yu Zhengxin, 1979–1994* [CITIC and I, 1979–1994] (Beijing: CITIC Press) pp. 1–3.

Welch, Lawrence S. and Reijo Luostarinen (1993) 'Internationalisation: Evolution of a Concept', in Peter J. Buckley and Perez N. Ghauri (eds), *The Internationalisation of the Firm: A Reader* (London: Academic) pp. 156–71.

Wells, Louis T. (1982) *Technology and Third World Multinationals*, Multinational Enterprises Programme Working Paper Series No. 19 (Geneva: International Labour Office).

Wells, Louis T. (1983) *Third World Multinationals: The Rise of Foreign Investment from Developing Countries* (Cambridge, Mass.: MIT Press).

Wells, Louis T. and Alvin G. Wint (1991) *Facilitating Foreign Investment: Government Institutions to Screen, Monitor, and Service Investment from Abroad* (Washington, DC: World Bank).

Wen Jinping (ed.) (1990) *Wo yu Zhongxin, 1979–1989* [CITIC and I, 1979–1989] (Beijing: CITIC Press).

Wen Jinping (ed.) (1995) *Wo yu Zhongxin, 1979–1994* [CITIC and I, 1979–1994] (Beijing: CITIC Press).

Wilkins, Mira (1970) *The Emergence of Multinational Enterprise: American Business Abroad from the Colonial Era to 1914* (Cambridge, Mass.: Harvard University Press).

Wilkins, Mira (1977) 'Modern European History and the Multinationals', *The Journal of European Economic History*, 6, 575–95.

Wilkins, Mira (1986) 'The History of European Multinationals: A New Look', *The Journal of European Economic History*, 15, 483–510.

Wilkins, Mira (ed.) (1991) *The Growth of Multinationals* (Aldershot, Hants/Brookfield, Va: Edward Elgar).

Wilson, Dick (1996) 'China Goes Transnational', *Hong Kong Business* (September), 6–8.

Womack, Brantly and Guangzhi Zhoo (1994) 'The Many Worlds of China's Provinces: Foreign Trade and Diversification', in David S. G. Goodman and Gerald Segal (eds), *China Deconstructs: Politics, Trade and Regionalism* (London/New York: Routledge).

Woo, Thye Wing (1999) *The Economics and Politics of Transition to an Open Market Economy: China*, Technical Paper No. 153 (Paris: OECD Development Centre).

World Bank (1988) *China: External Trade and Capital* (Washington, DC: World Bank).

World Bank (1997a) *China Engaged: Integration with the Global Economy* (Washington, DC: World Bank).

World Bank (1997b) *China 2020: Development Challenges in the New Century* (Washington, DC: World Bank).

World Bank (2002) *Annual Report, 2001* (Washington, DC: World Bank).

World Trade Organisation (2000) *International Trade Statistics, 1999* (Geneva: World Trade Organisation).

World Trade Organisation (2001) *International Trade Statistics, 2000* (Geneva: World Trade Organisation).

World Trade Organisation (2002) *International Trade Statistics, 2001* (Geneva: World Trade Organisation).

Wu, Fredrich (1994) 'China's Dirty Little Secret', *The International Economy*, (May/June), 22–6.

Wu Kuang (1994) 'Wukuang Kuaguo Jingying Zhilu' [MINMETAL Goes Transnational], in Zhu Ronglin (ed.), *Kuaguo Jingying: Zhongguo Jingji Fazhan Xinde*

Zengzhang Dian [Transnational Operations: The New Growth Point of the Chinese Economy] (Shanghai: Shanghai Far East Press) pp. 200–7.

Wu Zuyao (1994) 'Zhongguo Qiye Liyong Meiguo Gushi Rongzi de Shijian yu Tujin' [How Chinese Enterprises Raise Funds on the American Stock Exchanges], *Guoji Maoyi* (Intertrade), 2, 12–14.

Xie Kang *et al.* (1994) *Ruhe Chuangban Haiwai Qiye* [How to Start China's Overseas Enterprises] (Shanghai: Shanghai Communications University Press).

Xu Kangning and Luke Chan (1995) *Kuaguo Gongsi yu Zhongguo Qiye Kuaguo Jingying* [Multinational Corporations and International Business of Chinese Enterprises] (Nanjing: Dongnan University Press).

Xu Xianquan and Li Gang (1991) 'International Operations of Chinese Enterprises', *Intertrade* (January), 7–8.

Xue Shengbo, Guan Lihua and Xie Jianru (1995) 'ADR: Zhongguo Qiye Zai Meiguo Zhengjuan Shichang Rongzi Zhuyao Fangshi' [ADR: A Main Channel for Chinese Enterprises to Raise Funds in the American Securities Markets], *Xiandai Jingrong Daokan* (Modern Financial Herald), 6, 22–4.

Yamazawa, Ippei (1992) 'Gearing Economic Policy to International Harmony', in Glen D. Hook and Michael A. Weiner (eds), *The Internationalization of Japan* (London/New York: Routledge) pp. 119–30.

Yan Gonghua (1994) 'Sinotrans' Practices on Transnational Management', *Intertrade* (April), 18.

Yang, Dali L. (1996) 'Governing China's Transition to the Market: Institutional Incentives, Politicians' Choices, and Unintended Outcomes', *World Politics*, 48(3), 424–52.

Yang Jiong (1997) 'Zhongguo Zhengjuan Shichang de Guojihua Jinzhan ji Duice Jianyi' [The Internationalisation of China's Securities Markets and Policy Proposals], *Shijie Jingji Wenhui* (Essays on the World Economy), 1, 3–9.

Yang Xiaokai (2000) 'China's Entry to the WTO', *China Economic Review*, 11, 437–42.

Yasumuro, Ken'ichi (1998) 'Japanese General Trading companies and Free-standing FDI after 1960', in Geoffrey Jones (ed.), *The Multinational Traders* (London/New York: Routledge) pp. 182–99.

Ye Gang (1993a) 'Chutan Zhongxin Xianggang Gongsi Fazhan Zhanlue' [A Preliminary Study of the Corporate Strategy of CITIC Hong Kong], in Wang Chuntao and Wu Zhongshu (eds), *Zhongguo Qiye Kuaguo Jingying Lilun yu Shijian* [Transnational Operations of Chinese Firms: Theory and Practice] (Beijing: Foreign Languages Press) pp. 306–16.

Ye Gang (1993b), 'Jiefang Sixiang, Zongjie Jingyan, Jiji Fazhan Kuaguo Jingying' [Emancipate Our Thought, Learn from Our Experiences and Actively Develop Transnational Operations], in Wang Chuntao and Wu Zhongshu (eds), *Zhongguo Qiye Kuaguo Jingying Lilun yu Shijian* [Transnational Operations of Chinese Firms: Theory and Practice] (Beijing: Foreign Languages Press) pp. 28–44.

Ye Gang (ed.) (1990) *Zongjie Jingyan Banhao Haiwai Qiye* [Learning from Our Experiences in Order to Manage Well Overseas Enterprises] (Shanghai: The Chinese Association of International Economic Cooperation Studies).

Ye Gang and He Zhizhong (1993) 'Shenzhenshi Jituan Qiye Fazhan Kuaguo Jingying' [Group Companies in Shenzhen Develop Transnational Operations], in Zhu Ronglin and Ye Gang (eds) (1993) *Jiushi Niandai Zhongguo Qiye Kuaguo*

Jingying [Transnational Operations of Chinese Firms in the 1990s] (Shanghai: Shanghai Science and Technology Document Press) pp. 170–84.

Ye Yuansheng (ed.) (1994) *Zhongguo Jingji Gaige Lilun Liupai* [Contending Schools of Economics in China's Economic Reform] (Zhengzhou: Henan People's Press).

Yoshihara, Kunio (1982) *Sogo Shosha: The Vanguard of the Japanese Economy* (Tokyo: Oxford University Press).

Yuan Mu (1992) 'Guanyu Zhongguo Qiye Kuaguo Jingying de Ruogan Zhengce' [Policies Concerning the Transnational Operation of Chinese Firms], *Guanli Shijie* (Management World), 1, 29–32.

Yuan Wenqi (1991) 'Nuli Chuangjian Shehuizhuyi Kuaguo Gongsi', [Strive to Build up Socialist Transnational Corporations], in Zhao Kunbi and Li Zheng (eds), *Kuaguo Jingying Zhi Lu* [The Pathway to Transnational Operations] (Beijing: China Social Sciences Press) pp. 50–5.

Zhan, James Xiaoning (1995) 'Transnationalization and Outward Investment: The Case of Chinese Firms', *Transnational Corporations*, 4(3), 67–100.

Zhang Han-Yan and Daniel Van Den Bulcke (1994) 'International Management Strategies of Chinese Multinational Firms', in John Child and Yuan Lu (eds), *Management Issues in China*, Vol. 2, pp. 141–64.

Zhang Han-Yan and Daniel Van Den Bulcke (1996) 'China: Rapid Changes in the Investment Development Path', in John Dunning and Rajneesh Narula (eds), *Foreign Direct Investment and Governments: Catalysts for Economic Restructuring* (London: Routledge) pp. 380–422.

Zhang Jijing (1998) *Xiangmu Rongzi* [Project Financing] (Beijing: CITIC Press).

Zhang Qing and Bruce Felmingham (2001) 'The Relationship between Inward Direct Foreign Investment and China's Provincial Export Trade', *China Economic Review*, 12, 82–99.

Zhang Xiaoguang (1993) *Reforming a Centrally Planned Trade System: The Chinese Experience*, Economics Division Working Papers 93/6 (Canberra: Research School of Pacific Studies, Australian National University).

Zhang Yangui (1997) *Zhongguo Qiye de Kuaguo Jingying* [Transnationalisation of Chinese Firms] (Guiyang: Guizhou People's Press).

Zhang Yanxi (1991) 'Makesi Lienin Guanyu Shangpin Jiaohuan he Ziben Shuchu de Lilun yu Guojihua Jingying' [The Marxist-Leninist Theory about Commodity Exchange, Capital Export and Internationalisation], in Zhao Kunbi and Li Zheng (eds), *Kuaguo Jingying Zhi Lu* [The Pathway to Transnational Operations] (Beijing: China Social Sciences Press) pp. 43–9.

Zhang Yongjin (1997) 'China's Multinationals in the World Economy – A Preliminary Research', in Joseph Chai, Y. Y. Kueh and Clement A. Tisdell (eds), *China and the Asian Pacific Economy* (Brisbane: Department of Economics, University of Queensland) pp. 429–42.

Zhang Yongjin (1998) *China in International Society Since 1949: Alienation and Beyond* (London: Macmillan in association with St Antony's College, Oxford).

Zhao Jinxia and Yu Xiongfei (1996) 'Waizi Yinghang de Jinru yu Zhongguo Jingrongye Duiwai Kaifang' [Foreign Banks' Entry into China and the Opening Up of China's Financial Sectors], *Guanli Shijie* (Management World), 5, 41–9.

Zhao Kunbi and Li Zheng (eds) (1991) *Kuaguo Jingying Zhi Lu* [The Pathway to Transnational Operations] (Beijing: China Social Sciences Press).

Zhao Shuming and Lu Minghong (eds) (1993) *Qiye Kuaguo Jingying Yanjiu* [Studies of Transnationalisation of Firms] (Nanjing: Nanjing University Press).

Zhao Suisheng (1993) 'Deng Xiaoping's Southern Tour: Elite Politics in Post-Tiananmen China', *Asian Survey*, 33(8), 739–56.

Zhao Yunsheng (ed.) (1995) *Zhongguo Gongshangjie Sida Jiazu* [The Four Famous Families in China's Commerce and Industries] (Beijing: Central Party School Press).

Zheng Dunxun (1991a) 'The Internationalisation of China's Enterprises', *Intertrade* (January), 9–10.

Zheng Dunxun (1991b) 'Shehui Zhuyi Guojihua Jingying de Lilun yu Shijian' [Socialist Theory and Practice of Transnational Operations], in Zhao Kunbi and Li Zheng (eds), *Kuaguo Jingying Zhilu* [The Pathway to Transnational Operation] (Beijing: China Social Sciences Press) pp. 18–24.

Zheng Dunxun (1994) 'Zhongguo Zonghe Shangshe de Zujian yu Fazhan' [Establish and Develop China's Sogo Shosha], *Guojihua Jingying Zhanlue Yanjiu* (Studies of Strategies for Internationalisation), 25 (August), 1–7.

Zheng Dunxun (1995) 'Lishi de Zeren Shinshiye de Qidian: Zhonghua Gongsi Zonghe Shangshe Fazhan Zhanlue de Xingcheng yu Shishi' [Historical Responsibilities and the Start of a New Venture: The Evolution and Implementation of Sinochem's Strategy to Build Itself into a Sogo Shosha], *Guojihua Jingying Zhanlue Yanjiu* (Studies of Strategies for Internationalisation), 1 (March), 1–6.

Zhou Guanwu (1992) 'Shougang Gaige de Jiben Jingyan' [Basic Experiences of Shougang's Reform], in Hao Zhen *et al.* (eds), *Shougang Gaige*, vol. 2 [The Reform of Shougang Corporation, Vol. 2] (Beijing: Beijing Press) pp. 3–17.

Zhou Mingchen (1994) 'Ceroilfood's Transnational Operations', *Intertrade*, April, 12–15.

Zhou Xiaochuan (1997) 'Jiji Tuijin Waihui Tizhi Gaige, Wenbu Shixian Renminbi Ziyou Duihuan' [Actively Facilitating the Reform of the Foreign Exchange System and Steadily Moving Towards the Convertibility of RMB], *Guoji Jingrong Yanjiu* (Studies of International Finance), 1, 6–10.

Zhu Rongji (2001) *Gunayu Guomin Jingji he Shehui Fazhan 'Shiwu' Jihua Gangyao de Baogao* [Report on the Tenth Five-Year Plan for the National Economic and Social Development] (http://dp.cei.gov.cn/lszl/report07.htm).

Zhu Ronglin (ed.) (1994) *Kuaguo Jingying: Zhongguo Jingji Fazhan Xinde Zengzhang Dian* [Transnational Operations: The New Growth Point of the Chinese Economy] (Shanghai: Shanghai Far East Press).

Zhu Ronglin and Ye Gang (eds) (1993) *Jiushi Niandai Zhongguo Qiye Kuaguo Jingying* [Transnational Operations of Chinese Firms in the 1990s] (Shanghai: Shanghai Science and Technology Document Press).

Index